"Just the introduction is worth the price of this book. The Disciplers' Model provides a framework for understanding the components of transformational change. Some books appeal to the head and others to the heart. This book touches both head and heart, providing both strategic understanding and practical application for fulfilling our God-given mandate to make disciples of all nations. Some well-intentioned missionaries have 'toxic character traits' that erode their ministries. Here is a book to address those issues if the reader has the humility to listen and learn."

Albert Ehmann
President, World Team
http://www.worldteam.org

"Today's great omission in the Great Commission is 'make disciples.' The church is effective in going and baptizing, but it is failing at discipleship, the main imperative of our Lord's command. Rick Yount and Mike Barnett provide a practical, working model for helping people to 'obey everything' our Lord taught. *Called to Reach* is a must read for those who want to know how to turn converts into committed followers of Christ."

Daryl R. Eldridge
President, Rockbridge Seminary
Springfield, Missouri

"This book will be around for a long time! Yount and Barnett have made an invaluable contribution to discipling and equipping missionaries. *Called to Reach* offers insights, tools, and guidance for every Christian facing the challenge of 'becoming all things to all people in order that by all means they might reach some.' This book will bless and benefit anyone who takes seriously the Great Commission mandate to 'make disciples of all nations.'"

David Garrison
Regional Leader, South Asia
International Mission Board, SBC
Author, Church Planting Movements

"This book is a welcome read for those who care deeply about cross-cultural ministry. *Called to Reach* helps us escape from a 'seven techniques' kind of ministry mind-set and focus instead on our own characteristics . . . used by God to help others know him and grow in faith and faithfulness. It hits home at critical foundational elements of who we are . . . as we seek to become flexible servants/instruments for God's kingdom purposes. Written with insight and passion, this book will challenge and encourage readers regarding what is at the heart of effective cross-cultural ministry."

Kevin E. Lawson
Director, Ph.D. and Ed.D. Programs in Educational Studies
Editor, Christian Education Journal
Talbot School of Theology, La Mirada, CA

"We all struggle with how to effectively disciple others for Christ. *Called to Reach,* written by two who are practitioners, not theorists, is a great how-to book in that regard. But it takes the discussion an important step further, teaching us how to make disciples cross-culturally. It teaches us how to connect with and disciple those of other cultures whose thinking, values, and worldview are so different from our own. I especially appreciate the authors' emphases on character and relationships vis-à-vis techniques and methods."

George W. Murray
President, Columbia International University
Columbia, South Carolina
Former CEO of TEAM

"God is moving in unprecedented ways to reach a lost world. Western Christians often make an assumption that communication of biblical truth is the same everywhere. Rick Yount and Mike Barnett are experienced missiologists who understand the challenge of cross-cultural discipleship. With an impressive mix of academic integrity, spiritual sensitivity, and practical application, they have provided a volume that will aid those who witness among other cultures. Here you'll find understanding of all that must be involved in leading a believer to growth and effectiveness in their Christian life."

Jerry Rankin
President, International Mission Board
Southern Baptist Convention

"In *Called to Reach: Equipping Cross-Cultural Disciples* two veteran missionaries focus the spotlight on the key to effective missions: the character of the messenger. Character anchored in long-term scriptural principles will far surpass short-term techniques. Making room for God's Manual in life and work will result in the messenger's transformation as well as the hearer's. Essential reading and application."

Tom Steffen
Professor of Intercultural Studies, Biola University
Missionary in the Philippines for fifteen years
Author of several books on missions and cross-cultural ministry

CALLED
TO REACH

CALLED
TO REACH

Equipping Cross-Cultural Disciplers

WILLIAM R. YOUNT
& MIKE BARNETT

ACADEMIC

NASHVILLE, TENNESSEE

Published by B & H Publishing Group
Nashville, Tennessee

Dewey Decimal Classification: 266
Subject Heading: MISSIONS\ DISCIPLESHIP

1 2 3 4 5 6 7 8 9 10 11 12 • 15 14 13 12 11 10 09 08 07

Contents

Educator's Foreword, *Michael J. Anthony*   xi

Missiologist's Foreword, *James E. Plueddemann*   xiii

Preface   xv

Acknowledgments   xix

1. Introduction to Cross-Cultural Discipling   1
   Rick Yount

2. Developing Spiritual Character   14
   Rick Yount

3. Developing a Biblical Character   36
   Mike Barnett

4. Developing a Rational Character   66
   Rick Yount

5. Developing a Compassionate Character   104
   Mike Barnett

6. Developing an Impassioned Character   126
   Mike Barnett

7. Developing a Relational Character   148
   Rick Yount

8. Developing a Maturational Character   186
   Mike Barnett

9. Godly Influence: The Synergism of Discipling   210
   Rick Yount

Appendix 1: Insights into Cultural Differences   233

Appendix 2: Illustrations from Dr. Jeff Ritchey   241

About the Authors   243

Index   245

Educator's Foreword

Michael J. Anthony, Ph.D., Ph.D.

Professor of Christian Education, Talbot School of Theology
La Mirada, California

The Great Commission was given by Jesus to the church. It is his order of march, and it is nonnegotiable. His expectation is that we will busy ourselves with the task of leading a lost and needy world into a personal relationship with the God of all creation. However, he never intended for us to stop there. Fulfilling the Great Commission goes beyond spiritual rebirth. The Commission includes intentional engagement with those we have won to faith in Christ. Intentional engagement is the substance of discipleship. The challenge becomes even more difficult when we try to accomplish this in a cross-cultural setting. Words are misunderstood, and essential concepts can get lost in translation. Our best intentions may not be enough.

So stop! Don't board that plane just yet! Go back to the departure lounge, grab a cup of coffee, and sit down with this book. Believe me, it will be worth your time, and it may save you countless hours of frustration when you arrive at your final destination.

Rick Yount and Mike Barnett are seasoned travelers with well-worn passports to prove it. These are men on a mission themselves! That mission is to provide well-honed tools that cross-cultural disciplers will need when they find themselves face-to-face with the people to whom they are called to serve. Yount and Barnett do not write from the purely academic perspective of seminary professors cloistered away in an ivory tower. No, you'll find far more than abstract platitudes and mind-numbing theories here.

I know from my own experience how valuable these insights can be. Having led more than seventy-five short-term mission trips to countries all over the world, I can't imagine training my next team without this book. But this text does more than feed the mind; it also provides nourishment for the heart. Indeed, both clear mind and warm heart are needed if we are to achieve a lasting impact on the world in Jesus' name.

While leading a team of university students on a short-term trip, I saw a Haitian mother hand her young baby to one of the team members. The malnourished child was hours away from death, and the mother was desperate. She must have thought, *Surely this wealthy American girl can afford to care for my child.* We left the child and walked back to the bus with tears in our eyes. How easy it is to create children, but how terribly difficult it is to care for them once they're born.

Sadly the church is guilty of doing the same thing. We create spiritual children by the hundreds at crusades and other large event gatherings. But once born, we abandon them with little thought about what it takes to nurture them to spiritual adulthood. That's the substance of discipleship, and it is irresponsible to ignore the newly born. Responsible ministry sees spiritual birth as the first step on a lifelong journey of spiritual maturity. But oh, how we lack training in how to disciple those who come to faith in Christ!

If you've ever found yourself frustrated when trying to explain the fundamentals of the faith to someone from a different culture, then you know what I mean. At last we have some help. Rick and Mike speak to us from the trenches. They know what they're talking about. Principles and practices of cross-cultural disciple-making are supported and explained with stories of application from their own experience. They teach us lessons from their mistakes as well as their victories. This book is destined to become a classic in the realm of missionary training. How I wish I had read this book years ago!

As a seminary professor for nearly twenty-five years, I've seen many books come and go. Some provide valuable insights that challenge the status quo, that create intellectual disequilibrium in the mind of the reader. Other books sit on shelves, gathering dust, providing silent testimony to the lack of engagement between author and readers.

Called to Reach, on the other hand, lays a solid biblical and theoretical foundation for making disciples in the cross-cultural world in which we live, both here and abroad. What really resonates with me when I read this book is the way it connects theory to practice. The personal illustrations are shared in ways that will literally engage the souls of readers.

I have often wondered what it was like for those Emmaus disciples to discuss life's meaning with Jesus as they walked down a dusty road. As I read this book, I could almost taste what that was like, as the Lord taught me from these pages. May God bless your reading, as well as the cross-cultural ministry of discipleship that will be yours beyond the text.

Missiologist's Foreword

James E. Plueddemann, Ph.D.

Former International Director of SIM (Serving in Missions)
Professor and Chair of the Missions and Evangelism Department
Trinity Evangelical Divinity School

A book that links disciple-making with missions seems to be a "no-brainer." But such a book is hard to find and is urgently needed. Missions includes evangelism and church planting, but it is much more. Interestingly, Jesus didn't command his disciples to reach the unreached or plant churches. He commanded them to make disciples in the whole world by teaching new disciples to obey everything he had commanded. *Called to Reach* fills a critical gap for both Christian educators and missionaries.

Let me illustrate. All my life I wanted to be a missionary. That's all I ever wanted to be. Missionaries were my heroes. As a boy I observed missionaries in our home, and in a rather naive way I tried to be like them. I realized that missionaries in Asia ate a lot of rice, and I hated rice. So in order to be a better missionary, I learned to eat rice. Most missionaries I knew played tennis, so I learned to play tennis. I attended Wheaton College and read in the catalog that Christian education would be a good major for those wanting to be missionaries, so I majored in Christian education.

I married an MK from Ecuador, and for thirteen years Carol and I served with SIM in Nigeria under the Evangelical Churches of West Africa (ECWA) in Christian education. We wrote Sunday school materials and traveled with a Nigerian team holding Christian education conferences. I soon realized that many of the things I studied as a Christian education major were inappropriate for a cross-cultural missionary. I had studied important problems such as how high to hang the coat hooks for preschool children, how many square feet were needed per child, and whether to divide Sunday school classes by age or by year in school. When we arrived in Nigeria, few people wore coats, more than two hundred children of all ages were packed into one room, and monitors walked up and down the aisles with long sticks hitting children who misbehaved. Older sisters carried baby brothers on their backs. As I watched the bedlam called Sunday school, I bit my fingernails and wondered what I had learned in my Christian education courses that would help me teach in Nigeria. I realized for the first time how monocultural my Christian education really was. I tried to find people who could help me or books I could read. I found none. Missiologists seemed to be myopically focused on evangelism and church planting while Christian educators had yet to discover culture. I desperately needed a book like *Called to Reach.*

Called to Reach is a bit iconoclastic in today's world of missiology. Some of the most prestigious missiologists assume that numerical growth genuinely reflects inner qualities, and thus they sacrifice qualitative church growth on the altar of numbers. People with a mechanistic world-view don't pay much attention to the inner qualities of a disciple. It is refreshing that Yount and Barnett make growth in Christ the capstone of missions. Missions should not merely be defined as world evangelization or as reaching the unreached. While it is important to reach and evangelize, neither of these is the ultimate goal of missions. Worldwide disciple-making is a much better definition of missions.

Disciple-making takes time; in fact it is a lifetime process. Yet the church today is looking for quick and easy results. Each year several million people are sent by local churches on short-term mission trips. Billions of dollars are spent by people looking to get a lot of "bang for the buck" from each missions trip. When they arrive home, these missionaries who were away for two weeks are asked, "How many people did you win for Christ? Did you plant any churches?" It is much less dramatic to ask, "How many disciples did you make?" because discipleship is lifelong and time-intensive. I trust that *Called to Reach* will not only be used to prepare missionaries for ministries in cross-cultural discipleship but will also be used to challenge many who have had short-term experiences to give their whole lives to fostering growth in Christ in worldwide disciple-making.

The book is a delightful balance between biblical principles and social science research interspersed with dozens of real-life experiences. Such a book is long overdue both in the field of Christian education and in missions.

I pray that the Lord will use this book to influence thousands of cross-cultural disciplers and to make a powerful impact on the worldwide church.

Preface

Though I am free and belong to no man, I make myself a slave to everyone, to win as many as possible. To the Jews I became like a Jew, to win the Jews. To those under the law I became like one under the law (though I myself am not under the law), so as to win those under the law. To those not having the law I became like one not having the law (though I am not free from God's law but am under Christ's law), so as to win those not having the law. To the weak I became weak, to win the weak. I have become all things to all men so that by all possible means I might save some. I do all this for the sake of the gospel, that I may share in its blessings.
—1 Corinthians 9:19–23

The apostle Paul was a cross-cultural discipler. He was raised in a Jewish home and into a Jewish heritage, but because his father was a Roman citizen, Paul lived in two divergent cultures. "If anyone else thinks he has reasons to put confidence in the flesh, I have more: circumcised on the eighth day, of the people of Israel, of the tribe of Benjamin, a Hebrew of Hebrews; in regard to the law, a Pharisee; as for zeal, persecuting the church; as for legalistic righteousness, faultless. But whatever was to my profit I now consider loss for the sake of Christ" (Phil. 3:4–7).

The apostle Paul drew people to faith in Christ—"first for the Jew, then for the Gentile" (Rom. 1:16)—planted churches, and equipped "God's people for works of service" (Eph. 4:12). He preached the gospel, trained leaders, wrote instructive letters, and established a seminary in Ephesus for the training of pastors. He traveled and taught throughout Asia Minor, Macedonia, Greece, and Rome, going first to the local synagogues but moving from there into marketplaces and stadiums. He discussed the law with Jews in Galatia, philosophy with the Greeks in Athens, and secret knowledge with the early Gnostics in the Lycus Valley of southwestern Asia Minor. He supported the work of Lydia in Philippi and Priscilla, as well as Priscilla's husband Aquila, in Corinth and Ephesus. He gathered a love offering from Greek Christians for the persecuted and impoverished Jewish Christians back in Palestine, while supporting himself by making tents. He mentored younger leaders like Silas and Timothy. He convinced the runaway slave, Onesimus, to return to his master and then convinced his master, Philemon, to receive Onesimus as a brother in order to create a new kind of bond between Christian believers. In all these ways the apostle Paul crossed cultural divides, becoming "all things to all men" in order to communicate the gospel most effectively.

Given this fundamental principle of "all things to all men," I sat in my living room wondering where our missionary guest speaker was headed in his presentation. We had invited a dozen seminary students to our home for a "cultural experience" with a missionary just home on furlough. He had graduated from an accredited seminary. He had spent months in interviews and processing. He had worked his way through weeks of specialized training by his mission agency. But he had returned home from the mission fields defeated and bitter by culture shock. His "testimony" complained of hardship and loneliness, and his struggle with the language. He criticized the lifestyle of the people, using language I will not repeat here. Uncooperative national leaders. Disinterested church members. Hostile pagans.

As he talked, the students' eyes grew larger and larger. A knot formed in my stomach. This certainly had not been my experience in the few short-term trips I had made to the same area. Not wanting to embarrass our guest, I attempted to direct him to something more positive. I had eaten many different dishes in his adopted country and enjoyed them immensely. Perhaps a mention of the wonderful food would help nudge him back into a more positive presentation. And so I asked him to talk about the food. He snapped at the chance: "The food is awful. Everything is prepared from scratch. Very little meat. Mostly garden vegetables. I mean, cucumbers and tomatoes every day! And they don't even have restaurants to speak of. We had to buy our food in open markets, and we never knew what we were getting."

I interrupted him and announced that the presentation was over. My wife had prepared several dishes from the country, made from recipes she had collected on her visits. We spent the rest of the evening enjoying the food, talking with students, and keeping the missionary from saying much else. It was obvious he had not learned the lessons of Paul, or much of anything else relating to gospel ministry in another culture. He was suffering from extreme culture shock and had actually damaged the mission cause where he worked. I learned later that he and his family never returned to the field.

Engaging the lost and equipping the saints is difficult, even in our own culture. But crossing into another culture to evangelize and disciple makes the difficulties far more extreme. This text applies principles of the Disciplers' Model and the Christian Teachers' Triad to cross-cultural ministry.

We will use the term *disciplers* in this text to refer to followers of Jesus Christ who cross cultural and language barriers at home and abroad to share the gospel, plant and strengthen churches, and equip future leaders to carry on the work long after their tour of duty is over. A discipler may be a missionary, a minister, a tentmaker, or a church member. A discipler is more than a teacher, more than a teller, more than a leader. Disciplers are those who are growing toward spiritual maturity. They are biblically grounded, able to think clearly, value passionately, and relate warmly with others. Disciplers are learners who have not stopped growing in the Lord and whose focus is the needs of those they teach.

In this text we define seven characteristics that enhance the effectiveness of disciplers in overcoming cultural barriers which stand against the gospel, the Lord, and the Lord's family. Here at the outset, however, we make the following disclaimer: we are not saying that one must possess all seven of these characteristics in order to succeed on the mission field. God will take all of our inadequacies, as we depend on him, and make us effective in spite of our shortcomings. Leaders and teachers often succeed even when they do not possess abilities most would agree are necessary for success. Was Abram honest (think of Sarai)? Or David chaste (think of Bathsheba)? Was Moses a good communicator (think of his stutter)? Or Paul gentle (think of Barnabas)? And yet we know that if they had avoided their shortcomings, their lives and work would have been better. But we all have shortcomings! So we labor in this solid hope: the intentional cultivation of the seven qualities of character represented by the Disciplers' Model will help leaders improve their ability to connect with others—head, heart, and hand—across cultural divides.

We both love teaching and have years of experience teaching seminary and Sunday school classes and leading conferences. We both love missions, moving across cultures and languages to assist brothers and sisters in Christ as they serve the Lord among their own people.

For the past five years we met to pray and share ideas, traveled and interviewed as often as possible, and wrote down what the Lord impressed on us from within and without. We did all of this for you—dear student, missionary, pastor, educator, tentmaker, church worker—to enable you to cross cultural barriers in the name of the Lord, whether these barriers are found in your own town or around the world.

Find a place of quiet peace, ask the Lord to open your heart and mind to his direction, and receive what he has prepared to help those serving as the Lord's special agents of the gospel.

Rick Yount and Mike Barnett
January 2006

Acknowledgments

We wish to thank Dr. Jerry Rankin, president of the International Mission Board of the Southern Baptist Convention, for his encouragement in this task.

We appreciate the comments of Dr. Andy Leininger, a missionary-discipler with the International Mission Board (SBC) working in Siberia, Russia, and former student of Dr. Yount's discipling approach to teaching. He first suggested using the Disciplers' Model in a "character development approach" to cross-cultural discipleship. Dr. Leininger's doctoral research (D.Ed.Min., 2005) focused on a practical system for creating self-reproducing Christian cells in Belarus, which he is using now to extend church planting teams across Siberia. You will find Dr. Leininger's comments in endnotes identified by "AL."

We are grateful for the contributions of fifty-five students at Southwestern Baptist Theological Seminary (Fort Worth, Texas) who, in the fall of 2003, worked through the initial concepts of this text in an experimental cross-discipline course entitled "Discipling across Cultural Divides." We further appreciate the specific comments of the sixteen students of Columbia Biblical Seminary and School of Missions (Columbia, South Carolina) who, in a January 2006 one-week intensive, used the present manuscript as a course text for the first time.

1

Introduction to
Cross-Cultural Discipling
Rick Yount

It was he [Christ] who gave some to be apostles, some to be prophets, some to be
evangelists, and some to be pastors and teachers, to prepare God's people for works
of service, so that the body of Christ may be built up until we all reach unity in the
faith and in the knowledge of the Son of God and become mature, attaining to the
whole measure of the fullness of Christ.
Ephesians 4:11–13

Then Jesus came to them and said, "All authority in heaven and on earth
has been given to me. Therefore go and make disciples of all nations,
baptizing them in the name of the Father and of the Son and of the Holy Spirit,
and teaching them to obey everything I have commanded you. And surely I am with
you always, to the very end of the age."
Matthew 28:18–20

W e sat drinking tea and eating bread with jam. He was so frustrated.
Oh, it wasn't the strange food, the colder weather, or the long
dark nights. It wasn't even the daily strain to wrap his mind around verb
conjugations, case endings, and idiomatic speech. No, his frustration
came from the lack of success in repeatedly banging his head against
the unbending cultural wall that separated him from his ministry goals.
He had come to Russia with visions of mass evangelism, young national
pastors-to-be eager to learn, and a church planting movement sweeping
across eleven time zones. What he quickly found was indifference among
the masses, rock-hard tradition among believers, and pastors who were
slow to embrace the ideas he'd brought to Russia—giving up home in
America to do so.

"If only I could get one pastor to help me start a new church . . . If
only I could get inside the leadership circle . . . If only I could . . ." He
had overcome culture shock and language shock. He loved the people
with a supernatural love and certainly enjoyed the slower pace of life.
But he was caught in the "if-onlys" and was suffering pains of perceived
failure and despair. He was thinking of returning home.

His experience is not unique. I suppose every minister has had feelings like these from time to time. Even seminary professors fall prey to the idea that we could teach so much better "if only" our students were more creative or motivated or something. It is a fantasy of the imagination. We are not called to some abstract ideal. We are called "to prepare God's people for works of service" (Eph. 4:12). We take them as they are and lead them to become what they can. That is our calling.

It is hard enough within our own culture—leading those who think and feel and act like we do to think more clearly, value more deeply, and minister more skillfully. But to reach, teach, and equip leaders who are conditioned by a culture different from our own to think differently, value differently, and behave differently is another matter altogether.

A special something bridges the gap between people who are framed by differing cultures. I've seen it—*felt it*—while working with deaf people in the United States, Brazilians in São Paulo and Brasilia, and Russian-speaking peoples in Russia, Ukraine, Kazakhstan, and Kyrgyzstan. That something is an almost mystical connect that snaps across cultural divides to bind together people heart to heart and mind to mind. Those who can make this connection live by definable principles. They avoid cultural trip wires that cause explosions. Those who violate these definable principles hit cultural trip wires, collapse relational bridges, and cut communication lines. It takes more than desire, more than language proficiency, more than ministry know-how to connect.

This text identifies, in terse, straightforward language, principles for connecting across cultures in order to win the lost and disciple believers. The principles in this text will help you negotiate cultural minefields more safely. We frame these principles by means of two diagrams, the Disciplers' Model and the Christian Teachers' Triad.

The Disciplers' Model—used for over twenty-five years in training lay teachers in churches across America, over twenty years in teaching future pastors and ministers of education at Southwestern Seminary, and over ten years in teaching national leaders in various mission fields—provides the structural framework for the text. We often find help for ministers and missionaries cast in terms of *techniques* that can be *employed*. We believe we need to take a different tack. We cast our principles in terms of *character*: what we must *become* in order to connect with—to reach, teach, equip, and transform—those God called us to strengthen in his name. The seven elements of character correspond to the seven elements of the Disciplers' Model.

The Christian Teachers' Triad consists of three interrelated circles, each representing an aspect of human learning essential to discipleship. Let's look at each of these in turn.

The Disciplers' Model

Missionaries are disciplers who carry the good news across linguistic and cultural barriers. Our primary directive comes from Jesus' Great Commission recorded in Matthew 28:19–20. We are to "go and make disciples of all nations." The Christian faith is not bound by any culture, any language, any socioeconomic strata, gender, color, or age.

We make contact with unbelievers. Build bridges of relationship. Invite them to "taste and see that the LORD is good" (Ps. 34:8a). Bless them by leading them to faith in Christ ("blessed is the man who takes refuge in him," Ps. 34:8b). Encourage them to seal their faith commitment through public profession of faith and baptism. Equip them to disciple others. Finally, we release them to the Spirit of God for their quickening and direction that they may disciple others, who in turn disciple others until those of "every nation, tribe, people and language" stand before the throne and worship Jesus the Lamb of God (Rev. 7:9).

We go as God leads. We go despite earthly barriers. We go where God has already gone: to the ends of the earth. And having gone, we disciple all nations by "baptizing" and by "teaching them to obey everything . . . [Jesus] commanded." Those who are most effective in this process of transforming unbelievers into disciplers follow principles illustrated by the Disciplers' Model.

The Disciplers' Model takes the form of a temple, consisting of foundation stones, pillars, a capstone, and a synergizing circle. The foundation stones represent the Bible, God's eternal truth, and the needs of the people we reach.

These two foundation stones are essential to reaching across cultural divides: God's eternal Word relates to every culture. As we focus on biblical principles, we lessen the risk of stumbling

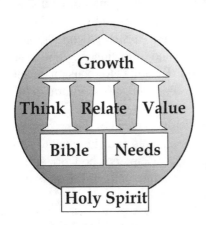

Disciplers' Model

3

over our own cultural biases. Further, meeting the needs of learner-leaders within their cultural context is the quickest way to build bridges. Chapter 3 builds on "Bible" to focus on developing a biblical character, and chapter 5 builds on "Needs" to focus on developing a compassionate character.

The pillars represent the processes of "Thinking" (left pillar), "Valuing" (right pillar),[1] and "Relating" (center pillar).

Cultural mistakes can result from misunderstandings and misconceptions (thinking). Concepts of time, relationships, success, and ministry vary from culture to culture. Disciplers are able to see the world from others' viewpoints and can then create ways to build bridges between themselves and others. We solve real problems in practical ways in the appropriate biblical and cultural contexts. Chapter 4 builds on "Thinking" to focus on developing a rational character, which helps us to connect across cultural divides mind to mind.

Cultural mistakes can result from differing values (valuing). Priorities, convictions, and the commitments to self, family, church, community, and the world vary from culture to culture. Disciplers love the people they equip and are passionate about building the Lord's kingdom by discipling others. We do far more than teach values; we model appropriate values for others to see the way we go about our everyday responsibilities. Chapter 6 builds on "Valuing" to focus on developing an impassioned character, which helps us to connect across cultural divides heart to heart.

Cultural mistakes can flow from an inability to meet people, build relational bridges, or embrace others as a meaningful part of God's flock (relating). Disciplers are sensitive to the viewpoints and values of others, working to build a family context in ministry. We strengthen relationships through humility, listening to wise advice and following the appropriate leadership of others. Chapter 7 builds on "Relating" to focus on developing a relational character, which helps us connect across cultural divides to build community and team.

The capstone represents growth in Christ. The end of the process of discipleship finds believers of all nations matured and equipped to serve the Lord in their world. This is the focus of disciplers who work effectively with nationals:[2] to help them grow, mature in the Lord, and become

---

1 If you have studied the Disciplers' Model in the past, you may have seen this pillar labeled "Helping People Feel." But the term *feelings* is used in such superficial ways today that I am compelled to lift the term from simple emotional responses to a level of heartfelt commitment and passion for the Lord and his work.

2 The primary focus of this text is to help Americans cross cultural barriers to reach those of other cultures. The examples emphasize this Ameri-centric view. However, the principles of the text apply

equipped to serve him as he leads in their world. This focus reduces cultural conflicts that grow from the frustration of "they will not do things our way."

Growth in Christ further reduces cultural conflict as we together grow away from our various conflicting cultures and toward a more godly culture. We will succeed to the extent we focus on our essential need (and our learners' essential need) to grow in the Lord and depend on him. Chapter 8 builds on growth to focus on developing a maturational character.

The circle represents the Holy Spirit, who, as Master Teacher, holds these elements together in a dynamic synergism (chapter 9). It sounds harsh, but until we succeed in becoming channels of the Lord's supernatural work, nothing of eternal substance will happen in our ministries.

Disciplers' Model

The fundamental importance of this element is underscored by its discussion before any of the other elements in chapter 2, which builds on "Holy Spirit" to focus on developing a spiritual character.

The Disciplers' Model reflects the Lord's answer to my prayers years ago while I was struggling to teach deaf college students in our church's Bible study program. Though my students seemed to enjoy the sessions, I saw little evidence of spiritual growth. And so I began to pray week after week, "Lord, how do I teach so that these students grow in you?" Over the next few years, through hundreds of teaching experiences with deaf youth and adults, seminary studies and discussions with deaf and hearing ministers, the Disciplers' Model took form.[3]

The model you see depicted here came together in the spring of 1977. Since that time I have used it with hundreds of lay teachers in local churches, thousands of seminary students, and many groups of pastors,

---

to believers of any culture reaching out to people of a culture different from their own.
3 Each chapter begins with an introduction to its element of the model, written by Yount. If you would like more information on the model, see chapter 1, *Created to Learn* (Nashville: Broadman & Holman, 1996) or go to http://members.aol.com/wyount and click on the Disciplers' Model icon.

teachers, and missionaries in the former Soviet Union (Ukraine, Russia, Kazakhstan, and Kyrgyzstan). It has been used by others, translated into Russian, Spanish, and Chinese. And so it forms the structural heart of this text.

The Christian Teachers' Triad: A Reflection of God's Design

The apostle John wrote his treatise on the life and work of Jesus so

that we might "believe that Jesus is the Christ, the son of God, and that by believing, you may have life in his name" (John 20:31). The word John chose for "life" in this verse was not *bios,* from which we get the word *biology,* but the richer term *zoē,* which refers to abundant, vibrant, spiritual life. John's focus was abundant, spiritual life in Jesus' name, and such should be our focus also.

The life we have in Christ can further be defined in three spheres which are revealed in the nature of God. God thinks. God loves. God acts. These spheres can be defined as the rational (thought life), the affective (emotional life), and the behavioral (skilled life).

The psychology of education has over the past one hundred years defined human learning theory in three major systems. These systems are generally known as the cognitive (mind), the humanistic (affect), and the behavioral (skills).

The Christian Teachers' Triad represents these three spheres of life as three interdependent circles. I developed this Christian Teachers' Triad in

Created to Learn (1996) as a way to integrate the major learning systems in educational psychology. The triad is shown in its simplest form here.[4]

Regardless of culture, language, religion, or region, every human being—created in God's image—thinks, feels, and acts skillfully. Concepts, values, and skills differ from culture to culture, from region to region and from person to person. But every human being thinks, values, and possesses skills.

In seminary classes and teacher conferences, I often ask participants to place themselves into one of three groups, defined by preferences in learning as thinkers, feelers, and doers. I've done this in several regions of the United States as well as in Russia, Germany, and Brazil. I've done this with groups of students, teachers, and musicians. Once I did this in a group of three hundred African-American Sunday school teachers in Oklahoma City.

From these repeated exercises I made a surprising discovery, producing our first principle: *learners consistently place themselves into three nearly equal groupings.* Men always outnumber women in the "thinkers" group, but the group consistently includes women. Women always outnumber men in the "feelers" group, but the group consistently includes men. The "doers" group divides into rough halves between men and women. Think of this! In every class, every conference, every group of human beings, we face roughly equal groupings of thinkers, feelers, and doers.

I further ask them to consider Bible studies they've experienced, and determine, as a group, their favorite characteristics and methods. Time after time the three groups report the same basic preferences. Thinkers like order, structure, in-depth lecture, context, "meat." Feelers like personal openness, freedom, spontaneity, sharing, "warmth." Doers like direction, usefulness, practical applications, "action."

When I ask them what they do not like, the groups consistently report dislikes in common with thinkers, feelers, and doers around the world. Thinkers dislike personal sharing, chasing rabbits, and shallow

---

4 The "Thinking" sphere reflects the same thrust as the "Thinking" pillar in the model. The "Valuing" sphere is the same as the "Valuing" pillar. While there is overlap between the two diagrams, each projects a different focus in the process of teaching and learning and, in turn, discipling and equipping.

applications (touchy-feely!). Feelers dislike lecture, analysis, and especially historical background (boring!). Doers dislike abstract analysis, historical background, and shallow emotion (waste of time!).

From this flows a second major principle: *Teachers operate primarily out of their own preferred circle.* Thinkers tend to teach as if all learners are thinkers. Feelers as if all are feelers. Doers—*doers.* And when we do this, we connect with roughly a third of the class. Even if we teach perfectly out of our preferred circle, we miss two-thirds of our learners! The only way to avoid this is intentionally to move out of personal comfort zones and into our weaker areas. Those who unwittingly teach out of their own circle—whatever circle it is!—inevitably produce imbalance in the classroom. How? While effective teaching must clearly define

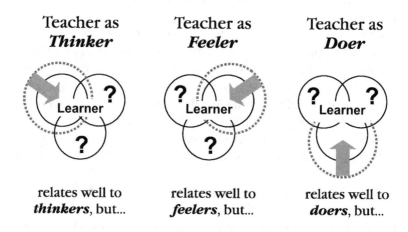

Teacher as *Thinker*	Teacher as *Feeler*	Teacher as *Doer*
relates well to *thinkers*, but...	relates well to *feelers*, but...	relates well to *doers*, but...

concepts and develop principles, too much emphasis here leads to academic intellectualism (cold dogma). While effective teaching must draw on learner experiences and encourage passionately held positive values, too much emphasis here leads to superficial emotionalism (warm fluff). While effective teaching must generate sharply defined skills, too much emphasis here leads to confused, uncommitted action, and eventually, exhaustion (burnout).

The exclamation points in the diagram reflect these extremes in the classroom. While thinkers revel in cold (objective) dogma (truths), feelers yearn for warmth, and doers look for praxis. While feelers revel in warm (subjective) fluff (personal experiences), thinkers search for meaning, and doers look for praxis. While doers revel in energized action, thinkers search for meaning, and feelers yearn for warm relationships.

Imbalance in disciplers yields imbalance in learning and growth.[5]

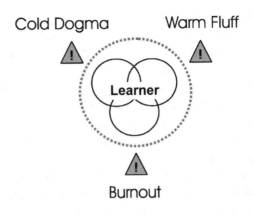

We face an even deeper problem when discipling and equipping across cultural divides. Deep differences exist in perceptions, values, and skills from culture to culture; and these differences undermine even the best of efforts.

The goal is to disciple and equip after the example of Jesus. He focused his teaching on the needs of his learners. He perfectly melded thinking (parables, illustrations, interpretations), feeling (love, care, support, choosing "twelve to be with him"), and doing (demonstrations, modeling the role, practical guidance) elements as they were needed to transform the lives of his disciples. And he taught perfectly, whether his learners were Jewish, Roman, or Syro-Phoenician.

Throughout the text we will build on these simple interlocking circles as we promote transformational principles which can reach and equip thinkers, feelers, and doers around the world.

The Essential Role of Character over Technique

Missions agencies tend to be pragmatic problem solvers, seeking effective ways to motivate, enlist, organize, and replicate success in ministry. It is easy, however, for these ways to be reduced to techniques. The implication is clear: Follow these specific steps and you will succeed. Worse, missionaries too often carry these techniques overseas and tell national leaders the same: follow these steps and you will succeed. More often than not, the specific techniques do not fit other cultures.

When old techniques fail to produce expected results, we are tempted to discard them in favor of something new, anchored in nothing more than disdain for the same old thing which no longer "works." Change

---

5 For a more detailed discussion, see chapter 11, "The Christian Teachers' Triad," in *Created to Learn* (Nashville: Broadman & Holman, 1996) and chapter 1, "Teacher as Dynamic Synergism," and chapter 2, "Teacher as Mature Person," in *Called to Teach* (Nashville: Broadman & Holman, 1999).

for change's sake. While techniques can be helpful in the short-term and have the advantage of quick development and distribution, life-changing ministry requires more than technique.[6]

Character, on the other hand, is solid and consistent and requires consistent effort over time to develop. Character anchors itself in unchanging principles. It is constant even when circumstances and methods change. It is the difference between those who are in their hearts friendly, prayerful, creative, humble, and caring and those who merely clothe themselves in these behaviors—much as one might don an ill-fitting winter coat. Artificial techniques of ministry may be a reasonable beginning point. But disciplers move beyond techniques to grow, under the Lord's mighty hand, solid character traits—traits which are expressed in and through everything we think, feel, and do.

In this text we will develop seven character traits which flow directly from the seven elements of the Disciplers' Model. We see these characteristics in Jesus, in the apostle Paul, in Barnabas, and in John. They are found throughout history and in those who are even now crossing cultural barriers to disciple and equip others. We believe you will become more effective in any ministry endeavor as you allow the Lord to develop these traits in you. Here again are the seven character traits:

1. The *Spiritual* Character of the Discipler (Holy Spirit)
   The effective discipler is a flexible, surrendered instrument in the hands of the Lord (chapter 2).
2. The *Biblical* Character of the Discipler (Bible)
   The effective discipler lives out biblical truth in tangible ways (chapter 3).
3. The *Rational* Character of the Discipler (Thinking)
   The effective discipler creates viable, local solutions to problems/ barriers (chapter 4).
4. The *Compassionate* Character of the Discipler (Needs)
   The effective discipler cares about the needs of learners (chapter 5).
5. The *Impassioned* Character of the Discipler (Valuing)
   The effective discipler commits to whatever it takes to share the gospel (chapter 6).

---

6 Whenever techniques have an inappropriate emphasis, it is usually at the expense of the *principles* that once made the techniques successful. Effective principles are built upon true, consistent character. The act of love done by an unloving person is not perceived as love. AL

6. The *Relational* Character of the Discipler (Relating)
   The effective discipler builds teams of learners and trains team builders (chapter 7).
7. The *Maturational* Character of the Discipler (Growth in Christ)
   The effective discipler stimulates personal spiritual growth in learners, groups, and churches (chapter 8).

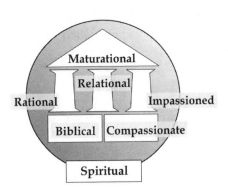

Character Traits
drawn from the
Disciplers' Model

Some might read these initial definitions and see nothing more than platitudes. Looking at these same principles from a negative point of view may help. We will call these insights "The Toxic Flipside" of each chapter's theme. They reflect possible reasons some struggle, even fail, in their attempts to cross cultural barriers with the gospel. Perhaps these teachers are . . .

1. Unspiritual—Using human know-how, in their own strength
2. Unbiblical—Preaching biblical truths but living by their own cultural norms
3. Unrational—Pushing their own (American) solutions and perspectives
4. Uncompassionate—Ignoring needs of disciples, focusing on their own agenda
5. Unimpassioned—Seeking first their own convenience and welfare in ministry
6. Unrelational—Insisting learners become like them before accepting them
7. Unmaturational—Measuring success in terms of *bigger* rather than *better*

These toxic character traits eventually destroy the best efforts, the best plans, even the best techniques, to carry the gospel across cultural divides and to disciple those we reach and teach in Jesus' name.

Through the following seven chapters, I will provide a general overview for each of the seven model elements. Then Mike and I will employ the model and triad to define specific characteristics for discipling and equipping saints of other cultures. We will illustrate the principles through stories of those who have already lived out these truths in effective cross-cultural ministry.

May God richly bless you as you read, as you absorb, as you open yourself to God's Spirit to mold you into one who can improve "connectedness" in real and tangible ways with those God has called you to reach, teach, and transform in his name.

Spiritual

The Spiritual Character
of cross-cultural
Disciplers

Holy Spirit

Disciplers' Model

2

Developing Spiritual Character
Rick Yount

Flesh and blood hath not revealed it unto thee, but my Father which is in heaven.
Matthew 16:17 KJV

Disciplers develop a spiritual character—a perspective devoted to on-going surrender to the Holy Spirit's leadership—and as a result they are better able to "connect" with cross-cultural learner-leaders than those who do not. Chapter 2 defines the circle of the model: the Holy Spirit as discipler. We then describe how Jesus exemplified a spiritual character through prayer, position, and priority. Finally we suggest ways to develop a spiritual character, one that allows the Spirit freedom to lead and work through us to accomplish his ends.

The Toxic Flip Side

Depending on our own know-how, ministering in our own strength

George and Lorene in Ecuador

George and Lorene Joslin are part of a handful of pioneers of ministry among the deaf. They served with the Southern Baptist Home Mission Board (now North American Mission Board) as missionaries to the deaf in California, Texas, and Virginia from the 1960s to the 1990s. George was one of my first mentors in deaf ministry beginning in 1970. They are now retired and, like Caleb of old, spend their retirement years not in porch rockers but on the front lines of missions among the deaf. If there are any living persons with more know-how about barrier-crossing be-tween deaf and hearing cultures, I don't know who they are. Despite their expertise their ministry focus remains spiritual. George and Lorene wrote the following in one of their prayer letters in 2001: "We face the diffi-culty of finding people, learning where they live, and then finding them at home. With no car it takes a lot of walking and taxi time to look for them. We have learned that it is better to prepare to talk with them and pray that they will come to us. And they do! They show up. The spontaneous leading of God in these situations is not a substitute for the work of going to where they are, but in these circumstances we depend heavily on the Holy Spirit to bring them to us."

In January 2002, I received a request from George—a request for advice on how to help mentor a deaf man named Pedro. Pedro had emerged as the leader of the deaf group in Ecuador. He could not read or write. He had little or no education. George wanted me to suggest ways he could develop Pedro as the primary leader-teacher in seven months—the time he and Lorene had before leaving for home. I felt so inadequate to respond, but this was the response I sent him:

George—

If you do not know how to transform Pedro into a leader in seven months, what can I say to help? You are my teacher! But I'm praying about it and will just write some things that come to mind, ignoring the gut feeling that everything I'm saying you already know.

Pedro does not need to be a leader as we define the term. He needs to be a leader among the deaf, a Christian leader through whom God can speak. It may be that he will not become the leader he needs to be until the month after you leave.

So we need to pray. We need to pray for Pedro to be open to the Lord of the universe and make real connection with him. That connection made, the Lord can yoke him (Matt. 11:29-30) and teach him day by day.

We need to pray for you as you "story" your way through basic doctrines, leader skills, and people skills. You have seven months left to love him, grace him, and grow him in the Lord. God is more interested in Pedro's success than you are, so give him free reign and give Pedro freedom to develop according to his timetable. Get yourself ready to leave seven months from now still feeling that he isn't ready yet.

You asked how to get new information across to him in a form he can preserve. Can you create pictures, even abstract depictions, of concepts around which you explain principles? Teach a principle or skill around the depiction. When he sees the depiction, he will remember the teaching. Small thumbnails of the depictions can be copied and given to learners. Those who can teach can use the books of depictions to share information with others.

Better still. Are there any deaf artists who can help create the depictions? Their ministry would be to put on paper the essence of a principle as you explain it.

Whatever you do, it will be more than would have been done had you not gone. You are an angel, come to shine light in a dark part of a silent world. The supernatural, eternal part of your work is done by prayer and prayer alone. Simply lay yourself before the Lord and pray that he will make the connection necessary for Pedro (and others) to become what is needed.

I've joined you in prayer for Pedro. I'm also praying that the Lord will give you the joy of seeing some of what he is doing in his life before you leave.

What a commitment you and Lorene have made! What a change you are making! Ignore the undermining thoughts from Satan, who wants nothing more than to make your work seem hopeless.

Grace,
Rick

"Christ in you, the hope of glory" (Col. 1:27).

The Circle:[1] Holy Spirit as Discipler

The circle of the Disciplers' Model represents the surrounding and indwelling presence of God's Holy Spirit in our lives and our work. If we ever expect to be associated with anything supernatural in process and eternal in impact, it will happen to the degree that we are surrendered to the directing of the Holy Spirit. The moment-by-moment direction of the Holy Spirit, blowing this way and that (John 3:8), is more important to

---

1 Chapters 2–8, regardless of author, contain introductions to elements of the Disciplers' Model. These are drawn from Yount's earlier writings, *The Disciplers' Handbook* (self-published, 1st ed., 1979; 9th ed., 2006), and chapter 1 of *Created to Learn*. Yount adapted the material to the present theme of cross-cultural implications for this text.

Holy Spirit

Disciplers' Model

our success as God's ministers than any religion or any ritual because these are our own creations. How do we open our lives and our ministries to the Holy Spirit? What do we do to open up the spiritual communication lines? How do we become channels of his blessing to those we teach? Prayer, priority, and position are the three essentials that determine how we answer each of these questions.

Prayer

If we want the Lord to have freedom to work in and through our ministries, we must invite him. Remember the Lord's words to the Laodecian church? "I stand at the door and knock. If anyone hears my voice and opens the door, I will come in and eat with him, and he with me" (Rev. 3:20). The presence of the Lord is not automatic, even in church. The Lord had been shut out of the Laodecian church, but he beckons to individuals in the church who desire fellowship with him. He tells them how to have that fellowship. We must ask him, invite him, welcome him into our lives, into our work. Day by day. Moment by moment.

Priority

Spiritual ministry has an insidious enemy, the notion of "turf." By "turf" I mean the *personal* kingdoms we build "in the name of the Lord." We may begin our ministries out of pure motives to leave home and comfort to go into the world to reach and help people. But somewhere along the line spiritual ministry may become "my ministry." Then "my ministry" slides into turf to protect. Turf turns us from outward-looking spiritual explorers to inward-looking turf defenders. Such self-centered defensiveness short-circuits the spiritual.

Disciplers, however, work in support of goals larger than self. We see our work as part of the worldwide work of God. If a request is made that will help the overall ministry plan, disciplers do all they can to support that decision. We model the role of cooperation for colleagues and learners and are positive in support of the bigger picture. Disciplers are mature enough to forgo turf as we maintain the proper priority of "seek ye first the kingdom." In doing this, channels open for the Holy Spirit to work in and through us.

Position

From the world's view, the most powerful position is at the top: rank has its privilege. The higher the position, the more power one has to control others. We Evangelicals exegete passages on servanthood and sacrifice better than most, but the natural human desire for high position and power will affect any of us who do not consciously, intentionally, regularly surrender self to the Lord. And not only to the Lord but also—and this is impossible in our own human strength—to those God called us to serve. Jesus said it this way: "Whoever wants to become great among you must be your servant, and whoever wants to be first must be slave of all" (Mark 10:43–44).

These aspects of spiritual teaching—prayer, priority, and position—rise directly out of our dependence on and submission to the Holy Spirit. Programs come and go, plans succeed and fail, gimmicks thrive and fade. But through all of this runs the golden thread of God's work: the drawing, winning, and maturing of people in Christ. This holy work proceeds only as the Holy Spirit, the Spirit of Christ, freely moves through us as surrendered disciplers.

◆ ◆ ◆

The Spiritual Character of Jesus

We find the three dimensions of spiritual character—prayer, position, and priority—in the day-to-day life experiences of Jesus. He was called "Lord" *(kurios)* because he did what only God could do.[2] Yet we find in him, the second person of the Trinity, the vital spiritual characteristic of submission to the Father.

---

2 Even Nicodemus, a Pharisee and a member of the Sanhedrin, said to Jesus, "Rabbi, we know you are a teacher who has come from God. For no one could perform the miraculous signs you are doing if God were not with him" (John 3:2).

The Prayers of Jesus

At the beginning of his ministry, Jesus appointed twelve to be "with him" (Mark 3:14). The appointments were preceded, however, by a night spent in prayer. "Jesus went out to a mountainside to pray, and spent the night praying to God. When morning came, he called his disciples to him and chose twelve of them, whom he also designated apostles" (Luke 6:12–13).

This prayerful consideration included the choice of Judas Ischariot, the one who would steal from the disciples' purse, pursue worldly political ends, and finally betray his Master to the authorities. Prayer is not a means of directing God to fulfill our desires, an essential tenet in most world religions, but rather a submissive act in which we allow God to direct our lives for his purposes.[3] "Very early in the morning, while it was still dark, Jesus got up, left the house and went off to a solitary place, where he prayed. Simon and his companions went to look for him, and when they found him, they exclaimed: 'Everyone is looking for you!' Jesus replied, 'Let us go somewhere else—to the nearby villages—so I can preach there also. That is why I have come'" (Mark 1:35–38).

Why had Jesus come? To preach the good news of the kingdom. What was prominent in his preparation for this task? Self-sacrificing prayer. Not just in this instance, but "Jesus often withdrew to lonely places and prayed" (Luke 5:16).

When Jesus finished his farewell to the disciples (John 16), He prayed: "Father, the time has come. Glorify your Son, that your Son may glorify you" (John 17:1). Matthew Henry comments as follows: "Those we preach to, we must pray for. . . . And the word preached should be prayed over, for God gives the increase." "Then Jesus told his disciples a parable to show them that they should always pray and not give up" (Luke 18:1).

The decision to give up, whether a difficult task or a disappointing pursuit, comes at the losing end of a struggle between our best efforts and a seemingly irresolvable barrier. We labor faithfully over a long period of time, without success. The intensity of the struggle increases as we apply more of our attention to removing the barrier until there is no more to give and we collapse under the barrier and our own intense efforts to remove it. Jesus explains that our burdens in ministry are not ours alone. They are laid across our shoulders by the hand of God, our God who will

---

3 In essence Jesus spent an entire night being with God in prayer before he began making disciples by being with the twelve. Ministry is being with God and then being with people. AL

not burden us beyond our ability to
Through prayer.

Conflicts at work? Strife at home
ing results? Self-doubts and fears? A
not give up! *Pray.* Lift every conflict
render to his solution whatever is req
der God's mighty hand, that he may
An authenticating mark of *spiritua*
them surrendered to the Lord through
ter requires cultivation of a self-sacrif

The Servanthood of Jesus

The second dimension of spiritual character—position—is defined by
the servant role Jesus embraced. The apostle Paul moves us beyond the
apparent contradiction of surrender and power in God's scheme of things
as he considered the life and work of Jesus: "Your attitude should be
the same as that of Christ Jesus: Who, being in very nature God, did not
consider equality with God something to be grasped, but made himself
nothing, taking the very nature of a servant, being made in human likeness. And being found in appearance as a man, he humbled himself and
became obedient to death—even death on a cross!" (Phil. 2:5–8).

The Lord of the universe, second person of the Trinity, gave up his
rights as God, took on servant flesh, and gave himself away in discipling,
equipping, and ultimately in crucifixion. In doing so he overcame the
incessant human drive to win over others. The result was a hideous death,
but death was not the end of the story. "Therefore God exalted him to the
highest place and gave him the name that is above every name, that at the
name of Jesus every knee should bow, in heaven and on earth and under
the earth, and every tongue confess that Jesus Christ is Lord, to the glory
of God the Father" (Phil. 2:9–11).

Satan uses our own human weaknesses—ambition, power, pleasure,
and comfort—as points of temptation to draw us away from the Lord.
Beginning with seemingly innocent, albeit self-serving behaviors, we are
pulled toward destruction like canoes swept downstream by the rapids.
Those in ministry and missions are not immune. The ambitious desires
for power, pleasure, and comfort can find their way into the most devoted
lives. Our only defense is living submitted lives: "Yet not my will, but

---

4 "But when you pray, go into your room, close the door and pray to your Father, who is unseen.
Then your Father, who sees what is done in secret, will reward you" (Matt. 6:6).

42). Jesus did this not only at the end of his
in the garden of Gethsemane, but at the beginning
ell. "The devil led him up to a high place and showed
all the kingdoms of the world. And he said to him, 'I
all their authority and splendor, for it has been given to me,
give it to anyone I want to. So if you worship me, it will all be
Jesus answered, 'It is written: "Worship the Lord your God and
e him only"'" (Luke 4:5–8).

The *first battle* for spiritual character is with the self. Having overcome the demands and desires of self, having submitted ourselves
under the mighty hand of God, we find ourselves lifted up by him into
increasingly higher positions of responsibility over others. Here we
find a *second battle* for spiritual character. How will we relate to those
we lead? Does God call us to leadership as missionaries (with people
groups), pastors (with congregations), or teachers (with classes) in order
to "lord it over them"? Or does spiritual leadership call us to self-sacrificing servanthood? Jesus made the point painfully clear: "Jesus called [the
disciples] together and said, 'You know that the rulers of the Gentiles
lord it over them, and their high officials exercise authority over them.
Not so with you. Instead, whoever wants to become great among you
must be your servant, and whoever wants to be first must be your slave—
just as the Son of Man did not come to be served, but to serve, and to
give his life as a ransom for many'" (Matt. 20:25–28).

When we lord it over others, whatever the level of leadership, we can
be sure that we operate out of human power concerns and not spiritual
character concerns. However, this is not to say that Christian leaders
are powerless. As a seminary professor, I hold students accountable for
course requirements. This is not "lording it over them." Holding students
accountable to course requirements is part of the professor's responsibility in an academic process. Failure to do so amounts to dereliction of
duty, leading to unjust treatment of students. Sacrificial service to my students involves such things as personal preparation, course guidelines, fair
examinations, openness to questions, clarity in explanations, availability,
and a heartfelt desire that students in my classes succeed. A lord-it-over-
them attitude translates into personal defensiveness ("*I* am the professor
in this class!"), student abuse ("Your question is not worth a response.
Let's get back to the point."), unclear instructions ("Just know everything
in the text."), arbitrary examinations ("Explain the nature of God and
give two examples."), and a lack of availability and openness.

Similar scenarios can be constructed for missionaries, pastors, and lay leaders. Do missionaries give themselves away for the peoples to whom God called them? Do pastors give themselves away to the congregations God sent them to serve? Do lay leaders give themselves away to the betterment of the followers involved in their ministries? If we can answer a resounding "yes!" then we line up well with the model laid down by the Lord. "You call me 'Teacher' and 'Lord,' and rightly so, for that is what I am. Now that I, your Lord and Teacher, have washed your feet, you also should wash one another's feet. I have set you an example that you should do as I have done for you. I tell you the truth, no servant is greater than his master, nor is a messenger greater than the one who sent him. Now that you know these things, you will be blessed if you do them" (John 13:13–17).

An authenticating mark of *spiritual disciplers* is the degree one finds in them a heart for service to the Lord and others. In order to grow in spiritual character, we must cultivate a self-sacrificing life of service to those God calls us to lead.

The Priority of Jesus

The third dimension of spiritual character is defined by our priorities in life. "So do not worry, saying, 'What shall we eat?' or 'What shall we drink?' or 'What shall we wear?' For the pagans run after all these things, and your heavenly Father knows that you need them. But seek first his kingdom and his righteousness, and all these things will be given to you as well. Therefore do not worry about tomorrow, for tomorrow will worry about itself. Each day has enough trouble of its own" (Matt. 6:31–34).

Our *natural* tendency is to build kingdoms for ourselves—*my* class, *my* church, *my* students, *my* mission. Those who develop a spiritual character intentionally engage a *supernatural* tendency: seeking God's kingdom first. Classes do not exist to give teachers a platform of power. Teachers exist to help students learn and grow for the kingdom's sake. Churches do not exist to give pastors a healthy benefit package and golf on Fridays. Pastors exist to "equip the saints" to help churches learn and grow for the kingdom's sake. People groups do not exist to give missionaries a reason to travel the world. Missionaries exist to help people groups find the Lord, grow in the Lord, and share the Lord with others for the kingdom's sake. As we grow in spiritual character, our priority becomes the Lord's priority, which is doing the will of God.

Jesus gave them this answer: "I tell you the truth, the Son can do nothing by himself; he can do only what he sees his Father doing, because whatever the Father does the Son also does" (John 5:19).

So Jesus said, "When you have lifted up the Son of Man, then you will know that I am the one I claim to be and that I do nothing on my own but speak just what the Father has taught me. The one who sent me is with me; he has not left me alone, for I always do what pleases him." Even as he spoke, many put their faith in him (John 8:28–30).

Jesus replied, "If I glorify myself, my glory means nothing. My Father, whom you claim as your God, is the one who glorifies me" (John 8:54).

Don't you believe that I am in the Father, and that the Father is in me? The words I say to you are not just my own. Rather, it is the Father, living in me, who is doing his work (John 14:10).

So we see painted clearly our Master's perspective of speaking and doing only that which he was led to say and do by the Father. This priority finds its fruition in dying to self. "I tell you the truth, unless a kernel of wheat falls to the ground and dies, it remains only a single seed. But if it dies, it produces many seeds. The man who loves his life will lose it, while the man who hates his life in this world will keep it for eternal life. Whoever serves me must follow me; and where I am, my servant also will be. My Father will honor the one who serves me" (John 12:24–26).

"Lord, I really want a pay raise." No, death to self. "Lord, these people do not appreciate me." No, death to self. "Lord, I'd really like that promotion." No, death to self. "I'd be glad to come and help, but I require travel expenses and honorarium." No, death to self. "Listen! *I* am the expert in this area." No, death to self.

"Lord, my life is yours. My future is yours. Show me what you would have me do, and I will do it without reservation." Ah, *now* you can be exalted!

Spiritual Character and the Teachers' Triad

Chapter 1 introduced you to the Christian Teachers' Triad. In each chapter we will use the triad as a prism to split the dazzling light of discipling into its primary colors of thinking, valuing, and doing. Before considering the refraction of this light of discipleship, however, we need to pay homage to its Source. That Source is God himself, who shines into our lives by faith and brightens every part of our existence as we open ourselves before him. Let's look at the spiritual center of the triad.

The Spiritual Center

The human will exists at the center of the triad, where all three circles overlap. In the natural scheme of things, the "I" (the will) controls what we think, what we value, and what we do. "I'll study this subject until I understand it" (thinking). "This is important to me. I love it!" (valuing). "I want to do this well and will work at doing it better" (doing). There is nothing at all wrong with this. In fact, God created us in this way, enabling us to know him, love him, and serve him. The problem came in the garden, however, when Adam and Eve had some ideas of their own which violated their relationship with God. They valued what God commanded them to avoid. They rebelled against his loving and protecting guidance. When we sin in thought, desire, or action, we place ourselves in conflict with God's best for us.

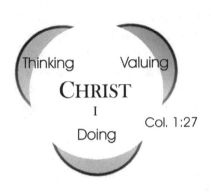

As Christians, we have given our lives—head, heart, and hand—to the Lord. Christ lives within us by the Holy Spirit, to guide us, teach us, comfort us, and equip us for kingdom service. But the development of spiritual character is not automatic. The apostle Paul struggled in the battle between "self-" and "Christ-control" in his own life (Rom. 7–8). His conclusion was that "there is now no condemnation for those who are in Christ Jesus" (Rom. 8:1).

For Paul, union with Christ stands at the center of spiritual growth: "Christ in you, the hope of glory" (Col. 1:27). What, then, must I do to grow in the Lord? I will grow spiritually, develop a more spiritual character, as I think as the Lord thinks, value as the Lord values, and do as the Lord does. Not robotically, of course, but as a person, a free moral agent, created in his image. To become like him, not by edict or threat but by love.

Having established the source of discipling light as the Christ who lives within, let's now refract this light into its three primary colors. We will be discussing each of these components in detail in later chapters. But in this present context, it is helpful to distinguish between natural and supernatural aspects of thinking, feeling, and doing.

Spiritual Concepts: Human Learning Versus Spiritual Thinking. There is a distinction between understanding "in the flesh" and understanding "in the Spirit," even in the context of discipleship. I often heard sermons extolling the virtues of living a "surrendered life" as I was growing up. Church leaders modeled for me the concept of "surrender" through their actions—pastors, teachers, and from time to time missionaries who visited our churches—and their words as they shared out of their own surrendered lives. I learned that an essential aspect of following Christ is to deny myself and take up my cross and follow Jesus. I sang, "All to Jesus I surrender, all to Him I freely give." I surrendered some of my allowance for offerings to help missionaries, the poor, or the building fund. I surrendered some of my time to participate in mission projects and work around the church.

Then at age twenty we faced a major crisis. My bride of six months made the surprising discovery that we were expecting. It was not part of our plan. It was 1969. My military draft number was thirteen. I had no job. I was in college and deeply involved in army ROTC. I was preparing for a career in the corps of engineers and maybe even the special forces! If I withdrew from college, I'd immediately be drafted, and how could I be a good father from Vietnam? All the army reserve units were full with long waiting lists. Yet I needed to secure a job and find a better place for us to live, which wasn't easy in New York City. How on earth could I prepare for the coming of our first child, provide for my family, and remain in school? Barb and I were "surrendered" to the Lord's will. But how were we going to manage this present situation? As we returned to New York from a visit to Barb's parents in northern Illinois, we discussed the problem from every angle.

When we arrived home ten hours later, we still had no answers. No solutions. No idea what to do. And so we did what should have been done at the beginning: we kneeled together before the Lord and surrendered. This surrender went far beyond loose change and an easy hymn-sing. We gave the Lord our lives. "Lord, we have no answers. We will accept any answer you provide. This situation is beyond us, but it is not beyond you. Thank you for the way you will lead us out of this present confusion into your own will."

I can tell you honestly that this was the most frightening prayer I'd ever prayed. It was frightening because I knew what the Lord would do with our surrender. He would send us to Africa as missionaries, which is why I had resisted such a prayer before this. I knew all about Africa because I'd seen several Tarzan movies. How petty those fears seem now, almost forty years later. But at the time I was caught between the harsh reality of an unknown future and the terror of total surrender. How foolish to fear the God who knows the number of hairs on my head.

Over the next three days, through friends and contacts, "coincidences," and "luck,"[5] the Lord walked us through the situation. The results were miraculous. I landed an instructional engineering job on Monday (a miracle for an undergraduate engineering student). I was accepted into an army reserve unit on Tuesday (a miracle at a time when waiting lists were long). But there were significant losses as well. On Wednesday I decided not to continue my education and did not enroll for classes. On Friday I resigned my prized position of commanding officer of our military fraternity—Company H–8, Pershing Rifles—a great honor. I had been on my way to a degree in systems engineering. Now that was suspended. I had every intention of becoming an army officer and serving with the special forces. Now that had been replaced by the humbling reality of being a clerk-typist private (the commanding general's secretary!) in the army reserves.

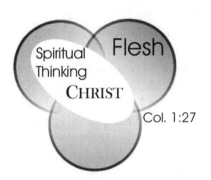

But the problem had been solved! I had a good job (income). I was not in school (time). I was in the reserves (no draft concerns). Everything was in order for the arrival of Tiffany Doran.

And then the greatest loss hit us: one month later Barb miscarried. The baby, the impetus for a complete change in life direction, was gone! "Lord, what was the point? What are you doing?" But we lifted our pain to the Lord and reconfirmed with him our commitment to accept whatever answer he had for us. We had never considered that part of the answer might be the loss of our child.[6]

---

5 I put these terms in quotes because, with God, there are no coincidences. There is no luck, only his will and our desire to live in it.

6 The loss was great, but as we were to learn over the next eleven years, it was not final. In 1978, Bonnie was born, and in 1981, Chris. They were pregnancy numbers six and eight.

A few months later Rodney Webb, missionary to the deaf with the North American Mission Board, came to our church and began a sign language class. We were drawn into the class and helped begin a ministry to deaf people in the area. This was the beginning of an exciting journey into deaf ministry. We moved to Gallaudet College for the Deaf in Washington, D.C., and began a new deaf ministry at Columbia Baptist Church in nearby Falls Church, Virginia. We experienced many joys and struggles in teaching Bible studies for the deaf. Then came the call to seminary training in 1973 and a return to Columbia Baptist as minister of education in 1976, then a return to join the faculty of Southwestern Seminary in 1981. The last four decades have revealed a continual unfolding of the lives God gave us in response to our heartfelt surrender on that single confused evening. My present teaching ministry at Southwestern, as well as my annual teaching trips to the former Soviet Union, can be traced back to the life-changing surrender to the Lord.

This was not my first experience of surrender: I had been saved at the age of six, and I had "surrendered to the ministry" at age fourteen at a summer camp. And there have been many experiences of surrender since that critical evening. But this first "total surrender" experience in the Lord forever redefined the meaning of the term for us. The Holy Spirit infused the term with new, supernatural meaning. This same distinction exists for every word we use in the church—love, joy, peace, justification, sanctification, glorification, prayer, ministry, offering, and on it goes. There are in-the-flesh meanings grasped by our own thinking, and then there are the in-the-Spirit meanings which are quickened by the Lord. Spiritual disciplers may begin with the former but strive toward the latter—strive by means of surrender to the only one who can teach these eternal truths.

God has given us minds by which to study and learn; he has also given us the Spirit to quicken our minds toward supernatural meanings and principles.

Spiritual Passion: Human Emotions Versus Spiritual Affect. A distinction must be made between natural human emotion and supernatural godly passion.[7] Natural human emotions exist as reactions to surrounding circumstances. We are happy when good things happen. We take pleasure in things that make us feel good. We value things that help us, bless us, and place us in better positions in life. On the other hand, we are sad

---

7 I am using *passion* here to mean "deep feeling, zeal, ardent affection, devoted pursuit." Later in the book we will use the term to mean "suffering." We will not use its negative meaning of "ambition, revenge, fear, or hatred"—as in, "His passion (i.e., lust) for money drove him to kill."

when bad things happen. We dislike and avoid those things that make us uncomfortable and uneasy. We detest things that hurt us, condemn us, or take away position or privilege.

Since the mid 1950s, American society has been on a journey through the subjective, a trek of emotion, a climb toward individual self-importance. Beatniks rejected traditional values of family, work, and community to create pockets of individual "coolness." The flower children of the 1960s embraced free love, the death of God, and the adage, "If it feels good, do it." Existential philosophy provided a platform for sub-

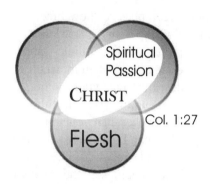

jective, individual choice. In the 1970s and beyond, *Star Wars* popularized the notion real truth could be found only by following one's feelings rather than reason ("Luke, let go of your mind. Feel your way. Let the force be with you!"). Popular culture was taught that human beings were not created, but rather we create ourselves through the choices we make. Reality is what I choose to see as real. Truth is truth that matters to me. Ethics is defined by how I choose to define right and wrong. Beauty is in the eye of the beholder. Humanistic psychology reinforced the "me-ist" perspective of existentialism by emphasizing self, free choice, and emotion. As a result, emotion has overtaken reason in our culture. "How I feel" carries more weight than "what I think." Entertainment has become our highest virtue—in television, in news broadcasts, in our churches.

Yes, even in our churches. Churches throughout history have always appealed to head (Bible, doctrine), heart (music and fellowship), and hand (ministry, missions, and evangelism). But as the culture moved away from reason toward emotion, so has the church. Services increasingly tend to be organized like television programs with segues from one element to another. Sermons increasingly tend toward more visualization with touching stories, video illustrations, PowerPoint slides, drama, and clever wordplays. Music increasingly tends toward performance with specialized praise teams, music synthesizers, dramatic lighting.

This move was inevitable, given our culture's swing, but there is danger here. The Holy Spirit certainly speaks to us through our emotions.

Spirit-filled, Christ-centered, Bible-based contemporary worship touches us at the center of our lives and lifts us up. Worship is not something we do for God but an experience with God. Still, God does not exist in emotions. Worship is more than enthusiastic singing, exciting visuals, and human interest stories. The point is that human emotion does not equate with spiritual affect. Human emotion reacts to external stimuli. Spiritual affect derives only from the internal stimulus, the Lord himself. Therefore, we, like Paul, can "sing psalms [Scripture], hymns [theological poetry] and spiritual songs [choruses] with gratitude in [our] hearts to God" (Col. 3:16).

Scripture, unlike our culture, does not overemphasize "how I feel." Feelings appear as by-products of our relationship with the Lord, not the source of that relationship. Scripture emphasizes how I understand and what I do. We find in Scripture hard commands, framed in harsh-sounding words: deny self, discipline, "follow me," hate your mother, pluck out your eye, cut off your hand, forgive, humble yourself, fulfill your vows, seek gifts that build up the church (rather than yourself), give freely of your time and money, and more. How can I engage in this kind of selflessness and still experience the joy of the Lord? Ah, this is just the point! In order to experience real joy, I must get myself and my own feelings out of the way, for the Lord gives me joy. From this joy grows commitment. And out of commitment, passion.

The writer of Hebrews calls on us to consider the example of the Lord: "Let us fix our eyes on Jesus, the author and perfecter of our faith, who for the joy set before him endured the cross, scorning its shame, and sat down at the right hand of the throne of God" (Heb. 12:2). The pain and shame of crucifixion is portrayed as the path to joy. This truth is central to supernatural affect, in-the-Spirit passion, godly values. God has given us hearts by which to feel, love, and experience life to the fullest. He has also given us the Spirit to quicken our hearts toward supernatural passion and values as we open ourselves to his work.

Spiritual Skills: Human Behavior Versus Spiritual Gifts. Finally, a distinction must be made between natural human work and supernatural ministry. My own human efforts are grounded in my abilities, experience, education, and planning. I can set out five-year plans and write specific life goals. I can focus my efforts in doing only those things which move me toward my goals. Through these principles of self-discipline and focus, I can accomplish a great deal in my life. And yet, if I am not careful, I can spend my whole life building monuments to my own in-the-flesh

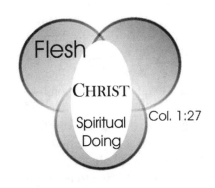

planning and miss the in-the-Spirit ministries that can move mountains in Jesus' name.

Spiritual gifts are discovered through faith-based risk by moving into situations that open to us whether or not we feel prepared for them. We depend on the Lord and do our best. The result is tangible help for others, heartfelt glory to God by those helped, and personal insight into the Lord's will for us. In-the-Spirit ministry can also happen in the moment by means of an unexpected request, unplanned open door, or a sudden problem.

The distinction between in-the-flesh and in-the-Spirit work is found in Paul's own description of how we build on Christ, the only foundation for our ministry.

> For no one can lay any foundation other than the one already laid, which is Jesus Christ. If any man builds on this foundation using gold, silver, costly stones, wood, hay or straw, his work will be shown for what it is, because the Day will bring it to light. It will be revealed with fire, and the fire will test the quality of each man's work. If what he has built survives, he will receive his reward. If it is burned up, he will suffer loss; he himself will be saved, but only as one escaping through the flames (1 Cor. 3:11–15).

In-the-Spirit actions produce spiritual gold, silver, and precious stones. Abel brought a blood sacrifice to the Lord. Noah built an ark on rainless land. Abram left his home in Ur for an unknown home in Palestine. Moses left the riches of Egypt for the wilderness. David trusted his life to God and became a man after God's own heart. Jesus rejected shortcuts to human power and accepted the cross. Stephen preached until he was martyred. Paul gave his life in carrying the gospel to the Gentiles. John was imprisoned on Patmos for his testimony about Christ. Every hero and heroine in Scripture demonstrated in-the-Spirit actions and so produced spiritual gold, silver, and precious stones.

In-the-flesh actions produce wood, hay, and straw. Cain brought a grain offering to God and then killed his brother when he found God was displeased with his offering. (Abel had brought his best to God.

Apparently Cain had not.) Noah celebrated his family's deliverance by drinking too much wine and exposing himself. Abram lied to the pharaoh of Egypt, saying Sarai was his sister and not his wife, to protect himself. Moses killed an Egyptian and fled for his life. David seduced Bathsheba and ordered her husband to the front lines where he was killed. Paul misjudged John Mark's potential and refused to take him along on his second missionary journey.[8]

In our culture today bigger is better. "Supersize it" is a way of life. Importance is measured in terms of salary, house size, or ticket sales. The materialism of our culture infects our churches as well: bigger is better.

God sees it differently. Large churches can be a blessing to many people, but if our goal is to build a large church, we sin. "Unless the LORD builds the house, its builders labor in vain" (Ps. 127:1). Speaking before large crowds of people can bless many, but if our goal is to speak before large crowds, we sin. Success, size, and fame are ego-driven goals. The results of such self-serving goals, even if accomplished, are wood, hay, and straw.

To engage in supernatural ministry, we work where we are, under God's hand, faithfully serving. At the proper time he will open doors to his opportunities of service, which are always more significant than those of our own choosing. The challenge is to maintain a willingness to minister in the smaller places, as the Lord leads. As one Ukrainian student once told me, "Most Americans only want to preach in the large downtown church. They are not interested in preaching in small village churches." Wood, hay, and straw.

God has given us hands with which to work, minister, and faithfully serve the Lord; he has also given us the Spirit to quicken our hands toward supernatural skills and ministry as we open ourselves to his work.

Spiritual maturation grows as Christ grows within us, influencing our thinking, values, and behaviors. Spiritual maturation is expressed well by the hymn "Let Others See Jesus in You." When others hear the truths of God coming from our lips, see the priorities of God flow out of our lives, and observe the manner of our life, that it is worthy of the Lord, they

---

8 John Mark gave up during the first journey and returned home to Jerusalem. Later Barnabas wanted to give him a second chance. Paul refused. So Barnabas, "son of encouragement," took Mark to Cyprus. There he discipled him into a mature leader. Paul chose Silas and set off, with Luke, on the second journey.

Years later, even Paul acknowledged John Mark's contribution to his gospel ministry. He was in prison awaiting execution and asked Timothy to "get Mark and bring him with you, because he is helpful to me in my ministry" (2 Tim. 4:11). John Mark later penned the first Gospel account, which bears his name, the Gospel of Mark.

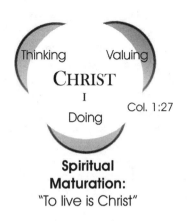

**Spiritual
Maturation:**
"To live is Christ"

know we have been with Christ and that Christ is living in and through us. "He must increase, but I must decrease" (John 3:30 KJV).

Let's pray constantly for an eye of discernment to see the monumental difference between human religion and godly faith, between natural human abilities and supernatural gifts, between human cleverness and godly insight, between manufactured emotion and an overflowing spiritual joy, between wood and gold. May God grant each of us, in our various places of service, an openness before him that he might teach us, shape us, equip us, place us, and use us for his purposes in this world.

George's Problem Revisited

In August 2002, seven months after I received George's request for advice, I received this note:

```
Rick,
    Thanks for the advice. I followed it. It worked!
    Remember a year ago I asked, "What can I do with
Pedro, the deaf leader? He knows little; he can't
read or write, but he is the leader. We leave in
nine months. What can we do to prepare him for our
departure?"
    I expected you to write me at least ten thousand
words of how-to. Instead, you said, "Pray. It is God's
work. He can do it."
    We prayed. We did some teaching. Pedro still can't
read.
    But a couple of Sundays ago he taught. We were not
there. I had not helped him with that lesson. Perhaps
his mother helped a little. She can sign a little bit,
and she is a believer. Monday night the deaf men met
at my house and said Pedro did a great job! They re-
told the story of Moses, the plagues, and crossing the
Red Sea. The fact that they had understood helps me to
know he did a good job teaching.
```

This past Sunday we met with the five deaf leaders who will have full responsibility for the work, along with Liz, a young hearing lady who helps them. They divided the responsibilities among them. Pedro said, "Pablo does not know how to do that, but I will teach him." Miguel said, "I can teach César to do his job." Then Pedro said to Liz, "I don't know how to teach very well, but you can help me." (He who knows not and knows he knows not . . .)

We leave here with the work in good hands, surrounded by the power of God's Holy Spirit. This is so because we and many others prayed. Just like you said we should do!

Thanks, friend,
George

Spiritual character is developed as we learn to die to self, depend on the Lord, and move into the unknown in his name. In practical terms we do this by laying our perceptions, wants, and behaviors against the plumb line of God's Word. God's Word exists in two forms, the living Word of God who lives within us (Christ, Col. 1:27) and the written Word of God (Scripture, 2 Tim. 3:15–16).

The living Word, like the wind, lifts us up, empowers us, leads us in his direction.

The written Word, like a kite string, anchors us, secures us.

Both wind and anchor are required for a kite to fly. Without the wind,  the kite flutters to the ground. Without the anchor, the kite flutters away and eventually falls to the ground. To fly, the kite needs wind and string.

Both wind and anchor are necessary for believers to grow straight and sure. Without the wind we fall into religious legalism. Without the anchor we flutter away into our own truths, our own ways, our own vain imaginations.

In this chapter we have emphasized the wind, the living Word within, in the development of our spiritual character. In the next we will discuss the role of the anchor, the written Word, in developing a biblical character.

Mike's Reaction

Rick's Disciplers' Model begins with the most profound aspect of discipling. The Holy Spirit is our Discipler! If we could just grasp this fact, if we could only grab hold of this one encircling principle, surely we would be well on our way to effective discipling cross-culturally. This is what a personal relationship with God through Jesus Christ depends upon. We are to be followers of Jesus. The Holy Spirit is our coach, our comforter, our teacher, our discipler. He will teach us to know and obey all that Jesus commanded. He will lead us to lead others. Wow! I want to be coached by the Holy Spirit.

Thanks, Rick, for reminding us that spiritual character grows through prayer. I know it. I want to experience it. I'm getting better at it. But I'm a thinker and a doer. My heart sometimes finds it difficult to connect with God through prayer. About twenty-five years ago I broke the first prayer barrier by learning that praying is both talking and listening to God. But I still find myself turning to him in prayer more out of a sense of desperation than a desire to learn or to be continually led by my coach. Father, help me to depend on prayer. Holy Spirit, help me become a better listener when we get together.

Servanthood—our "attitude should be the same as that of Christ Jesus" (Phil. 2:5). I am living this one out every day. The more I listen and learn from the Holy Spirit, the more I like, live, and thrive by serving others and him. Jesus' teachings on leadership didn't make sense in the first-century world of the Roman Empire. They don't make sense today either. His teachings about leadership turn global, universal concepts on their head. The first will be last, the great will be slaves, to live is to die. I cannot grasp this radical concept of leadership without the Holy Spirit instructing me along the way. I just cannot handle the temptations of power, recognition, ambition, and worldly position. I must be led by the Spirit of God.

Spiritual character encircles all that we are as disciplers. In the following chapters we will see the recurring reality that if we are not totally plugged in to God's Spirit, there is nothing we can do to make his kingdom happen. Developing Christlike character in the life of a discipler depends on the power and leadership of the Holy Spirit.

The Biblical Character
of cross-cultural
Disciplers

Disciplers' Model

3

Developing a Biblical Character
Mike Barnett

Whatever you have learned or received or heard from me,
or seen in me—put it into practice.
Philippians 4:9

The discipler lives a life of biblical character—putting into practice
the principles, teachings, and models of the Bible as demonstrated
through the life of Jesus Christ. Continually depending on the leadership
of the Holy Spirit, the discipler becomes more like Christ and, as a result,
is better able to connect with cross-cultural learner-leaders than those
who do not. Chapter 3 surveys one of the foundation stones of the model,
the Bible as God's eternal truth, and identifies how living a life of biblical
character communicates Christ across cultures.

The Toxic Flip Side

Preaching biblical truths while *living* by our own cultural norms
"Talking the Talk" without "Walking the Walk"

"A Very Religious Christian" in Somalia

Nathan was a young relief and development worker on a mobile im-
munization program in the rural villages of the bread basket of war-torn
Somalia. One night he and ten of his expatriate colleagues were rounded
up and taken hostage by the militia of a Muslim clan leader and warlord.
They were detained in a small UN residence. At first they were asked to
remain silent. As time went on, they began to get to know their captors.
Some of the hostages were held at gunpoint and roughed up a bit. At one
point Nathan was threatened with a bayonet held to his chest and throat.

One day a delegation from the warlord arrived with his son to talk with
the hostages. One man was obviously a bigwig. He was the warlord's
minister of foreign relations. Nathan's captor/guard friend, Abdul-ahi,
suddenly took Nathan's hand and presented him to the minister! When he

introduced him, he said, "This is Mr. Nathan, who is a religious Christian." Nathan nearly fell over in his tracks because he and Abdul-ahi had yet to talk about his faith in Jesus Christ. It was definitely on Nathan's to-do list, but the opportunity hadn't presented itself. Nathan wondered what possessed Abdul-ahi to do that. How had Nathan's biblical character shown through without a single spoken word of witness? More important, what was the Muslim minister going to do with Nathan?

The Left Foundation Stone: The Bible—
God's Eternal Word

The left foundation stone of the model represents the Bible, God's eternal Word. Missions and ministry involve all sorts of religious activities. But unless these efforts produce a clearer understanding of the Bible, with its call to personal commitment to Christ and his church, our efforts may produce little more than "wood, hay or straw" (1 Cor. 3:12). For teaching to be rightly called Christian, it must be built upon the sure foundation of God's Word. Theories of inspiration abound, conflicting interpretations thrive, but God's Word still speaks across the ages to people of all cultures today. How does the Bible define itself?

Disciplers' Model

The Bible is divinely inspired. Scripture emphasizes that the Lord, not man, speaks through the Word.

"Take a scroll and write on it all the words I [the Lord] have spoken to you" (Jer. 36:2).

The word of the Lord came to Ezekiel (Ezek. 1:3).

The Scripture had to be fulfilled which the Holy Spirit spoke long ago through the mouth of David (Acts 1:16).

All Scripture is God-breathed and is useful for teaching, rebuking, correcting and training in righteousness (2 Tim. 3:16).

For the prophecy never had its origin in the will of man, but men spoke from God as they were carried along by the Holy Spirit (2 Pet. 1:21).

The Lord spoke, and man recorded the message. The Lord revealed himself, and man recorded the experiences. The Bible exists above human culture, drawing believers from every culture into a new culture, the kingdom of God.

The Bible is sacred. Scripture warns its readers and teachers not to alter it by adding to it or taking away from it. "Do not add to what I command you and do not subtract from it, but keep the commands of the LORD your God that I give you" (Deut. 4:2). "Every word of God is flawless; he is a shield to those who take refuge in him. Do not add to his words, or he will rebuke you and prove you a liar" (Prov. 30:5–6). While Scripture is interpreted through cultural norms, care must be taken not to distort Scripture by cultural norms.

The Bible is powerful in its influence. Scripture is more than words and symbols. It is an extension of God's power. "The gospel . . . is the power of God for the salvation of everyone who believes" (Rom. 1:16). "Take the . . . sword of the Spirit, which is the word of God" (Eph. 6:17). "It judges the thoughts and attitudes of the heart" (Heb. 4:12). By implication we can declare scriptural power extending to every culture, to "everyone who believes" (John 3:15).

The Bible was written for a purpose. John wrote, "But these are written that you may believe that Jesus is the Christ, the Son of God, and that by believing you may have life in his name" (John 20:31). Later in life John wrote again, "I write these things to you . . . so that you may know that you have eternal life" (1 John 5:13). The purpose of Scripture is also our purpose as missionaries: that others may discover true life as we reach them in Jesus' name.

The Bible reveals eternal truth. Scripture moves us upward from our daily experiences within our own cultures to eternal principles. "Your Word, O LORD, is eternal; it stands firm in the heavens" (Ps. 119:89). "The word of our God stands forever" (Isa. 40:8). "My words will never pass away" (Matt. 24:35). "But the word of the Lord stands forever" (1 Pet. 1:25). When we properly understand scriptural truths apart from our own personal culture, we are more likely to find receptive ears for our reaching and teaching.

How Do Teachers Use the Bible?

God's Word is eternal truth. Few would argue about the nature of Scripture. But how do we handle Scripture as we teach? Whether we are effective in helping learners grow spiritually depends directly on how we handle Scripture. Even with the highest regard for Scripture, we may not help our learners grow in the Lord. What makes the difference?

Talk about it. A popular way to teach Scripture is to talk about it. I remember spending hours each week preparing to teach the lesson on Sunday. I read the assigned passage, studied the accompanying teaching helps, and wrote out several pages of notes: my lesson. On Sunday morning I stood behind a podium or at a desk and taught my lesson. Yet several days later members of my class remembered little of what I had worked so hard to teach. How could they become "doers of the Word" if they couldn't remember what the Bible said? Telling people about the Bible is a good first step, but there is a better way to help people grow as they learn.

"Let the Bible Speak." The better way to handle Scripture in teaching situations, and the approach I've found to be helpful in really changing learners, is to *let the Bible speak.* When I ask thoughtful questions and lead learners into God's Word for the answers, I find that they remember what we've studied far better than when I simply give them my own ready-made answers. They find answers to their own concerns within their own culture. The Bible, God's eternal truth, is the sure foundation of discipling Bible study. Let us unsheathe our swords! Let the Word speak across cultures that it may convict and comfort, warn and console, revive and refresh—so we might all become what he intends and do all he commands.[1]

---

1 I would take this thought one step further and say, "Let the Bible Teach!" One of the greatest ways to let the Bible speak is to teach our students to study the Bible for themselves. Helping students discover the Bible on their own gives them the skills to use the Bible anywhere at any time. There is nothing more freeing for disciplers than to rely on the wisdom and power of the Bible in all situations of life. When learners can personally apply the Bible to their lives, it will speak beyond personal and cultural barriers. When your students learn how the Bible can be their teacher, they can in turn teach others.

Common skills we try to teach cross-culturally are Bible reading and application. This does not have to be complicated to be effective. In several churches we encourage all of the members to read their Bibles daily, and then once a week we have a special sharing time where each person can share a favorite verse for the week. We encourage them to teach themselves, read the Word, and then compare their readings to find the verse that means the most to them. These habits over time build a church that knows and applies the Bible to their lives. AL

The Operating Manual

One would expect evangelical believers to build their ministries on a biblical foundation. "Fine," you may say. "I believe the Bible; now I am ready to get on with the part about discipling the nations." "Not so fast," I say. Remember the warning about "wood, hay, and stubble"? The minister who builds his or her life and ministry on a weak view of Scripture is a nonstarter. The tentmaker who neglects God's Word in his or her daily course of life is impotent. The missionary who fails to use God's Word as an operating manual for missions is foolish. On the other hand, disciplers build on the strong foundation of Scripture.

The most common mistake of a pastor, teacher, or missionary may be taking the Bible for granted. How important is this Bible foundation stone for the discipler? It defines God's mission and outlines the assignment of the discipler. It is the authoritative source of God's eternal truth. God's Word connects across all cultures. It is the primary tool of the discipler in equipping other disciplers. "In what way?" you ask. Let's look at three ways.

The Manual Protects Your Call

Much is made in missions circles about the call of God. This is the most critical question facing those applying for missionary service. What is God's call on *your* life? Where has he called *you* to go? What has he called *you* to do? Who has he called *you* to serve? Which agency has he called you to serve with? In the case of a young couple applying for missions service, the pressure is on *both* to communicate clearly God's call to be a missionary. Experts insist that if you don't nail down the missionary call you won't survive the tough times on the field. It's a critical issue. It's a tough question.

But for me the question is upside down! We should not be focusing on the *what, where, who,* and *which* that *we* are all about. We should focus on the what, where, who, and which that *God* is all about. You may say it's just semantics. I don't think so. I challenge my students to focus on *God's* mission and purpose and simply answer the question, "Where do I fit in *your* mission, God?" Once we realize that God's mission is to bless all peoples on earth, and once we understand that his purpose is to be worshipped by all peoples on earth, then the answers to the what, where, who, and which questions will come from the right perspective—God's perspective!

Where do we learn about God's mission and purpose. You guessed it—in his operating manual, the Bible.

God's Mission. The Bible reveals God's mission (*missio Dei*)[2] to reach his creation. It outlines his master plan or strategy to connect with every people on earth. This peoples-focused mission is based on a God-centered dynamic of God being glorified and thereby glorifying. The essence of God's mission is seen in his love for all peoples and their love for him and for one another. The result of this mission of God is that the Father's name is exalted, made famous, by the life and witness of the Son through the leadership of the Holy Spirit upon the lives of his people. Sound complicated? Let's dig into the Manual and learn more.

The Bible tells "The Story of God's Glory,"[3] from Genesis to Revelation. The strategy is rolled out with God's promise to Abraham of "a blessing for all peoples" (see Gen. 12:2–3). It is a drama about God—his blessing, his name, his honor, his fame, his glory. And God himself is the starring actor through the three-in-one cast of Father, Son, and Holy Spirit. God makes the promise. God provides the promised land (Gen. 13:14–16). God builds a nation (Gen. 13:16; 15:5). God gives the blessing (Gen. 17:7; 26:4). God sends his Son (John 3:16). The Holy Spirit connects with the nations through his church (Acts 1:8; Eph. 3:10). God fulfills his mission of a blessing for all peoples on earth.

God's Purpose. But there is more to the mission than the blessing! The dictionary defines *mission* as "an assigned or self-imposed duty or task," a "calling [or] vocation." If God's mission is his vocation or his task, and if it is based on his promise to Abraham, then *why* is this his mission? What is God's purpose in blessing all peoples? The answer: his glory! God *will* be glorified by all peoples on earth. This is the purpose behind the mission. That every people on earth would know and worship the one true living God, thereby blessing or glorifying God and receiving a blessing or glory in the process![4] God says, "Be still, and know that I am God; I will be exalted among the nations, I will be exalted in the earth" (Ps. 46:10). This is God's motive for the promise to Abraham. This is the reason behind the mission. God will not fail. He assures a stubborn Israel that he will not give up on them in spite of their faithlessness. He

---

2 For a complete discussion of *missio Dei*, see John A. McIntosh, "Missio Dei," *Evangelical Dictionary of World Missions,* ed. A. Scott Moreau (Grand Rapids: Baker Books, 2000), 631–33.

3 Steven C. Hawthorne, "The Story of His Glory" in *Perspectives on the World Christian Movement,* 3rd ed., ed. Ralph D. Winters and Stephen C. Hawthorne (Pasadena, Calif.: William Carey Library, 1999), 34–48.

4 John Piper, *Let the Nations Be Glad!: The Supremacy of God in Missions,* 2nd ed. (Grand Rapids: Baker Academic, 2003).

proclaims, "For my own name's sake I delay my wrath; for the sake of my praise I hold it back from you, so as not to cut you off. . . . For my own sake, for my own sake, I do this. How can I let myself be defamed? I will not yield my glory to another" (Isa. 48:9, 11).

God is on mission to reach all peoples on earth so he can be glorified. Sounds sort of self-centered on God's part, doesn't it? Yes and no. God-centered, yes. Self-serving, no. God doesn't need to be glorified by us. We need to glorify him! He desires that we glorify him, the one true living God. We were created to glorify him. The *essence* or nature of this mission of God is his love. God is not on mission to bless all peoples because he is obligated. Likewise we are not drawn to worship and glorify him out of a sense of duty. God so loves us that he is committed to connecting with us so we can love him and reflect that love to one another (John 3:16; 13:34; Matt. 22:37–40). And the good news is that he will accomplish his mission to bless all peoples. We don't have to wait for the end of the story of God's glory. It's already there! On that day God celebrates his final glory through the worship of "every nation, tribe, people and language" on earth (Rev. 7:9). This is God's mission accomplished across cultures. It is revealed in his manual, the Bible.

God's Perspective. OK, that's an interesting sprint through a theology of God's mission, but how does all of this protect our call? The answer: it keeps us focused on God's perspective, on his agenda more than ours. If we continuously feed off of God's story of his glory among all nations, if we understand the big picture of God's strategy, if we constantly tell the story, if our perspective is all about God's purpose not ours, if we naturally look to the Bible for lessons on how God fulfills his mission of a blessing for all peoples, then we will be less likely to fall into the pit of petty, self-centered, small thinking. We'll stay on track as we serve on mission with the master cross-cultural discipler!

The God-Sized Global Vision of Paul. The apostle Paul practiced this discipline of looking to God's Word for a constant reminder of God's mission. You can hear the excitement in his voice when he reports to the church at Colossae that "all over the world this gospel is bearing fruit and growing, just as it has been doing among you" (Col. 1:6). Paul wasn't exaggerating. He was telling the story. Paul was not a small thinker. He had God-sized vision. Even in the midst of a pastoral letter of instruction to the disciples of Colossae, he cast the big-picture vision of a God on mission throughout the whole world! God's mission was ingrained in Paul's talk and walk.

God's global vision is reflected in Paul's missions strategies. For two years in Ephesus, he preached and taught in the hall of Tyrannus in a way that the entire region of ancient Turkey heard the gospel (Acts 19:10). Paul was about more than planting a single church in Ephesus or even establishing the first Christian seminary on earth! He was on mission with God among all peoples, even from the city of Ephesus. He stays on task "to preach the gospel where Christ was not known." He was always headed to the "Spains" of his world—to the least-reached people on earth (Rom. 15:20–24). This was his call! This is where he fit on mission with God.

Where did Paul get this God-sized, global vision? And how did Paul protect his call to preach the gospel among the Gentiles? By holding tight to the biblical mandate, the mission of God, the promise to Abraham, the Great Commission. Paul taught the mission of God to those he discipled. He taught straight from the Bible. He reminded the "children of Abraham" in Galatia that the "Scripture foresaw that God would justify the Gentiles by faith, and announced the gospel in advance to Abraham: 'All nations will be blessed through you.' So those who have faith are blessed along with Abraham . . . in order that the blessing given to Abraham might come to the Gentiles through Christ Jesus, so that by faith we might receive the promise of the Spirit" (Gal. 3:8–9, 14). So Paul used Scripture to teach the mission of God to those he discipled. And he practiced what he taught. He "put . . . into practice" what he learned (Phil. 4:9). Paul's biblical character was reflected in his life and work. For him it was all about God's mission.

Case in Point: The Thirty-Year Legacy of Jim and Susan

They were well-known veteran missionaries. They had served twenty-five years in one of the least reached Middle Eastern countries on earth. And they were in big trouble! Their missions agency was in the midst of a major restructuring, and a new paradigm was being touted. Everything was being reassessed and evaluated. It had been a long time coming. Younger, less experienced missionaries from very different parts of the world arrived on the scene in new roles of strategy leadership. Everything was changing. New terms, new concepts, new policies, new procedures. Jim and Susan's world was crumbling around them. And now it was their turn to meet with the new leader and evaluate their past ministry and propose a future assignment.

The fact is, they had been dodging this strategic bullet for years. Looking back on their twenty-five years of international missions service was like remembering one career crisis after another. First they were assigned to evangelize an Arab Muslim minority population in their country. It started out well enough, but they just couldn't connect with the language and culture of the Arabs. They loved the international community and seemed to thrive in the expatriate ghetto of the capital city, but their work among the local people group was a nonstarter.

Next they were assigned to the majority population, again in the role of evangelist. It just wasn't a match. The language continued to be a challenge, and they were reluctant to leave the capital city, where better schools for their kids were available. The mission needed administrative help, so they found themselves increasingly immersed in the business of managing the mission and less involved in evangelizing the locals.

Every transition and reassignment was difficult. The mission met annually to review missionary assignments, approve resource allocations, and conduct peer evaluations. They did not look forward to these annual critiques. They knew deep inside their hearts that they were not serving according to God's plan.

Finally after about eighteen years, they seemed to find their niche. Jim was asked by some expatriates to pastor their small English-speaking church. At least he was able to be involved in ministry, and Susan worked alongside him as she led worship and played the piano. After all, this is how they had served years ago in the United States. The other missionaries knew that this did not fit their strategy to focus on the large numbers of unreached nationals in the land, but after all, Jim and Susan were veteran missionaries, and they had earned the right to enjoy this assignment.

But today they faced another day of reckoning! The new paradigm had arrived, and it didn't seem to have room for a twenty-five-year veteran North American missionary pastor of an English-speaking church made up of a few international expatriates.

So here they were, sitting in the fast-food restaurant with the new leader. After the cordial conversation the new leader cut to the chase. He only asked one question. "Jim, tell me, what is the legacy of your twenty-five years of missions work in this country?" Jim sat and thought about the question. Susan looked at him and waited hopefully for his response. They sat there, rewinding the tapes of their lives over the past twenty-five years. Jim looked at Susan, inviting her response. Nothing. Time passed, seconds ticked into minutes that seemed like an hour. Tears began to well up in both their eyes as they realized they could not answer the question.

It was a new question for them, one they had never really contemplated. The three of them sat there in the local hamburger joint. First they cried, then prayed, and finally began to talk out the significance of their inability to answer that one question.

Over the years Jim and Susan had forgotten why they came to this Middle Eastern country on the other side of the world. In fact, the more they talked, they realized they were so focused on themselves—their jobs, titles, status, recognition, kids, house, car, and ministry—they lost sight of their original call to be on mission with God as disciplers across cultures. They no longer saw the big picture, the biblical picture. They forgot that this was to be all about God's mission, not theirs! Their biblical character had suffered. They still claimed the promises of the Bible. Jim preached from God's Word every Sunday. But the essence of the message was not God centered but Jim and Susan centered. Their heads turned from God's mission to theirs. The pressure was on *them* to succeed rather than participate in God's success. They were stuck in the toxic flip-side mode of "talking the talk without walking the walk."

The good news is that it is never too late to return to the discipline of building biblical character. It is never too late to learn about God's mission. Jim and Susan revisited the biblical basics of God's plan for the nations and reconnected with their call of twenty-five years ago. It wasn't easy. But gradually they began to see the critical issues of the past in a different way. They recommitted their loyalties, not to the mission board, the ministry, the expatriate community of their country, or even their family but to the purposes of God. They accepted a new assignment in a new land. But it freed them to pursue openly God's mission in a new way. Jim and Susan recovered their call to missions.

The biblical narrative and mandate for God's mission keeps us on track as we disciple across cultures. It focuses us on God's mission, his purpose, and his perspective. It keeps us from falling into a self-focused world of small thinking. It puts the things of the world into proper perspective. It confronts us with the big picture of God's plan. It protects our call to be on mission with God among all nations.

The Manual Transforms Your Life and Empowers Your Witness

Not only does a strong biblical character keep us in touch with the big picture of God's mission and protect our call, but it also transforms our everyday life and empowers our witness. In the same way that prayer is the energy node for spiritual character development, God uses the Bible to grow and develop biblical character.

Case in Point: Rebooting Your Bible Program

I was an international missionary in the early 1990s assigned to provide strategy support for one of the most creative missions teams of the latter part of the twentieth century. My wife and I worked from our southeast England base and had the privilege of developing financial and logistical support systems for what became a force of over five hundred missions workers in the 10/40 Window. I traveled around the world, participating in cutting-edge strategy sessions that were truly creating the future of international missions. I met and worked with some of the most passionate people on mission with God among the least reached peoples on earth. It was the missions opportunity of a lifetime. Nothing is better than being plugged right in the middle of where God wants you. We were there.

But all was not well. I'm a strong doer and a thinker on the learner's triad. I was plenty busy doing things for God's mission. The hours were brutal, but the challenge was worth the effort. We were at the top of our game as missions workers. I cannot remember a time in my life when I was more fulfilled in my work. My time with family and church was also on track. I was worshipping, praying, and reading God's Word daily! I was not in some kind of missionary burnout syndrome. There was plenty of energy to spare. I was "in" God's Word, but something was missing.

I really noticed the problem at an annual conference of 10/40 Window workers. By the end of the meeting, I knew I had a problem. Many of my colleagues were connected spiritually to God's Word. The Bible was their operating manual for life and witness. Everything they were about was connected to God's Word in a way that I had not experienced for years in Christ. I wanted—I needed what my colleagues were experiencing. At the end of the conference, I planned to meet with my leader, Mike Stroope, and discuss my problem, but time didn't seem to allow it. Three hundred workers wanted to bend Mike's ear; and though we talked almost daily about work issues, it seemed I wasn't going to be able to confide in Mike about my situation.

The meeting was over. Families headed back to buses and trains after breakfast. The logistics teams that I led were fully engaged in moving everyone from the conference center to far points around the world. I was walking through the upstairs dorm rooms of the college campus where we met, just making sure that nothing was being left behind, and suddenly there was Mike, standing in the hallway. "Hey Barnett!" he greeted me in his characteristic coach mode. "Great meeting. You guys did a great job with the logistics." "Thanks," I replied. "So, how are *you* doing?" he asked. We sat together on a bench in the hallway upstairs in a dingy English dormitory, and I began to tell Mike about my problem. He knew exactly where I was coming from. My team leader and mentor led me to realize that all of us cross the path of disconnecting from God's Word at one time or another. Mike shared with me some secrets from his own life in the Bible. We made a mutual commitment that day to hold each other accountable to keep the connections between us and God's Word alive and well.

It was really that simple. It was a matter of encouragement, commitment, and accountability for me. I started out reading through Isaiah as Mike suggested. Nothing special happened for the first few weeks, but as I e-mailed Mike about business and we checked each other on our Bible reading and its relevance to our lives and work, I found that God's Word came alive for me once again. I came back to the biblical basis of my decision to follow Christ as a nineteen-year-old university student. I began to measure my life as a disciple, husband, father, and missions worker against the biblical standard of Christ. I found answers to the why questions regarding our missions strategies to engage the least reached peoples on earth. I rediscovered the purpose and nature of the church under Christ. The former boldness of my witness returned. I was able to tell others my story—the story of God's glory in my life. The doing and thinking parts of my life and work didn't let up. In fact, as I look back on it today, I realize that the months that followed were even more challenging. How could I have made it without a red-hot connection with the Bible?

As time passed, Mike and I ended up on separate paths. But the effects of that time in my life continue. That rebooting of my Bible program resulted in a season of intensive study regarding my missiology, my understanding of God's mission and how I fit into it. Now I teach and train others about the vital nature of the operating Manual for life, witness, and missions involvement. Mike and I stay in touch though we serve God's mission from separate platforms today. But I'll never forget how he walked me through that reboot experience. It made all the difference in the life of this cross-cultural discipler.

Make room for God's Word. It sounds too simple, but the first step for developing a biblical character that empowers our life and witness is simply to make room for God's Word! In a sense I had allowed my biblical database to become cluttered with other stuff to the point that I needed to purge some files, defragment some drives, and reboot my Bible program. I wasn't giving God's Word the time, space, and reflection it required.

Jesus taught the Pharisees a lesson on this same issue. In John 8, Jesus is teaching the crowds the gospel in a kind of temple court dialogue. The Pharisees are challenging Jesus' theology. Jesus is teaching these religious leaders the truth about the law, sin, and grace (vv. 34–36); but they cannot see it. They are bound by what they know. They only hear Messiah's words through the context of their version of faith and practice. They cannot escape their worldly understanding of God and his purposes. Jesus tells them straight up, "You have no room for my word" (v. 37). Nothing he says will make a difference in their lives until they stop and make room in their minds and hearts for a new Word from God. They are stuck in their self-perpetuating game of religious jousting. The databases of their souls are full. They need to reboot their Bible program.

An effective cross-cultural discipler continually makes room for God's Word. Just do it!

Be a learner, not merely a knower! Like the Pharisees, what we know often gets in the way of what we need to know. During that same theological dialogue in the temple courts, Jesus challenged the Jews who believed in him, "If you hold to my teaching, you are really my disciples. Then you will know the truth, and the truth will set you free" (vv. 31–32). But even those who believe struggle to learn and live the true Word of God. It's as though they are paralyzed and cannot do the will of the heavenly Father but are only doing "the things [their] own father does" (v. 41). They judge everything by the human standards that they themselves institutionalized (v. 15). They can't recognize God even when he stands before them. The Pharisees are caught on the "toxic flip side" of biblical character. They are "talking the talk without walking the walk."

Don't do it! Think *learner* not *knower*. At the Southern Baptist International Learning Center in Rockville, Virginia, hundreds of outgoing missionaries are consistently taught to be learners. It's the first step in the humbling experience of entering another culture and learning another language. The new missionaries are warned, "If you start thinking you're an expert, get ready, you're probably headed for a crisis." We should approach everyone we meet and everything we do as learners—disciples of God's Word—especially those we want to hear the gospel. We need to avoid the arrogance of theological and missiological self-indulgence.

God's Word is powerful. Let it teach us new things about God's mission among all peoples and where we fit. Let the Bible empower our life and witness.

Teach God's empowering Word. If we make room for God's Word as our manual for life and witness, if we approach God's Word as a learner more than a knower, then God's Word, the Bible, will transform our life and empower our witness. The apostle Paul says that he was "not ashamed of the gospel, because it is the power of God for the salvation of everyone who believes" (Rom. 1:16). It is the power of God, this story of God's glory! For those connected to God's Word, it is easier to tell the story. We have a real, up-to-date, alive story to tell. It is God's story about our life, not our story about God's.

Of course, the whole purpose of developing biblical character is to be effective disciplers. Discipleship involves teaching others about Jesus. When the Bible is central to who we are and how we live, our teaching will be powerful. It will impact more than the heads of those we are teaching. It will transform hearts and result in acts of obedience. Paul reminds Titus of this dynamic of biblical character and how it relates to our witness—to what we teach.

Paul outlines sound doctrines for Titus to teach the church. He should teach the older men to be worthy of respect in their behavior, doctrine, and service. Likewise, older women should model for the younger women how to live godly, biblical lives as faithful wives and mothers. Young men should set the example for others by living self-controlled lives and doing what is good. Then Paul coaches Titus, "In your teaching show integrity, seriousness and soundness of speech that cannot be condemned, so that those who oppose you may be ashamed because they have nothing bad to say about us" (Titus 2:7–8). In other words, Titus is to "talk the talk" of the Bible but also to "walk the walk"! Titus "must hold firmly to the trustworthy message" (Titus 1:9). He "must teach what is in accord with sound doctrine" (Titus 2:1). And as a result, those who receive his witness and teachings "may be careful to devote themselves to doing what is good . . . [what is] excellent and profitable for everyone" (Titus 3:8). If we make room for God's manual, if we learn it well, if we teach it to others, our life and the lives of others will be transformed. Our witness will be empowered.[5]

---

5 One observation from an experienced missionary is that the learners who stay learners on the field make it long-term. Ten, twenty, even thirty years later, they are effectively growing and ministering on the field. Those that are not continuing learners don't last long; and if they do, they become ineffective, like old, dried, inedible raisins. AL

This is how it works. This is the result of biblical character in the life of a cross-cultural discipler.

The Manual Informs Our Strategy

As I teach classes and seminars on strategic thinking, I am amazed at how few of those called to lead the church actually think strategically! There are always one or two nay-sayers in the group who criticize me for using corporate-speak and business tactics regarding spiritual matters. They protest that we shouldn't apply secular principles to God's work. They imply that God isn't a strategic thinker himself. This is simply wrong! If there is one thing the Bible reveals in its entirety, it's that God *is* a strategic thinker and planner. The Bible reveals his master plan for reaching the world. It tells us the entire story of God's glory beginning with Abraham, Israel, Messiah, the church, and God's eternal reign. The Bible provides a picture of that glorious day when all will be judged and all peoples will worship the Lamb at the foot of the throne of God. The Bible is all about God's plan, his strategy.

So it stands to reason that if we want to learn how to be on mission with God, we should learn from him, from his manual! I'm not just talking about learning the great theological truths about God. I'm talking about learning and practicing the patterns and methods that he models in his mission work. I'm talking about going to the Bible for methods for evangelism and church planting. We should learn from God's experiences in communicating the gospel across cultures. We must look to God's Word for examples and models of what the church is to be and how it is to disciple across cultures.

If we cling to the practical principles, patterns, and methods of the Bible, we will be better disciplers. I've seen it many times on the mission fields. Let's look at just one example of what happens when we base our discipling strategy on God's manual.

Case in Point: The Watsons and the Man of Peace Model

In 1989 Southern Baptists appointed strategy coordinators David and Jan Watson to serve among the millions of Bhojpuri-speaking people of northern India. Their task was to develop and implement a strategy that would result in a church planting movement of hundreds of churches planting churches among this unreached people. Their initial strategy was to use experienced evangelists from southern India to preach the gospel in northern villages. It had worked well in southern India. They expected a good result in the north. The Watsons were devastated when their first six evangelists were brutally murdered.[6]

David spent the next two years struggling with feelings of guilt and discouragement. He searched his soul and every source of missions strategy available and could not see a way forward in the work among the Bhojpuri. Desperately he began to search the Scriptures for answers. One day God spoke to him. He should not abandon the Bhojpuri because of this tragic martyrdom of six faithful Indian brothers in Christ. He should use the same strategy that Jesus did in a similar situation. In the Bible Luke 10 reports that Jesus sent out seventy-two disciples two by two "like lambs among wolves" (v. 3). He instructed them, "When you enter a house, first say, 'Peace to this house.' If a man of peace is there, your peace will rest on him; if not, it will return to you. Stay in that house. . . . Do not move around from house to house [but when you] are welcomed, eat what is set before you. Heal the sick . . . and tell them, 'The kingdom of God is near you'" (Luke 10:5–9).

Watson reequipped and facilitated dozens of Indian evangelists to take the gospel back into the north. They didn't preach openly in public. They watched and waited for men and women of peace; and when they found one, they stayed and discipled. The results of this "man of peace" strategy among the Bhojpuri are well documented today. In the year 2000 moderate estimates indicated some forty-three hundred Bhojpuri churches with approximately 300,000 baptized members. David Watson's biblical character drew him back to Scripture to search not just for some theological principle but to find a practical model for discipling across hostile cultures. The result was a church planting movement among the Bhojpuri.

Observe people-to-people patterns. The Bible is full of practical patterns and methods for discipling across cultures. One of the most consistent patterns of New Testament discipleship involves God's method of resource management. It takes resources to bless all people on earth! And God's Bible consistently reveals that the primary resource in his strategy is *people*. This is the mystery of God's plan. He uses his fallen creation to reach his fallen creation. He uses "jars of clay" to carry the precious treasure of the gospel of "the glory of God in the face of Jesus Christ" (2 Cor. 4:6–7) to all creation. Of course, the end result is that he is glori-

---

6 This story is based on the author's firsthand knowledge and David Garrison's *Church Planting Movements: How God Is Redeeming a Lost World* (Lubbock, Tex.: WIGTAKE Resources, 2004), 33–35.

fied because we realize that clay pots can't claim the credit. And isn't this mystery revealed even in that first promise from God to Abraham—"and all peoples on earth will be blessed through you" (Gen. 12:3). Those who receive the blessing will be the conduit through which the blessing flows to all peoples on earth!

So God's number one resource in accomplishing his mission is people. Not money, buildings, endorsements, media exposure, programs, political influence but people. Surely the best biblical model for this people strategy of God is seen in Jesus' approach. Though he preached and ministered to thousands, he invested his life and ministry in the discipleship of the twelve. And it was this small band of Galileans plus Paul the apostle whom God used to change the world.

The greatest evangelist of the twentieth century, Billy Graham, was asked in an interview by *Christianity Today* what his strategy would be if he were the pastor of a large church. Graham replied that he would follow the pattern that Christ set. Graham explained that Jesus "spent most of his time with twelve men. He didn't spend it with a great crowd. In fact, every time he had a great crowd . . . there weren't too many results. The great results . . . came in his personal interview and in the time he spent with his twelve."[7] Even the premier mass evangelist understands that the pattern projected by the Bible is people-to-people discipling.[8] Jesus was the master cross-cultural discipler. His life is characterized by a passion to serve people. This is a prominent aspect of the biblical character of a discipler.

Teach them to walk the walk! Aren't you glad that the manual really does have everything we need to disciple others effectively! Jesus taught the great truths and principles of the kingdom of God. He modeled these principles as he lived among the disciples. He taught the disciples how to pray—"your kingdom come" (Matt. 6:10). Notice, it's still all about God. He coached them as he sent them out into the masses to tell the story of God's glory. He commanded them to be witnesses to all peoples—in their Jerusalem, Judea and Samaria, to the ends of the earth (Acts 1:8).

---

7 Ken Adams, "He Said 'Go and Make Disciples!'" Impact Ministries Web site, www.impactdiscipleship.com/pdfs/; Patrick M. Morley, "The Five Defining Disciplines of Growing Men," Man in the Mirror Web site, www.maninthemirror.org/alm/alm14.htm, accessed 19 December 2003.

8 "Second Timothy 2:2 is a little like a mathematical formula for spreading the gospel and enlarging the church. Paul taught Timothy; Timothy shared what he knew with faithful men; these faithful men would then teach others also. And so the process goes on and on. If every believer followed this pattern, the church could reach the entire world with the gospel in one generation! Mass crusades in which I believe and to which I have committed my life, will never finish the Great Commission; but a one-by-one ministry will." Billy Graham, *The Holy Spirit* (Waco: Word, 1978), 147. AL

But he didn't stop there. He also left them with specific instructions on how to disciple!

Matthew 28 is much more than a Great Commission. It is an instruction manual for discipling. The text clearly defines and delineates what we are to do as we go among the nations. Jesus said to "disciple all peoples"[9] by "baptizing them . . . and teaching them to obey everything [he] commanded" (Matt. 28:19–20). Jesus wrapped what we call evangelism and discipleship all together into one task called discipling! But notice what discipling entails. We enlist followers (literally "students" or "learners"[10]) of Jesus. We seal their commitment to follow by the culturally familiar and symbolic act of baptism. We teach these students of Messiah all that he taught his disciples (that's you and me). But wait! We don't just teach them to know. We teach them to obey. We teach them with words and deeds. We teach them to "talk the talk" *and* "walk the walk"! How do we do that? The way Jesus did. We walk the walk alongside them. We invest in their lives. We mentor them. We let them see our vulnerability. We model for them a Christlike life. We live a life of biblical character as we disciple across cultures—just as Jesus did!

The resources are in the harvest. But where do we find all these people? Simply put, the resources are in the harvest! These are important watchwords for strategy coordinators who focus on facilitating movements of churches planting churches around the world. It takes us back to the biblical character and practices of the discipler. In other words the way we disciple all peoples on earth is by making disciplers of all peoples on earth! Jesus could have summoned thousands to serve as disciplers, but he focused on twelve. Yet he equipped these twelve (though they were young and slow to learn) to equip others who would equip others. The disciplers who were needed to complete the task of the Great Commission would come from the harvest of disciples themselves.

This sounds so simple that it's easy to miss the point. The resources are in the harvest. Focus on the harvest for our people resources. Make sure that as we are on mission with God among all peoples on earth, everything we do is reproducible. Teach and model for others how to obey everything Jesus taught—including this command to disciple all peoples!

Paul got it. He read his Bible. He lived and breathed biblical character. He understood the genius of God's strategy. We already saw how he un-

---

9 Steven C. Hawthorne, "Mandate on the Mountain" in *Perspectives on the World Christian Movement*, 3rd ed., ed. Ralph D. Winters and Stephen C. Hawthorne (Pasadena, Calif.: William Carey Library, 1999), 110. I like Hawthorne's translation of this pivotal text. See also his note 3. on page 112.
10 Robert E. Coleman, *The Master Plan of Discipleship* (Grand Rapids: Baker Books, 1998), 9.

derstood the big picture of God's mission, but he also caught the practical details. He was no mobilizer of mass numbers of Messianic believers to take the gospel to the Gentiles. He equipped Gentiles to take the gospel to Gentiles. I teach my students to search Paul's letters carefully, especially the "headers" and "footers" of his first-century e-mails. Every now and then he slips in a tiny strategic tidbit worth noting.

Paul ended his letter to the Colossians in his traditional way: by commending the saints to one another. In this way he modeled the biblical character traits of mutual support and prayers for the team. He sends greetings from his fellow prisoner Aristarchus and his coworkers Mark and Justus. Then he muses to himself, "These are the only Jews among my fellow workers for the kingdom of God, and they have been a comfort to me" (Col. 4:11). By this time in his missions work, Paul is coordinating a vast complement of church planters and workers throughout Asia Minor and beyond. Yet among all of his coworkers, he lists only these three as Jews! Only three "foreign missionaries" as it were. The rest were Gentiles, people like Epaphras, who was a Colossian church planter himself (Col. 4:12; 1:7). Paul was discipling new disciplers among all the peoples of Asia Minor. He was not simply relying on existing believers to import their version of the gospel and establish God's church. He was relying on the harvest, new believers, to be agents of communicating the gospel and establishing the church "all over the world" (Col. 1:6), as he liked to put it!

Who better to communicate the gospel to peoples of Asia Minor than people of Asia Minor! Surely Paul learned this people-to-people pattern from the Bible—God's story of his mission. No doubt, the Holy Spirit led Paul to rely on the harvest to plant churches in Asia Minor. This was God's method: people-to-people resources in the harvest. Paul understood it. Paul modeled it.

The Indigenous Church. Another basic strategy addressed in the Bible is the issue of church and culture. This is perhaps the greatest challenge of the missionary, the cross-cultural discipler. How much of the discipler's culture of faith and church must be assumed by the new disciples?

Throughout history the church has struggled with this one. For example, for hundreds of years Roman Catholics imposed their Latin language on all peoples they discipled. Worship services were limited to Latin. There was no room for "foreign" languages. Of course they didn't consider the fact that Latin was a foreign language relative to the Bible culture of the Near East! It took a few exceptional sixteenth-century

Jesuit missionaries to impress upon the leaders of the Roman Catholic Church that Latin was not the exclusive language of God's Word. This was not God's plan but man's. God's plan concludes with "every nation, tribe, . . . and *language*" worshipping the Lamb (Rev. 7:9). The gospel of Jesus Christ transcends culture. It is not limited by culture. The church has been plagued with controversy upon controversy surrounding the culture question. What is a cross-cultural discipler to do?

Go to the manual! Perhaps Peter was the first of Jesus' disciples to face this issue of God's plan for those from other cultures. It took a vision from God and an encounter with Cornelius, but Peter finally realized "how true it is that God does not show favoritism but accepts men from every nation who fear him and do what is right" (Acts 10:34–35). The issue came to a head in Acts 15 when the council in Jerusalem called a meeting to discuss just how "Jewish" one must become in order to be a follower of Jesus. Brothers from the Pharisees were concerned that these new Gentile believers needed to be circumcised and follow all the laws of Moses. Peter, Paul, and James contended that God's grace saves, not laws. They argued in effect that the Jewish church should not burden the Gentiles with "a yoke" of cultural practices that were not central to the gospel itself. They won the day for the Gentiles; and though this issue was hardly settled once and for all in Jerusalem that day, it laid the basis for seeking to plant churches that are true to the gospel but indigenous or "homegrown."

To summarize, we have discussed just a few of the ways the Bible reveals strategic patterns and methods for discipling across cultures. To be effective disciplers we need to understand God's mission and purpose. We need to have the big picture ingrained in our thinking. This will protect our call, our reason for being on mission with God among all peoples. It will get us through the tough times.

But biblical character is more than knowledge. It reaches beyond the big picture. We need to develop a Christlike character that empowers our life and witness and results in a disciplined life based on biblical values and motives.

Finally, as effective cross-cultural disciplers we need to apply what we know and how we live to our role on mission with God among the nations. This is God's plan after all. Why not use his methods? If we have vibrant biblical character, we will more likely stay on God's track for our life and missions work.

How to Get and Keep Biblical Character

We defined the Bible as the left foundation stone of the Disciplers' Model. We discovered the necessity of using the Bible as our operating manual for discipling across cultures. Now let's look at the how-to questions of biblical character. How do we get it? How do we keep it?

Own It!

The first thing we have to do to develop biblical character is to own the Bible. I don't mean just possess one physically but really *own* it in our life and work. We need to take responsibility for God's Word in our lives. We need to *depend* on it as our operating manual for life and work. It's what we do when we make room for God's Word. It's a commitment that we make to God to be a discipler of biblical character. A major part of having biblical character is wanting it, insisting on it, seeking it, owning it. Make the Bible ours. It's nonnegotiable. It's a part of who we are in Christ Jesus. The psalmist makes the Bible his own. Listen as he takes possession of God's Word:

> How can a young man keep his way pure?
> *By living according to your word.*
> I seek you with all my heart;
> do not let me stray from your commands.
> I have hidden your word in my heart that I might not sin against
>   you.
> Praise be to you, O Lord;
> teach me your decrees.
> With my lips I recount
> all the laws that come from your mouth.
> I rejoice in following your statues as one rejoices in great riches.
> I meditate on your precepts and consider your ways.
> I delight in your decrees;
> I will not neglect your word (Ps. 119:9–16).

I suggest finding an accountability partner for owning biblical character. Just as I connected with Mike Stroope, all believers can benefit from a mutually supporting accountability relationship with a friend in Christ. It helps us to own God's Word in our life and work. It's the first step.

Learn It!

We've decided to own the Bible in our life and work; now what? We need to learn it. Learning involves more than knowing concepts or content. We also learn values and behavior (more on that later), but I am speaking about learning what the Bible says—what it teaches. This is the trickiest part of getting and keeping biblical character. You see, the church has become pretty good at teaching us the Bible. We've had about two thousand years of practice. The problem is that we often learn what the church teaches more than what the Bible teaches. How does that happen?

Some of us are like the Pharisees in John 8 who see themselves as knowers rather than learners. We often use Scripture to test or prove our existing beliefs more than to teach us about God and our relationship with him. As a result we sometimes miss out altogether on the teachings of God's Word. As Jesus put it to the Pharisees, some "have no idea where [Jesus comes] from or where [he is] going" (John 8:14). They rely on others to teach them the truth. They trust in church doctrine and tradition more than God's Word and, in the process, add much to the teachings of Christ. Others are either too lazy or simply afraid to trust his Word to speak the truth. Some can't hear his Word, only their own replayed tapes of what they think the Bible teaches. They've lost the ability to learn God's Word!

Inductive Bible Study. One of my teachers and mentors, Dr. Tommy Lea, taught us to study the Bible inductively. Simply put, we should study the Bible by starting with the particulars and working our way to the general truths. A simple three-step approach to inductive Bible study includes:

Step 1 (synthetic)—Assume little as you approach Scripture. Start with a broad search of a book or section of Scripture. Read the text straight through more than once and don't rely on outside sources— just stick to the Bible. Identify the context, setting, theme, and basic outline of the text. Trust the Holy Spirit to teach you something new. Let the Bible speak for itself.

Step 2 (analytical)—Select one verse or paragraph of Scripture. Determine the main point of the text. Identify key characters and events. Determine obvious teachings from implied teachings of the text.

Step 3 (devotional)—Determine how the text relates to life and work today. Identify the intent and purpose of the message for its original recipients in their day and time. Then decide how that message relates to today. Test your conclusions with other related passages of Scripture.[11]

This simple model for interpreting God's Word has many variations. By carefully committing yourself to a balanced approach to Bible study, you begin to learn God's Word.

Scripture Memory. The psalmist says, "I have hidden your word in my heart" (Ps. 119:11). Once you have studied God's Word, you should memorize it as well. Scripture memory is another proven discipline which stores up the teachings and truths of the Bible in our hearts and minds. It provides a ready reference for walking the walk. It adds to your knowledge and use of God's Word as you disciple across cultures. It provides a basis for learning God's Word.

If we take seriously the study of God's Word, if we discipline ourselves to a life of consistent, effective Bible study and Scripture memory, we will not only own it, but we'll begin to learn it! We'll learn more about how we learn in chapter 4.

Teach Others to Teach It!

Paul is clear about what we are to do with the teachings of the Bible. He instructs his student and "dear son" Timothy to build upon the spirit of power, love, and self-discipline. He coaches him to "fan into flame the gift of God, which is in you . . . [and] do not be ashamed to testify about our Lord. . . . Be strong in the grace that is in Christ Jesus. And the things you have heard me say in the presence of many witnesses entrust to reliable men who will also be qualified to teach others" (2 Tim. 1:6,8; 2:1–2). In short, teach others to teach others!

As disciplers we are to be about teaching others to teach others. The commission from Christ to teach others to obey all that he commanded includes this concept of reproducibility. God is on mission to reach all people with the gospel. He will bless them, and they will worship him. He chose to use people-to-people methodology. He reveals his truth through the Bible, and he equips effective disciplers by growing in them biblical character. What better way to develop—to get and keep—biblical character than to teach others to teach it!

---

11 Tommy Lea, "Inductive Bible Study Methods," *Biblical Hermeneutics: A Comprehensive Introduction to Interpreting Scripture,* 2nd ed., eds. Bruce Corley, Steve W. Lemke, and Grant I. Lovejoy (Nashville: Broadman & Holman Publishers, 2002), 39–53.

One of the newest training models for facilitating church planting movements around the world is called "T4T," "training for trainers." It has been developed by missions workers in East Asia. The house church movement of China has been the testing lab. It provides a method for rapidly multiplying the number of Bible trainers and church planters among a given population segment and beyond.

My students are perplexed when I invite a T4T equipper to share with them about this cutting-edge training tool. I see the looks on their faces. "Is that all there is? Can it be that simple?" Yes. It is that simple. One T4T module includes seven basic lessons on salvation, prayer, daily devotions, the church meeting, God our heavenly Father, and spreading the gospel. God's global mission among all people is the theme. It includes the roles of the Father, Son, and Holy Spirit and challenges the trainer to plan for creating their own "Acts 29" event as the church continues to expand. The genius of T4T is not the profound content of the training tool or the slick media presentation. The secret is its chronic obsession with reproducibility. It focuses on training to train. Everything, everybody, everywhere is about training trainers.

What better way to get and keep biblical character than to teach others to teach it! What better way to disciple across cultures!

Of course, even the best discipleship method can become the end instead of the means for discipleship. A warning is in order at this point. I can become the most unbiblical, arrogant, self-serving, condescending teacher of the gospel if I lose sight of the basics we have already discussed. Always approach God's Word as a learner more than as a knower. Expect the Holy Spirit to teach you something new. And most important, model biblical character as you live it out before those you are teaching to teach.

Live It!

Look closer at the operating manual to learn how to get and keep biblical character. Luke reports that the Bereans of the first century "received the message with great eagerness and examined the Scriptures every day to see if what Paul said was true." They took seriously the teachings of God's Word. As a result, the Bereans were "of more noble character" than others, and as a result many Jews and prominent Greeks believed the gospel (Acts 17:11). Once again we see that the power of biblical character is not so much in what we know but who we are as people of the Bible.

Biblical Character and the Teachers' Triad

Remember the Christian Teachers' Triad? How does it apply to the biblical character of the cross-cultural discipler? To develop and maintain biblical character, our whole person needs to invest in God's Word. A discipler with strong biblical character thinks, feels, and acts according to the teachings and practices of Scripture. We learn and teach God's truth as revealed in the Bible. We respect and cherish the supernatural mystery of the gospel itself, the story of God's glory. And we obey his Word; we live it through our life and work for the honor and glory of Christ Jesus.

Biblical Concepts

Did you make the connection to the triad when we discussed what it takes to get and keep biblical character? Remember, we need to *learn it*—that is, learn what it says. This is the thinking circle of the triad. God intends that we learn and follow the teachings of Scripture. The early Christians "devoted themselves to the apostles' teaching" (Acts 2:42). It was a priority. Paul coached Timothy to "correctly [handle] the word of truth" (2 Tim. 2:15). He clearly instructed Titus that he "must teach what is in accord with sound doctrine" (Titus 2:1) as he discipled the men and women of Crete. The Bible is our manual for understanding who God is, who we are, our relationship to God, what church is all about, what God's mission is, and where we fit in his mission to reach all peoples on earth. As cross-cultural disciplers on mission with God, we must learn what the Bible teaches. It's the thinking part of biblical character.

Biblical Values

But biblical character takes more than head knowledge of the Bible. Remember, we need to own it! We need to decide to make it a complete part of our life and work. When we own God's Word, we trust it, we cherish it as our manual for life and work. The author of Hebrews says that those of us "who have once been enlightened, who have tasted the heavenly gift, who have shared the Holy Spirit, who have tasted the goodness of the word of God and the powers of the coming age" will not be forgotten by God and will receive his blessing (Heb. 6:4–5). Have you tasted the goodness of God's Word? Is it good? This is our heart, our feelings, the affective part of our person responding to God's Word.

How else do we value God's Word? We recognize and feel its power. Paul said it more than once, "I am not ashamed of the gospel, because it is the power of God for the salvation of everyone who believes" (Rom. 1:16). You can almost hear his hilarious tone of voice as he proclaims to the Colossians, "All over the world this gospel is bearing fruit and growing, just as it has been doing among you" (Col. 1:6). The gospel is powerful. It bears fruit. Around the world we hear testimonies of the power of God's Word. We learn about people who are isolated from the church for geographical or political reasons; but somehow through the written Scriptures, an audiotape, or perhaps a video like the Jesus film, their lives are transformed as they become disciples of Jesus Christ. Effective disciplers appreciate the power of the gospel. We've seen its power. We've experienced it. We know it in our hearts.

Biblical Behavior

Finally, the learner's triad applies to the development of biblical character at the point of obedience. We must live it! Talk the talk *and* walk the walk. Paul preaches this message to his teams repeatedly. He pleads with the Messianic believers of the early church, "Do not merely listen to the word, and so deceive yourselves. Do what it says" (James 1:22). He instructs Titus to "encourage the young men to be self-controlled. In everything set them an example by doing what is good" (Titus 2:6–7).

Paul's charge to Timothy goes beyond learning the teachings of Scripture. It includes the heart values of faith and love but requires more. It moves Timothy to faith in action. As Paul mentors Timothy, he continuously encourages him to live the biblical life that he teaches others. He acknowledges that Timothy knows Paul's teachings and his "way of life, [his] purpose, faith, patience, love, endurance, persecutions, [and] sufferings." He calls upon Timothy "to live a godly life in Christ Jesus" in spite of the persecutions that will follow (2 Tim. 3:10, 12). Paul encourages Timothy in the midst of trials to "continue in what you have learned and have become convinced of, because you know those from whom you learned it, and how from infancy you have known the holy Scriptures, which are able to make you wise for salvation through faith in Christ Jesus. All Scripture is God-breathed and is useful for teaching, rebuking, correcting and training in righteousness, so that the man of God may be thoroughly equipped for every good work" (2 Tim. 3:14–17). A discipler with biblical character lives a life of biblical behavior, a life of every good work.

The psalmist describes the three aspects of the learners' triad when he sings to God, "How can a young man keep his way pure? By living according to your word. I seek you with all my heart; do not let me stray from your commands. I have hidden your word in my heart that I might not sin against you. Praise be to you, O LORD" (Ps. 119:9–12). The psalmist has learned what God's Word says; he has hidden it in his heart. He passionately pursues God through his Word; he seeks God with all his heart. And he knows that he must live the biblical life by living according to God's Word. This is biblical character.

A Very Religious Christian in Somalia—What Happened?

Remember Nathan, the young relief-and-development worker taken hostage in Somalia? Whatever happened to him? Abdul-ahi had introduced him to the bigwig minister as a "very religious Christian." What now? The minister smiled politely, shook Nathan's hand, and, after a few words of conversation, moved down the line of hostages. At the end of the day, the hostages were released and all was well. But Nathan wondered what possessed Abdul-ahi to introduce him in this manner.

After the minister left, Nathan pulled Abdul-ahi aside and asked him why he introduced him the way he did. Abdul-ahi replied, "You know your friend Abdul-kadir?" Nathan said, "Yes." Abdul-ahi went on, "Every day your friend Abdul-kadir comes and wants to see you, but you know I can't let him in. He told me that you were a very religious Christian and that you don't drink alcohol, you don't smoke, you don't say bad words, and you are a man of your Book. He told me to watch you and see for myself. I have watched you, and he is right."

Abdul-kadir worked for Nathan handling logistical tasks in the clinics. He had been with Nathan nearly every day for months. They had a few good conversations about faith, but Nathan never pressured Abdul-kadir about the subject. Unaware that he was being watched, Nathan had been labeled as a man of the Book. He was a man who followed the teachings and lived a life worthy of his Book. Years later Nathan described his reaction to this event in an e-mail to me: "Whatever these two men saw in me was revealed to them simply by the grace of God. What's interesting is that sincere faith, in their eyes, is proven genuine by observable action or behavior. Somalis are well-known for and take pride in their ability to read a person's character quickly. They even have a proverb that states something to the effect that 'to talk/walk with a man for an hour is to know him.'"

This experience and others have given me glimpses into the worldview of the Somali Muslim. I continue to learn about those external indicators that a Somali looks for in order to make a judgment about a person. As a result, I work at making my faith known by what others see and hear of me. For example, I want to be seen reading my Bible and praying. I want to be heard as one who recognizes the hand of God at work in my day, in my life, as I go about living the life that he has given me. I try to let this come out in my conversations naturally and regularly.

Nathan's biblical character revealed itself through his talk and walk in the most difficult of times. How do we get and keep biblical character. We decide to own it in our lives. We discipline ourselves to learn it, teach others to teach it, and struggle each day to live it.

Biblical character is foundational for the cross-cultural discipler. You cannot stand without it. When we rely on the Bible as our operating manual for life and work, God will protect our call to be on mission with him. The manual keeps us focused on his story of his glory. As we connect with its message and power, the Bible transforms our life in a way that empowers our witness to others.

We saw in chapter 2 how a solid foundation of biblical character is impossible to get and keep without the encircling of the Holy Spirit. As we surrender to the Spirit, he directs us in our commitment to own and learn the teachings of the Bible. As the Holy Spirit empowers our thoughts, feelings, and actions, we are better able to teach others to teach God's good and perfect Word. And as we live out the life of Christ as revealed in the Bible, we are more effective at communicating the gospel across cultures.

The Thessalonians experienced this dynamic of the encircling Holy Spirit and empowering gospel. They knew how to get and keep biblical character. God used them to communicate the gospel to their world. Paul commends them:

> We always thank God for all of you, mentioning you in our prayers. We continually remember before our God and Father your work produced by faith, your labor prompted by love, and your endurance inspired by hope in our Lord Jesus Christ.
>
> For we know, brothers loved by God, that he has chosen you, because our gospel came to you not simply with words, but also with power, with the Holy Spirit and with deep convictions. You know how

we lived among you for your sake. You became imitators of us and of the Lord; in spite of severe suffering, you welcomed the message with the joy given by the Holy Spirit. And so you became a model to all believers in Macedonia and Achaia. The Lord's message rang out from you . . . your faith in God has become known everywhere (1 Thess. 1:2–8).

May we also be encircled by God's Holy Spirit and founded upon the left foundation stone of his biblical character as we disciple all peoples for his glory and honor, Amen.

Understanding God's message is essential. But communicating God's truth to people of another culture, a different language, and exotic customs requires the ability to think well in order to apply biblical truths in ways not done before. We next delve into the rational character of cross-cultural disciplers.

Rick's Reaction

The first time I heard Mike refer to the Bible as "the manual," long before he wrote this chapter, it made me nervous. It sounded flippant, as if he were reducing "the marvelous majestic Word of God" to a how-to book. But I knew him and knew that flippancy was not in his heart, and so I looked deeper into what he meant. What I found *then* is what he has presented clearly *here* in this chapter. The Bible is not a holy book to be defended but God's Word to be lived. Mike mirrors Paul's view of Scripture: "useful for teaching, rebuking, correcting and training in righteousness, so that the man of God may be thoroughly equipped for every good work" (2 Tim. 3:16–17).

Mike has done more than explain the *what* of the manual. He has helped us focus on the practical *hows* of becoming biblical. Own it! Learn it! Teach others to teach it! Live it! Mike confessed his struggles to engage these stages in his own life, struggles we all live through if we take biblical character seriously. In doing so, he takes us beyond platitudes to spiritual power as we submit the growth of our own concepts, values, and actions to the freedoms and constraints of the written Word.

Some may use the Bible to extend their own personal power, building kingdoms of their own. Mike shows us in this chapter "a more excellent way" (1 Cor. 12:31 KJV), how to become more godly in our influence by living the truth for the extension and promotion of God's kingdom to all nations.

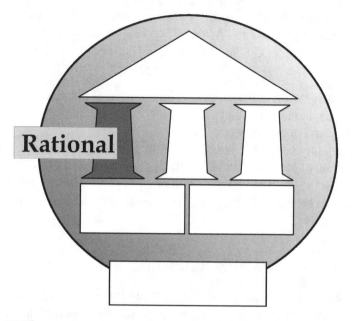

The Rational Character
of cross-cultural
Disciplers

Disciplers' Model

4
Developing a Rational Character
Rick Yount

Do not conform any longer to the pattern of this world,
but be transformed by the renewing of your mind.
Romans 12:2a

We have not stopped praying for you and asking God to fill you with the knowledge
of his will through all spiritual wisdom and understanding. And we pray this in
order that you may live a life worthy of the Lord and may please him in every way:
bearing fruit in every good work, growing in the knowledge of God, being strengthened with all power according to his glorious might so that you may have great
endurance and patience, and joyfully giving thanks to the Father, who has qualified
you to share in the inheritance of the saints in the kingdom of light.
Colossians 1:9–12

D isciplers develop a rational character that is devoted first to understanding the perspectives of national learner-leaders, then to helping
them solve problems both biblically and creatively in their own cultural
context. Chapter 4 defines the role of thinking and problem-solving in
discipling across cultures. We then describe how to develop a rational
character as a pillar of discipling ministry.

The Toxic Flip Side

Pushing *our* solutions, ignoring *their* perspectives.

Strong Tea, Tapioca, and Bread Crumbs

Misunderstandings about things and between people happen within
any culture, but the possibilities for misunderstanding across cultural
barriers grow exponentially. The first time I taught in the former Soviet
Union was at Odessa Theological Seminary in Odessa, Ukraine. My wife
and I made our way to the dining hall for breakfast the first morning and
saw at one end of the room the largest samovar we'd ever seen. The metal
electric water heater stood four feet tall and was shrouded in roiling
steam. On top of the samovar was a large white ceramic pitcher—tea!
We each got a small tea cup from the table and poured a dark liquid from
the pitcher. We added two teaspoons of sugar and sat down to wait for
our breakfast of fried eggs and cheese. We took a sip of our tea and were

shocked to find it bitter, so strong as to be undrinkable. My conclusion was, "Ukrainians like their tea strong!"

George Joslin told me a story, years ago, about visiting a deaf residential school. As they went about the school, the director mentioned to George that they would have tapioca pudding for lunch. This was good news to George, who likes tapioca pudding. But the director was not so positive. "Deaf people just don't like tapioca pudding."

After lunch George and the director sat and talked over coffee. Students excused themselves as they made their way past them. After the students were gone, the director apologized for the students' bad behavior. George told him that he had not noticed any bad behavior. "Oh yes," he said. "Every one of those students brushed the bread crumbs off their hands as they passed us! I was so embarrassed and hope you'll forgive their rudeness."

These three stories illustrate misconceptions generated across cultural barriers. We'll return to them later in the chapter.

The problems we face are monumental. Our intentions are good. The results, despite smiles and polite expressions of thanks, may be less so. In a candid moment of openness, a university professor, a Ukrainian Baptist, told me, "Americans come to us with their 'five ways to do this' and 'seven ways to do that,' all framed within their own cultural context. Rarely do they ask us about our own needs. They tell us how they do it back home, thinking all the while that if we imitate their lists, we will have the same success. Their lists are useless to us."

A Ukrainian professor-friend told me of a highly publicized teacher training event he had recently attended. "For four days, one Westerner after another stood before us and gave us lists of things to do. Most of the information was unnecessary because we were already doing these things. The rest was inappropriate because it did not address our frame, our history, our mind-set. The lists were considered both *unknown* and *universal*. The Americans considered the lists unknown to the Ukrainian professors seated before them—so it was necessary for them to be told—and universal, appropriate to everyone everywhere. They were not. Not once were we asked what we already knew or what we needed. The conference was basically a waste of time for us."

In yet another conference, in St. Petersburg, Russia, Westerners provided "cutting-edge advice" on setting up Internet access and using the Web to provide theological education across the former Soviet Union. They shared their insights into the intricacies of using Web-based learning for theological education by extension. After the two-hour conference, I asked one of the Russian participants what he thought of the presentation. "Well," he said dryly, "it might be helpful in twenty years when we have a telephone system that will support these levels of data exchange. For now it is a problem because there is simply too much noise on the lines to permit the level of access necessary for consistent educational use."

"So did these men just waste your time?" I asked.

"No, not really, I suppose. It gives us something to dream about for the future. But the reality is this: when we have data lines to support such instant communication, the technology will have leaped over itself several times, making the specifics of their presentation today ancient history."

In each of these cases, presenters had not developed the rational character necessary to grasp real problems, real situations, and real needs from the point of view of their listeners. They did not provide solutions in context. Nor did they provide the rational foundation for nationals to make the applications themselves. Rather, they gave five ways to do this, seven ways to do that—all in a Western context.

Let's look again at the basics of helping people think in the Disciplers' Model and then pursue the development of a rational character.

The Left Pillar: Helping People Think

If we truly want to transform the people we teach, our task is to help them to think clearly within their own cultural context. Getting them to parrot our own answers, produced within our own cultural context, will not help. The biggest complaint I hear about Western (particularly American) missionaries and visiting teachers is our tendency to give nationals four ways to do this and seven ways to do that, all couched in our own culture. This is little more than tying oranges on apple trees. We need to help them weigh the evidence of Scripture, ask questions, and analyze their own situations in order to confront their own status quo with God's Word. The "thinking pillar" represents the disciplers' *objective focus* in teaching: helping learners translate the stories of the Bible (or any discipling content) into principles and standards by which they can make biblical decisions in their own everyday situations. How do we teach so that thinking skills are improved?

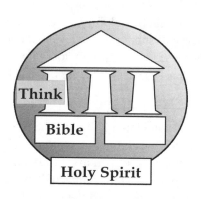

Disciplers' Model

Paul gave us a keen insight into the role of thinking in Christian growth when he wrote to the Colossian believers: "We have not stopped praying for you and asking God to fill you with the knowledge of his will through all spiritual wisdom and understanding" (Col. 1:9).

Here Paul presents us with three components of spiritual growth through using the mind. These are knowledge, understanding, and wisdom.

Knowledge

Philosophers and theologians commonly use the word *knowledge* to refer to the global result of rational processes such as knowing, comprehending, analyzing, synthesizing, and evaluating. For these global thinkers, knowing involves a range of cognitive functions from processing raw information to evaluating the most abstract principles.

Educational psychologists delineate these cognitive functions into levels of learning. In this taxonomy of levels, knowing is the lowest and refers to the process of committing facts to memory. To *know* John 3:16 means "to quote the verse from memory." To *know* the cities Paul visited on his first missionary journey means to be able "to identify the cities he visited from a list of New Testament cities." The process of helping learners establish knowledge (teaching for knowledge) requires more than giving learners information, a common misconception of teaching. We know we have succeeded in teaching for knowledge when our learners actually remember what we've taught. Information will be quickly forgotten unless we do more than talk through the lesson. Teaching, even at the level of basic knowledge, requires more than talking.

We help learners convert information into knowledge by the use of specific principles shown below.

By using principles such as these, we help learners commit factual information to memory. Teaching for knowledge requires more than giving facts; it means helping students reinforce what they learn so they can remember it. The example in the sidebar on the facing page may seem

Principles of Teaching for Knowledge (recall)

Preview key points. That is, show learners what they will be learning. For example, draw the Disciplers' Model on the blackboard and say, "In this session we will learn the seven elements of the Disciplers' Model."

Break material into small units of material (chunks) to memorize, then lead the learners in memorizing the whole, one chunk at a time. For example, "Let's say the first two elements together." (Students say, "Bible" and "Needs"). After explaining these two, say, "Let's say the next three together." (Students say, "Thinking," "Feeling," "Relating".) Later, "Let's say the final two together." (Students say, "Growth" and "Holy Spirit.")

Use drill and practice cycles to reinforce memory of each chunk in turn—*alternate repetition of chunks with explanations of items.* After explaining each item, repeat the entire set (two elements, three elements, two elements).

Keep drills short but repeat them frequently. The process of establishing knowledge—helping learners memorize—is innately monotonous and soon leads to boredom. Reduce monotony by keeping the drills short.

Space practice cycles over the entire teaching period—*alternate explanations with repetition of chunks of items.* Do not concentrate the practice cycles in one part of the session, but intersperse explanations of the elements with the drills so that brains can rest. This reduces boredom and makes each practice cycle more effective. Further, the mind can remember meaningful elements better than raw facts. Avoid trivia by providing clear explanations in the spaces between practice cycles.

Use active recall (learners recall for themselves) more than passive recall (teacher reminds learners what they should know) to reinforce key points. Active recall is more effective in establishing knowledge.

Provide feedback on students' performances. Test learners' ability to remember by giving a memory quiz near the end of the session. "OK, now take out a sheet of paper, draw the Disciplers' Model, and label each part." Then lead learners to compare their answers to see how well they recalled the seven elements.

simplistic, but the house church movement in China is known for this type of knowledge-building teaching with their Scripture and doctrinal memorization, recitations, blackboards, handouts, slogans, and so on.

In fact, Brother Yun testifies how he began what became part of a vast house church movement in Henan province, China, in 1974. He was a half-starved sixteen-year-old boy. After miraculously receiving a copy of the Bible, he began to read and memorize it.

> In the beginning, reading my Bible was not easy because I had only received three years of education. Furthermore, my Bible was in the traditional Chinese script, while I had learned to read simplified characters. I found a dictionary and painstakingly looked up one character at a time as I advanced through the Bible.
>
> Finally I finished reading through the whole Bible, so I started to memorize one chapter per day. After twenty-eight days I had memorized the whole Gospel of Matthew. I quickly read through the three other Gospels before proceeding to the book of Acts and started to memorize it.

Soon after this Yun had a dream in which the Lord told him to preach the gospel in villages to the west and south. The next morning Yun started walking west. He was met by a man who had been sent from the village of Gao to the west to find Yun and bring him to share the gospel.

> We went into the house. I sat down on the floor, and everyone crowded around me. I was nervous because I had never spoken to a group of people before. Thirty or forty people were all staring at me, searching me with their eyes, and longing to hear God's Word. They were so hungry for the truth. There were already a few Christians in Gao Village, but the majority of people had not yet believed.
>
> I sat there with my eyes tightly shut and held the Bible above my head. I declared, "This is the Bible. The angel of the Lord sent it to me in answer to my prayers. If you want to get a Bible, you will have to pray and seek God as I did." . . .
>
> They wanted me to teach them. At that time I didn't know what it meant to preach. I could only recite the Bible from the chapters I had memorized, so I recited the entire Gospel of Matthew out loud, from chapter 1 to 28.
>
> I didn't know if the people understood what I was saying. In order not to lose my place or forget anything, I recited what I had memorized quickly, like a flowing river. . . .

When I opened my eyes, I saw how God's Word had captivated everybody. The Holy Spirit was convicting them of their sins. They all knelt down and repented with tears flowing down their cheeks. That night, even though I was just sixteen years old, I learned that God's Word is powerful. When we share it [recite it!] with a burning heart, many people are touched. At that first meeting, thanks to the power of God, dozens of people had given their hearts to Jesus.[1]

The principles of knowledge-building are important, and the discipler who can help disciples commit God's Word to memory provide them a powerful tool for sharing the gospel. In higher levels of discipleship, memorization of diagrams, charts, formulas, and whole systems provide a virtual living library of information to draw from, at any time.[2]

Now back to Colossians 1:9. Paul was more philosopher than psychologist and therefore goes beyond the idea of head knowledge in this passage. He does not use the more common word for knowledge, *gnosis*. He was writing against the forerunners of the Gnostics who held that without their secret knowledge believers could not get to heaven.

The word Paul used here for "knowledge" is *epignosis*. The word means "knowledge that reaches out and grasps its object and is in turn grasped by its object." As I have studied the Russian language—as I have reached out and grasped it—the Russian language in turn has reached out and grasped me. Now, even when I grow tired of studying verb forms and noun endings, Russian will not let me go. The term *epignosis* includes head knowledge (I must memorize verb forms) but moves beyond it into what we might call "heart" knowledge, a knowledge that affects the way we live. This is the kind of knowledge Paul prays for the Colossians, a knowledge of God's will which possesses them and changes them.

What does the Bible say? The *beginning point* for helping learners think biblically is to convey what the Bible says (see chapter 3). They cannot interpret Bible teachings without correct knowledge of Bible persons, terms, places, and events. Without an adequate background in the setting of a given Bible passage and the meanings of words, learners will interpret the words of the Bible incorrectly in light of their own culture and experience.

---

1 Brother Yun, *The Heavenly Man: The Remarkable True Story of Chinese Christian Brother Yun,* with Paul Hattaway (Grand Rapids, Mich.: Monarch Books 2002), 33, 37–38.

2 Rote memorization is common in the former Soviet Union and results in people knowing the Scripture but never being forced to interpret it in light of itself. Paul chides Timothy and us to "correctly [handle] the word of truth" (2 Tim. 2:15). Knowing Scripture does not mean we are correctly using Scripture. AL

One of the interesting discussions I've had with Russian students in my teaching classes is on honesty in testing. As an American, I put a lot of importance on students doing their own work and answering test items on their own. To "borrow" another's work or get answers from another's test is cheating and rightly condemned. In one such discussion a Russian pastor said, "When my brother asks me for help, what can I do but help him? To refuse to help him will break fellowship between us, and surely God is not pleased with that." He makes a good point but one which does not apply to an academic test.

I answered, "If fellowship is broken, it is your brother's fault because he is attempting to steal from you. And this God condemns. You studied. He did not. He is attempting to steal your understanding and make it his own. His grade will not reflect what he truly understands. And he will not learn the importance of studying for himself."

God himself said, "You must have accurate and honest weights and measures, so that you may live long in the land the LORD your God is giving you. For the LORD your God detests anyone who does these things, anyone who deals dishonestly" (Deut. 25:15–16). This is not American (versus Russian) truth; it is God's truth.

Overemphasis on Information. No matter what learners need, what questions they ask, or what problems surface, some teachers focus on conveying their own factual agenda. Yet covering background facts can absorb so much time that we lose the opportunity to address higher stages of thinking. We will not establish knowledge. We will not help learners integrate new information into their own perceptions. We merely flood learners with unstructured information, and this they soon forget.

I recently discovered a Russian phrase used commonly among students: *Zu-bree-YOSH-ka, zdal, zabil* which literally means, "cramming, passed, forgot." Or more loosely translated: "Don't worry about studying until the night before the exam, then study all night in order to pass the exam, and then forget it." This is not a Russian flaw but human sin, a shortcut. The results are self-evident. Exams may be passed, but little fruit remains. The thinking of the students who behave this way has not been changed by the facts we've showered over them.

God has called us to a more important task than talking through a set of notes in front of a group of people. We are called to lead learners from information to clear understanding.

Understanding

Learners *understand* what we teach when they organize established knowledge into concepts and principles that can be used. They can explain it to others in their own words. They have the ability to describe ideas and terms, give examples of what words do and do not mean, and create examples and illustrations to clarify the idea.

Paul knew the Old Testament well. He had studied under the Jewish philosopher Gamaliel. He was trained in the best pharisaical schools. He was zealous in his persecution of liberal Jews who were following a dead Nazarene carpenter. He demanded that they return to the culturally correct "old-time religion." But when he met the risen Lord on his way to Damascus, he saw things in a completely new way, and he was lifted out of his Jewish culture. During three years in an Arabian desert, he studied the Old Testament with a new perspective. The book of Romans gives us the result of his thinking. Before, he knew what the Old Testament said in his cultural context; now he understood what it meant to the world in the light of the resurrection of Jesus.

What does the Bible mean? I've had more than a few students who insist that there is no difference between what the Bible says and what it means. "The Bible *says* what it means, and it *means* what it says!" This often evokes a hardy amen! The only problem is that it isn't necessarily true. The first time I read Colossians 1:9 ("asking God to fill you with the knowledge of his will"), I misinterpreted the verse because I assumed the word *knowledge* meant just *what I understood the word to mean:* that is, knowledge equals memorization of facts or the ability to recall. That is not what Paul had in mind when he wrote that statement under inspiration of the Holy Spirit. I read my understanding into the text (*eisegesis*) and therefore misunderstood its true meaning.

One night, years ago, I learned how this kind of *eisegesis* can be dangerous. I was talking with a deaf man about the Lord after a deaf revival service in our church. His heart had been warmed by the message, but he wasn't ready to make a commitment. He wanted to end our discussion of his spiritual condition quickly, so he simply said, *"I can't be saved."*

"Why?" I asked.

Without hesitation he said, *"Because I'm deaf."*

"Because you're deaf? What makes you think that you can't be saved because you're deaf?"

In a blink of an eye he said, *"The Bible says so."*

"Where does the Bible say you can't be saved because you're deaf?"

He hesitated and then said, *"I don't know where exactly. But it says somewhere 'If you confess with your mouth, "Jesus is Lord," you will be saved.' I'm deaf. I can't confess with my mouth. God made me this way. See? I can't be saved. Because of God. That's what the Bible says!"* He was quoting Romans 10:9: "If you confess with your mouth, 'Jesus is Lord,' and believe in your heart that God raised him from the dead, you will be saved."

"But that's not what that passage means," I heard myself say, wanting to reassure him that despite his deafness he could be saved. With great finality he looked me in the eye and with conviction said, *"That's what the Bible says!"*

When learners read their own definitions into Bible passages and then interpret what the Bible "says" accordingly, *they make the Bible reflect their own ideas.* They are not letting the Bible speak to them. Jean Piaget calls this process "assimilation," but we'll get to his helpful discoveries in a few minutes.

This confirmed for me in a practical way that what the Bible says— that is, what it seems to say to us—may not be what the Bible actually means. It is a natural human tendency to process information according to what is already known. The words I hear are processed by the concepts I've already established, and these concepts may not correspond to new meanings. I've made this distinction in the past by contrasting words and concepts. Knowing words and understanding concepts are two different things.

Holiness. Salvation. Prayer. Ministry. Church. Sin. Sacrifice. Faith. Hope. Patience. Anger. What do these and hundreds of other biblical terms *mean?*

Mercy and truth. Love and wrath. Free will and predestination. Holy anger and forgiveness. Grace and conviction. These biblical concepts pull us in two directions at once. Only clear understandings of their individual and paired meanings will lead our leader-learners to biblical, Christlike action, growth, and maturity.

It is my personal conviction that teachers could improve their teaching tenfold simply *by giving attention to this area of conceptual understanding.* It is far better to help learners master a single biblical concept that they will remember for years than it is to tell them thirty-five facts that they will forget in a few hours. *Zu-bri-yosh-ka, Zdal, Zabil.* But even proper understanding isn't sufficient for growing learner-leaders. We have one step yet to take: helping learners grow in wisdom.

Wisdom

Jesus said, "Everyone who hears these words of mine and *puts them into practice* is like a wise man who built his house on the rock." And further, "Everyone who hears these words of mine and *does not put them into practice* is like a foolish man who built his house on sand" (Matt. 7:24, 26).

The clear distinction between wise and foolish in Jesus' definition is the phrase "puts them into practice." My American students know what cheating is and understand that it is wrong. Are they wise or foolish? It depends on whether they cheat. Pastors know what adultery is and understand it is wrong. Whether we are wise or foolish is determined by our behavior. Spiritual wisdom emphasizes *what we do* more than what we know or understand.

Rational Growth Is an Upward Spiral

Knowing, understanding, and wise-doing carry us upward toward spiritual maturity. Learners discover and remember what the Bible says (knowledge). They process this knowledge in order to establish clear Bible concepts (understanding). As they use these biblical concepts to make decisions (wisdom), they grow spiritually. As they grow in wisdom, they learn more about what the Bible says about life (knowledge increases), which in turn allows them to deepen their understanding of life in Christ, which enables them to live as citizens of the kingdom, which in turn produces spiritual wisdom, and so on throughout life. Paul exhorts, "Do not conform any longer to the pattern of this world, but be transformed by the renewing of your mind" (Rom. 12:2). Christians put off purely cultural perspectives and take on "the mind of Christ" (1 Cor. 2:16) as they spiral upward through knowledge, understanding, and wisdom.

What is the goal of this growth in thinking? Paul tells us it is to "live a life worthy of the Lord," and then he defines that life. "We pray this in order that you may live a life worthy of the Lord and may please him in every way: bearing fruit in every good work, growing in the knowledge of God, being strengthened with all power according to his glorious might . . . giving thanks to the Father, who has qualified you to share in the inheritance of the saints in the kingdom of light" (Col. 1:10–12).

A life *worthy* of the Lord's mercy!
A life *pleasing* to God!
A life *bearing fruit*!
A life *growing* in experience with God!
A life *being strengthened!*
A life fortified with *endurance and patience!*
A life of *joyful thanks to God!*

This is the left pillar of the Disciplers' Model. Teach in a way that helps people think biblically. Over time learners will develop lives "worthy of the Lord." Lives pleasing to God. Fruitful and strong.

Insights from Jean Piaget

As we consider reaching across cultural barriers with the gospel and biblical discipleship, we will find helpful some of the ideas of cognitive psychologist Jean Piaget. Piaget demonstrated that mental functioning develops as individuals interact with their environment. The processes by which all humans learn to think are the same, regardless of culture. But since environments differ from culture to culture, the *content* of thinking varies. That is, all humans think (process), but what we think (content) differs from culture to culture. Our goal is to use universal processes to introduce learners to God's way of seeing things. We will disciple more effectively if we tap into the universal process of human thought. Further, we will minimize mental clashes and misunderstandings as we approach the process aware that deep differences exist between ourselves and our learners in the content of what is thought.

> Our goal is to use universal processes to introduce learners to God's way of seeing things.

Piaget believed, as do all cognitive psychologists, that the human mind is active and seeks to arrange experiences in the world so that they make sense to us. We automatically try to make sense of what does not make sense in an unfamiliar culture. Piaget called this natural, innate drive to understand our world "organization." Piaget developed a number of technical terms like this to describe the complex process by which humans construct intelligence. His terms have been translated from French into English, but the special meanings need careful definition. While an in-depth analysis of Piaget is beyond the scope of this book,[3] the following terms will prove helpful.

Organization

Organization, briefly mentioned above, is the *natural tendency to make sense of experiences by creating and modifying logically related cognitive structures.* These cognitive structures are simple early in life but are built up into ever

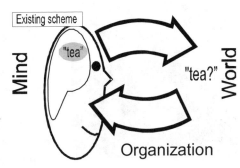

more complex, coherent mental systems over time. The natural tendency of our minds to make sense of the world continues as long as we live, regardless of culture, language, or education. When I confronted the unfamiliar samovar, I attempted to understand it with my previous experience. I attempted to embrace this "tea" and make it part of my conceptual world. I did not analyze the situation. I simply reacted out of the natural tendency to mentally organize the world as I experience it—organization.

Schemes

The "logically related cognitive structures" mentioned above are called "schemes" (*schema, schemata*). Schemes are *organized patterns of behavior or thought which represent, in our minds, the world as we have experienced it in the past.* My scheme of "tea" was built from having used tea bags back home to brew tea in a pitcher or cup. My "hometown-tea" scheme did not fit the situation with the samovar. The dark liquid in the pitcher seemed to be tea but very bitter tea!

The picture is a souvenir version of the mammoth samovar I saw in Odessa. It boils water with an electric coil. The bitter tea concentrate held in the pitcher, called *zavarka,* is diluted with boiling water from the *samovar* to make tea *(chai).* This pitcher sits in the brass ring on top.

Schemes change as we grow. Schemes increase in number, allowing us to recognize differences among similar objects, and become more

3 For a fuller discussion of Piaget and stages of development, see William R. Yount, *Created to Learn: A Christian Teacher's Introduction to Educational Psychology* (Nashville: Broadman & Holman. 1996), chapter 4, "Cognitive Development."

complex, allowing us to recognize similarities among different objects. Since perception of the world depends on one's level of cognitive development, it is reasonable that children are not able to learn and think like adults.

Further, we will find differences in cognitive development even between adults which exist because of differing developmental patterns. This is especially true across languages and cultures. Disciplers detect these differences and adjust their understanding *of others* as well as their explanations and illustrations *to others* accordingly.

Equilibration

Equilibration is the *natural tendency to maintain a balance between what we already know and understand (our cognitive network) and what we experience in the world.* When we experience something that does not fit what we know, the balance between known and experienced is disturbed. This disturbance is called disequilibrium and causes anxiety, discomfort, or confusion. Equilibration compels us to reduce the disequilibrium by restoring the balance, or *equilibrium,* between our understanding of the world and experiences in the world.

The samovar created disequilibrium for me. I knew about tea, but my knowledge did not include Ukrainian methods for making it. My best attempt to solve my disequilibrium created sweet but very bitter tea.

George Joslin thought it strange that deafness should cause a dislike for tapioca pudding (disequilibrium). When they went through the lunch line, he noticed that, true enough, none of the students took the tapioca pudding. Now his disequilibrium was stronger, and he wanted to discover why (organization).

In another example of disequilibrium, George was puzzled over the director's apology for "the rudeness of the students." He thought the students had been well behaved and polite. His disequilibrium caused him to ask what the director meant.

Disequilibrium motivates us to change our thinking (or the experience) in order to relieve the mental anxiety and thereby produce equilibration between thinking and experience. The process by which equilibration is achieved is called adaptation.

Adaptation

Adaptation is the *natural process of adjusting our schemes, or our environment, so that balance exists between what we know and what we experience.* Adaptation creates coherence between our concept of reality and real-life experiences. Adaptation consists of two parts. The first part, called *assimilation,* reduces disequilibrium by *interpreting experiences so they fit what we know.* "Ukrainians like bitter tea." The second part, called *accommodation,* reduces

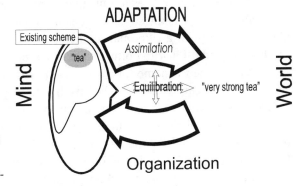

disequilibrium by *adjusting schemes* to fit our experience. "Mix a little *zavarka* with a cup of boiling water to make tea." Adaptation combines these two processes so that we maintain a state of equilibrium between our thinking and the world.

Assimilation means to "interpret experiences to fit what is known."

When an experience does not fit an existing scheme, we can easily (mis)interpret the experience and connect it to the scheme which provides the closest fit. In doing so, we often modify or distort what we've experienced.

I assimilated Ukrainian tea: "They really like their tea strong!" The director assimilated deaf behavior: "They don't like tapioca pudding." "How rude to brush their bread crumbs on us." Westerners assimilated student needs in their conferences: "The to-do lists we have are what these national professors need."

In each of these situations, equilibration was established by changing the experiences in the world according to what was already known. And yet the results were incorrect. Ukrainians do not drink bitter tea. The deaf students actually had good reasons for not eating the tapioca pudding (see below) and were not "brushing off bread crumbs" on the principal and his guest. The "essential to-do lists," expensive to the Westerners in time and money, had little value to the Eastern professors receiving them. The misconceptions resulted from forcing preconceived notions on present situations.

Some writers consider one other sense of assimilation, which refers to the *reinforcement* of existing schema. Each time I see Russians, Ukrainians, or the Kyrgyz make tea by adding a cup of boiling water to several tablespoons of *zavarka,* my Ukrainian tea scheme is reinforced.

Accommodation means to adjust schemes to fit experiences.

When an experience does not fit an existing scheme, we can either adjust an existing scheme so that it does fit, or we can create a new scheme. When I saw a Ukrainian student pour a small amount of *zavarka* into his cup and fill it with boiling water, I learned a new way of making tea. I created a new scheme for *zavarka* and modified my "tea scheme" to include "Ukrainian," which is delicious, by the way!

George solved his dilemma with deafness and pudding when he and the director went through the lunch line. He took some tapioca to taste. When he tried to eat it a little later, he found that it was as hard as a rock. The pudding had been made and set out early that morning and had hardened. Students had learned that the tapioca pudding is always inedible and didn't bother to take any. The fact that the pudding was inedible had nothing to do with their deafness.

George helped the principal understand (correctly) that the deaf students were actually being polite as they passed, saying, "Excuse me." The sign for "excuse (me)" is made by sliding the right hand, palm down, across the left hand, palm up, several times. The students were saying, "Excuse me" as they passed, not brushing crumbs on visitors, as he had thought. They were actually being polite!

As far as I know, none of the Westerners

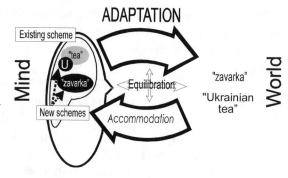

realized that their lists and presentations were essentially a waste of time for the Russian participants. They most likely assume to this day that their work was more useful than it really was.

The concepts of assimilation and accommodation (more commonly called "contextualization"[4] by missiologists) are central to cross-cultural discipling. We do well to avoid misinterpretations of other cultures (assimilation) which cause culture clashes and distort our message. We do well when we learn from other cultures, changing the way we think, or at least adding new ways of thinking to what we already have (accommodation), so we can convey meaning more consistently.

Accommodation: Understanding Versus Believing

One concern raised by students goes like this: "How do we keep from accommodating our thinking to worldly ideas or New Age religions?" They have a tangible fear that accepting the idea of accommodation may result in compromising their thinking, attitudes, and lifestyle with the world around them. But there is a difference between *understanding* and *believing*.

If I am to share the gospel with New Age devotees, I need to understand what New Agers believe. I accommodate my thinking—that is, create appropriate schemes—in order to understand New Age teachings. This is not the same as accepting New Age beliefs or accepting New Age as appropriate teaching. Does understanding Hitler's *Mein Kampf* make me a Nazi or studying Marx's *Das Kapital* make me a Communist? For that matter, does understanding Jesus' teachings make me a Christian? Of course not. Cognitive understanding and heart commitment are two different animals altogether.

Should we study evolutionary theory? If we want to be able to speak intelligently on the subject, we must. We should accommodate our thinking to evolution to understand what evolution really teaches rather than make it into what we think it is (assimilation). Understanding evolution has nothing to do with committing myself to, or even accepting, its tenets. Believers have the greatest opportunities to share the gospel with others when they understand, when they have accommodated themselves to, the viewpoints of others. The apostle Paul wrote:

---

4 It has been commonly reported that Francis A. Schaeffer, noted lecturer and author from L'Abri Fellowship in Switzerland, once said if he had only one hour to share the gospel with a person, he would spend the first forty-five minutes finding out what the person believed about God and the last fifteen minutes presenting Christ from that basis. For some the idea of "starting where they are" would seem a worthless exercise because the people they are working with come from the same background as they do so they are "starting where they are." But the need for this type of method comes in when the respondent is from a different background from the speaker. This process has been called contextualization or cross-cultural adaptation. See Michael Depew, "Paul and the Contextualization of the Gospel," at http://pages.preferred.com/~mdepew/mis1.html.

Though I am free and belong to no man, I make myself a slave to everyone, to win as many as possible. To the Jews I became like a Jew, to win the Jews. To those under the law I became like one under the law (though I myself am not under the law), so as to win those under the law. To those not having the law I became like one not having the law (though I am not free from God's law but am under Christ's law), so as to win those not having the law. To the weak I became weak, to win the weak. I have become all things to all men so that by all possible means I might save some (1 Cor. 9:19–22).

Paul accommodated himself, without compromising the gospel, to as many people as he could in order to present the gospel clearly. His goal was to help others accommodate their thinking to the gospel, the first step toward faith. But faith itself—believing in, committing to—is another matter entirely.

Stages of Cognitive Development: Keys to Effectiveness

Piaget proposed four major stages of development in thinking. For our present purpose we will discuss here only stages 3 and 4.[5] Although stage 3 develops between the ages of seven and eleven, most teenagers and adults "live" at this level. Piaget called this stage "concrete operational."

The term *concrete* refers to the ability to think logically about objects which have been physically handled or events which have been personally experienced. The term *operational* refers to the ability to handle operations—mental representations of actions—which have been personally experienced. Ask a four-year-old child whether he would like to have ten pennies or one quarter, and he will choose ten pennies. Why? Because it is "more money" (ten is more than one). The concept of "monetary value" has not been developed. Ten-year-olds will choose the quarter every time because they have had experience with pennies, nickels, dimes, and quarters and well know the difference in value!

Stage 3 thinkers learn better with the help of visual aids and props. Hands-on projects reinforce major ideas. Verbal instructions (words) can be confusing and should be kept brief and well organized. Find out what learners already know and use that to bridge to new material. Confront learners with logical problems which require them to use the information they're learning.

---

5 If you plan to work with children in different cultures, you will find help in Piaget's first two stages: "sensorimotor" and "preoperational."

Logical and *real* are defined in terms of what they have experienced for themselves. While teenagers and adults have the ability to think at stage 4, most choose to live at stage 3: "I know best what I have personally experienced." This has profound implications for evangelism and discipleship, especially across cultural barriers:

- Tradition (gods punish) is more powerful than (new) truth (God loves).
- A familiar ritual (lighting candles) is more comforting than an intangible relationship (with Jesus).
- Long-held family values (Muslims read the *Koran*) are more stable than new values (read the *Bible*) shared by strangers.

Jesus faced this challenge in the people he taught, as we shall soon see.

Piaget called stage 4 "formal operational." The term *formal* refers to the ability to think logically about abstract realities, such as *truth, justice,* and *liberty*. At this stage of development learners can think scientifically or hypothetically. They can consider ideas apart from personal experience. The following table focuses on the differences between the stages.

Stage 3	Stage 4
Visual (tangible) props	Mental images
Personal realities (subjective)	Abstract realities (objective, theoretical)
Rules (What *should* we do?)	Possibilities (What *can* we do?)
Hands-on projects	Mental reasoning
Rigid logic	Flexible hypothesizing
Correctly use stated procedures	Create innovative procedures
Application here and now	Universal principles
Concrete objects and events	Ideas
One's own perspective	Perspectives of others

Stage 4 is characterized by abstraction. Learners can examine abstract problems systematically and generalize results. They can operate with formal logic, constructing hypotheses (What if?) and testing them. They can isolate and control variables as well as evaluate their own reasoning and engage in introspection. They develop concerns about society. They can think logically about the possible as well as the impossible. Formal thinkers no longer need props or equipment to work out solutions to problems. They can manipulate objects in their minds. Without the ability to think abstractly, students must revert to memorizing what the teacher gives them.

However, formal thinking is not all positive. Without a concrete foundation, abstract thinking can lead to idealistic solutions which never touch reality. Having discovered the boundless freedom of the mind to see the ideal, adolescents create their mental Utopias. Then they rebel against the older generation that has not been able to make its own Utopias into realities.

Formal thinkers can create images of reality in their minds and find themselves hypocritically *thinking one way* and *living another.*

- A television evangelist enthusiastically preaches against every kind of moral evil and then cruises the red-light district of his city, paying call girls for pornographic poses.
- A pastor preaches a "salt and light" sermon decrying Christian Yellow Pages and exhorting the congregation to support the public school system while his own children attend an expensive private Christian school.
- A missionary preaches honesty and truthfulness while trading in the black market illegally "to stretch the Lord's money."
- A men's mission organization meets to eat breakfast and study missions around the world, but few engage in mission action.
- We sing "I Surrender All" with heartfelt emotion but live for the Lord as it is convenient.
- We powerfully proclaim the ideal but weakly live in the ordeal.

The Christ of the Book is not so concerned with abstract theologizing as he is with commitment to him in the realities of our day-to-day experiences. "Then he said to them all: 'If anyone would come after me, he must deny himself and take up his cross daily and follow me'" (Luke 9:23). We do his work his way. No red-light districts. No hypocritical preaching. No black market. Mission action more than mission talk. Living what we sing.

Formal thinking skills help learners understand the unconcrete world of spiritual things. But too much emphasis here can lead to idealized (and ultimately unworkable) solutions to problems. Concrete thinking skills help learners tie spiritual truths into solving real problems in a real world. But too much emphasis here can lead to rigid thinking which is resistant to change. What we must do is teach in a way that connects real-world issues to spiritual realities in mutually interactive ways.[6]

Jesus and the Rational

In the emotion-charged Middle East, with people suffering under Roman occupation, Jesus engaged the minds of listeners in several ways. "To the Jews who had believed him, Jesus said, 'If you hold to my teaching, you are really my disciples. Then you will know the truth, and the truth will set you free'" (John 8:31–32).

Parables

The parables of Jesus connected the real, experienced (stage 3) world of his Jewish listeners to the yet unexperienced truths of the abstract reality of the kingdom of heaven. The principles for living in the kingdom are abstract realities which must be connected to, or anchored into, the tangible world in which we live. Think of a boy flying a kite. He holds tightly to the kite by means of a string (anchor). The kite pulls against the boy under the power of the wind (lift). Both are needed for the kite to fly. If the wind stops blowing (no lift) or the boy lets go of the string (no anchor), the kite will fall. Kingdom truth lifts us to heaven and anchors us in the world.

> Jesus connected the stage 3 rational world of his learners to the stage 4 rational world of the kingdom by means of parables.

Principles such as *agape* love (meet the needs of others), justice (do to others as you would have them do to you), forgiveness (seventy times seven), long-suffering (carry the soldier's pack two miles rather than the

---

6 A challenge to formal thinking usually occurs for missionaries when they realize their idealized dreams will not work in the reality of their missionary setting. Missionaries are by nature idealists: they come to change their part of the world; they must see into the future; they see things that do not exist. However, their zeal does not include the skills and experience to make the dreams a reality. The true challenge of missions is taking these formal operations that exist in thought and finding ways to make them happen. AL

required one), inner joy (be happy when others abuse you for my sake), gentleness (return good for evil), and others are abstract realities. Even though we see them as ideals of the kingdom of heaven, which is itself an abstract reality, *Jesus modeled them* in his own earthly life and expects his followers to do the same. He connected the stage 3 rational world of his learners to the stage 4 rational world of the kingdom by means of parables. "The kingdom of heaven [abstract reality, stage 4] is like treasure hidden in a field [concrete reality, stage 3]" (Matt. 13:44).

"The kingdom of heaven is like . . .

- a man who sowed good seed in his field" (Matt. 13:24).
- a mustard seed, which a man took and planted in his field" (Matt. 13:31).
- yeast that a woman took and mixed into a large amount of flour until it worked all through the dough" (Matt. 13:33).
- a merchant looking for fine pearls" (Matt. 13:45).
- a net that was let down into the lake and caught all kinds of fish" (Matt. 13:47).
- the owner of a house who brings out of his storeroom new treasures as well as old" (Matt. 13:52).
- a king who wanted to settle accounts with his servants" (Matt. 18:23).
- a landowner who went out early in the morning to hire men to work in his vineyard" (Matt. 20:1).
- a king who prepared a wedding banquet for his son" (Matt. 22:2).

Jesus began with realities familiar to his listeners (stage 3), then used those concrete realities to express truths about the intangible, spiritual, invisible kingdom of heaven (stage 4). What are the concrete realities of Russians? or Asians? or Africans? or Hispanics? Can we use a schema that they already possess to convey gospel truths? With the Jews, Paul argued from Scripture. With the Greeks he quoted poets and philosophers. With the Romans he argued from natural law. We begin with stage 3, helping leader-learners connect what they know to what God has said about himself and his kingdom. Parables are a powerful point of connection.

Direct Experience

Jesus was not content to gather his disciples in a classroom and talk *at* them. He chose twelve to be *with* him. They observed his miracles and his teachings. They engaged in ministry with real people. He gave them instructions (Matt. 10) and then sent them out to surrounding villages. He also went out (11:1) and then debriefed them when they all gathered together. Such practical ministry experiences converted abstract theory into real-world practice and changed their thinking.

Social Interaction

Again, "He chose twelve to be with him." For three years Jesus and the twelve lived together, traveled together, prayed together, served together. What Jesus said around the campfire at night was mirrored by what he had done during the day. Zealots and fishermen learned from each other and from the Lord.

Questions

He asked questions. He did not have to ask questions, for he "knew what they were thinking" (Luke 5:22) and "knew what was in a man" (John 2:25). But he asked anyway, if for no other reason than to reveal to others what they were thinking. In the act of formulating and expressing an answer to a teacher's question, learners search their schema and organize their thinking.

The Learning Environment

Jesus created an environment where questions could be asked and opinions shared. Sometimes the disciples abused this freedom and expressed themselves inappropriately: "Also a dispute arose among them as to which of them was considered to be greatest" (Luke 22:24). But this discussion prompted one of the greatest teachings about who Jesus considered "great" in the kingdom: Jesus said to them, "The kings of the Gentiles lord it over them; and those who exercise authority over them call themselves Benefactors. But you are not to be like that. Instead, the greatest among you should be like the youngest, and the one who rules like the one who serves" (Luke 22:25–26).

Or remember when James and John began to argue (with the help of their mother) about who would sit at Jesus' right hand (the place of power)? The disciples became indignant over this. Jesus did not fuss at them for their childishness. He simply explained how misguided their thinking was. "Jesus called them together and said, 'You know that those who are regarded as rulers of the Gentiles lord it over them, and their high officials exercise authority over them. Not so with you. Instead, whoever wants to become great among you must be your servant, and whoever wants to be first must be slave of all. For even the Son of Man did not come to be served, but to serve, and to give his life as a ransom for many'" (Mark 10:42–45).

The learning environment Jesus created for his disciples was warm and demanding, loving and shaping, tender and tough; and by this process rational seeds were planted that would later bloom and bear fruit by the Holy Spirit. Jesus' teachings were the iron ore of the kingdom, which, when later smelted by the fire of the Spirit, would form the structural steel of a new way of thinking.

Revelation

Jesus asked his disciples one day about their views on his identity: "Who do you say that I am?" Peter responded, "You are the Christ, the Son of the living God" (Matt. 16:15–16). Jesus said to him, "Blessed are you . . . for this was not revealed to you by man, but by my Father in heaven" (Matt. 16:17). Spiritual truth is revealed by God, not "discovered" by natural biological processes. We will look more deeply at the teaching ministry of the Holy Spirit at the end of this chapter.

Jesus displayed rational character by his mastery of the Old Testament, his application of clear scriptural truths to real issues confronting his listeners, by his illustrations, questions, and explanations. He displayed flexibility in thinking as he connected with Jewish commoners, Pharisees, Romans, the Syro-Phoenician woman, and myriads of others. In fact, Dallas Willard makes a clear case for considering Jesus "the Smartest Man in the [history of the] World."

> [He] knew how to transform the molecular structure of water to make wine. That knowledge also allowed him to take a few pieces of bread and some little fish and feed thousands of people. He could create matter from the energy he knew how to access from "the heavens," right where he was. . . .
> He knew how to transform the tissues of the human body from sickness to health and from death to life. He knew how to suspend

gravity, interrupt weather patterns, and eliminate unfruitful trees with neither saw or ax. . . .

All these things show Jesus' cognitive and practical mastery of every phase of reality: physical, moral, and spiritual. He is Master only because he is Maestro. "Jesus is Lord" can mean little in practice for anyone who has to hesitate before saying "Jesus is smart."

He is not just nice, he is brilliant. He is the smartest man who ever lived. He is now supervising the entire course of world history (Rev. 1:5) while simultaneously preparing the rest of the universe for our future role in it (John 14:2). He always has the best information on everything and certainly also on the things that matter most in human life. Let us now hear his teachings on who has the good life, on who is among the truly blessed.[7]

Following this profound introduction to the brilliance of Jesus is four hundred pages of detailed analysis of the Sermon on the Mount.

Returning to Piaget

In Christian circles terms like *self-directed learning* and *inventing knowledge* cause a lot of disequilibrium. After all, don't we expect pastors to explain the Bible to their congregations? Don't we expect Bible teachers to teach the Bible, that is, to explain to learners what to believe? Don't we expect professors in Christian colleges to teach the truth so that students get it right? If so, then what has Piaget to say to us?

General Implications

For me teaching is more than talking at students. Teaching is more than presenting a lesson. It is more than transmitting content. *The evidence of effective teaching is found in the learning which occurs.* I can talk, but do my students listen? I can present a lesson, but do my students understand it? I can transmit facts, but do those facts have meaning for those I teach? Pastors explain, but do congregations understand? Bible teachers teach the Bible, but does their teaching ever make it into their learners' thinking, actions, or attitudes? College professors talk through their notes, but do their students grasp what those notes mean?

---

7 Dallas Willard, *The Divine Conspiracy: Rediscovering Our Hidden Life in God* (San Francisco: HarperSanFrancisco, 1997), 94–95.

A line from the hymn "People to People" expresses the problem Piaget addresses in teaching. The line reads, "How do you tell an orphan child about the Father's love?" The orphan has a scheme called "father." That scheme is different from the biblical image of God as Father. The biblical image is one of protection, guidance, strength, and discipline. The orphan's conception? It depends on his own experiences in being orphaned. But the one who teaches this orphan about God as Father must deal with the child's misconception of the term. The child can easily memorize the fact that the Bible says, "God is Father," but the *child's understanding of that term will never be biblical until he deals with his misconception first.*

Teacher and learners enter into conversations in which new material is related in meaningful ways to old ideas. Bible truths collide with learner perceptions and produce disequilibrium. Now if we provide the environment where the Bible speaks to our students, if we help them accommodate their thinking to its message, then they will begin to grow to be like him. This exegesis, this "reading out of" Scripture, in conjunction with the Holy Spirit's illuminating, provides light for the journey.

This light leads the bigot and the racist to learn to be "no respecter of persons" (Acts 10:34 KJV); it leads the materialist to learn to put his trust in the Lord, not possessions (Hab. 3:17–19); the power hungry to be a servant (Mark 9:35); the adulterer to be faithful (Matt. 5:27–28); the thief and liar to be honest (Hos. 4:2; Acts 6:3; 1 Pet. 2:12); and on and on, in a never-ending story, until we become as mature as the Lord (Eph. 4:11–13).

Beyond these general implications, what can we specifically do to energize a rational focus in our discipling and equipping ministry? Here are a few suggestions from Piaget's work.

Specific Implications

1. Optimal Discrepancy. *Optimal* means "best, most effective." *Discrepancy* means "difference" and refers to the difference between what learners know and what we are teaching. Put another way, we present ideas different enough to evoke curiosity about them but not so different as to provoke rejection of them.

Ask questions to find out what learners already know. ("Think about the best teacher you ever had." Pause. "How would you describe your best teacher?")

Tie new material to what learners already know. ("You will notice how your descriptions of your best teachers fall into three general areas. We can define these as a Triad.")

Illustrate principles with ideas that are already familiar to them. (I use the story of the samovar and bitter tea to illustrate the concept of assimilation. Not only does this connect with Russian students immediately; it does so with humor at my expense—stupid American doesn't know about zavarka? I am on their turf. My vulnerability also invites them to be honest and think of ways they have misunderstood (assimilation) things in their world. As they share these, the concept is reinforced naturally.)

Model the value of accommodation to new ideas by *learning from leader-learners*. For example,

- I graciously accept their corrections to my Russian slides, even though other groups of Russian speakers have corrected these same slides before.
- When they raise new ideas in class, I consider them carefully and attempt to see situations from their point of view.
- When they open themselves and their culture to me, explaining how they see things and do things, I treat their offerings gently and with heartfelt sensitivity.
- As I listen to them, I model the role of a thinker, which encourages them to consider my ideas as well.
- I constantly look for ways to express my ideas their way.
- I study indications of discrepancies in their thinking, as well as signs of resistance and, worse, rejection.

At the end of a course this past summer, I asked the students to evaluate my class on the basis of principles emphasized in class. One summary statement was this: "You haven't given us 'five ways to do something.' You have given us ideas, perspectives, ways to look at our problems within our own context. These we can use. These we need. *When can you come back and teach another class?*" This exercise of evaluation proved so effective in sealing the major emphases in the course that I have made it a regular part of every course I teach.

2. Direct Experience. Much of what we do in teaching is verbal—teachers telling learners about subjects. But real rational development in learners—that is, growth in understanding—occurs when learners engage subjects as active thinkers, not passive listeners.

I define the Teachers' Triad verbally and visually, but it is not until learners place themselves in one of the three groups and discuss their preferences in learning that the triad becomes a reflection of real differences among learners. I explain how to write instructional objectives, and my learners tell me they understand. But when they actually attempt to write objectives, few are able to do so. It is only through cycles of writing and correction that they master the process.

3. Social Interaction. Young learners are egocentric in their thinking. That is, they think that things *really are* the way *they see them.* Older learners may be egocentric. Social interaction—thinking, discussing, sharing with others—exposes learners to the ideas and opinions of others. One-way communication, teacher to student, needs to be supplemented with age-appropriate activities which encourage learner-to-learner interaction. Group projects and role-play scenarios are excellent ways to intersect the thinking of older children and youth.

Small groups of learners provide a better environment for interaction than large classes where individual differences are easily hidden. Learners will more likely admit confusion in a small group. More knowledgeable learners are better able to explain ideas in small groups. Some cultures place value on being part of the group (class, community), not standing out. These cultures view American individualism as a lack of respect for the group and in some cases as overt arrogance which deserves punishment. This is expressed nicely in the Russian proverb, "The tallest blade of grass is the first to feel the scythe." That is, don't stand out. Small-group activities permit opportunities for individuals to ask questions and process information more freely.

4. Thought-Provoking Questions. In processing a thought-provoking question, learners must consider what they know, decide what is relevant to the question, and then frame an answer. "How are 'to love' and 'to like' similar? How are they different?" Answers to such questions are windows into the minds of learners, allowing us to see what they already understand. Thought-provoking questions can certainly be answered incorrectly, but such incorrect answers are also important because they reveal where learners go wrong in their thinking.

Parroting back memorized answers to set questions does not reflect the understanding of learners. Memorized answers may hold no meaning for learners at all, and this leads to distorted memory.

Dog-ness. While these kinds of distortions are common among children, teaching across cultural gaps makes translation of concepts difficult even for adults. When teaching in western Ukraine, I found a class of adults who did not have the concept "concept." They understood facts. These they could memorize. And they understood values. These they could share. But "concept" was a concept they could not understand. I spent four hours giving them examples, asking questions, and working on the idea of concept. I finally broke through by using the made-up word "dog-ness" (*sabachnost,* from *sabaka,* dog) to differentiate between factual breeds (collie, dachshund, etc.) and the conceptual generic dog.

Preschoolers	Structured Play Creative Arts Music Nature Experiences Bible Thoughts
Children	Visual Aids Concrete Props Projects Learning Centers Bible Characters and Themes
Teenagers	Analytical Bible Study Drama and Role Play Hypothetical Situations Problem-Solving Testimonies of Christian Living Bible Concepts and Principles
Adults	Analytical Bible Study Specific Applications of Bible Truths Testimonies of Christian Living Practical Ministry/Mission Projects

Open-heart surgery? My first experience with this cross-cultural dilemma of understanding came in sharing the gospel with a deaf college student. I used the words I had learned growing up in Southern Baptist churches: "You need to open your heart and let Jesus come in." The deaf student looked at me and in all seriousness asked the following questions: "Do I have to go to the hospital for open-heart surgery? Is Jesus so small that he can live in my heart? Wouldn't he drown in the blood?"

I was speaking in "formal operational." He was hearing in "concrete operational." I could not explain the gospel to him. I asked the Lord to help me communicate with this deaf young man, and in a few days I got another chance.

"You are walking through life alone," I signed to him, drifting my upraised index finger outward, circling it, indicating *walking alone*. He immediately shook his head yes. "Jesus wants to walk with you and talk with you and live with you, but he is separated from you because of sin."

He said, "I've sinned a lot in my life."

"But if you repent of your sin," I explained, "and receive him into your life, he will come into your life and walk *with you* and talk with you, together, forever."

He looked at me and signed, "I want that." He prayed to receive Christ, and immediately there was a change in his eyes, in his face, in his understanding. A few weeks later I saw him talking with another college student: "You need to open your heart and invite Jesus to come in." The words now had real meaning for him. "Wouldn't he drown in the blood," his friend asked. "No, No! Let me explain this to you clearly." And he proceeded to share his newfound faith. Thought-provoking questions unlock the minds of our learners and help us establish clear meanings, even across cultural divides.

5. Learner Responses. Even students who answer questions correctly may not necessarily understand the answers. We will do better in crossing rational divides if we focus on the process of thinking and not just the product. Ask how learners arrived at their answers. Ask learners why they answered as they did. Focus on learners' meanings of words. What do learners mean by the words they've chosen?

Consider the common mistakes learners make in answering questions. Anticipate these and prepare explanations that target these problem areas. Remember, common mistakes in understanding will differ from culture to culture.

Discipling missionaries listen to others as intently as they speak to us. We cannot build a sturdy bridge from our cultural bank to theirs until we have theirs in sight. As we focus on learner responses, we seek the other bank.

6. Problem-Solving. "Teaching" for Piaget means creating situations where learners make discoveries. Problem-solving activities provide a rich environment for this kind of learning. Problems confront learners with unfamiliar situations and create disequilibrium. Solving the problem based on available resources brings about equilibration and a higher level of understanding.

The methodology of problem-solving encourages interaction among learners and with the teacher through discussion, questions, hypotheses, opinions, research, and teamwork. As disciplers listen to learners' solutions to problems, they not only determine how well they understand the material, but, further, they learn how their learners think.

The summer of 2005 was the first time, as I mentioned earlier, that I ended my Russian course, "Principles of Teaching and Learning for Pastors and Teachers," by having students (1) evaluate the course and the teacher, individually, based on course principles, (2) work in groups of four to five to summarize their evaluations, and (3) present their summaries to the class. As I listened to these group summaries, I learned more about how Ukrainian and Russian students think than in the previous eight years. For the first time I saw the course through their eyes, as they used the words and concepts I had taught them to express their views. I'll do this debriefing exercise from now on.

7. New Material. New material makes more sense to learners when it is connected to prior knowledge. Jesus "knew what was in a man" (John 2:25). We have to ask questions. The more we teach members of a given people group, the better we understand what they already know. As we teach them, we will do better if we integrate new material into what has already been learned. Specifically, use questions to link new material to past learnings.

In the introduction to the course, we discussed the Disciplers' Model. What was the left pillar called? "Thinking," they say. *Right!*

We discussed the importance of helping learners know and understand what we teach. We called this *what kind of focus?* "Cognitive," they say. *Very good!*

Today we will analyze six specific levels of learning within this general cognitive focus.

When we build rational bridges from established schemes to new material, learners see the new material as more meaningful and easier to master.

8. The Teaching Environment. Learning occurs as a result of interaction between learners and their learning world. Learners accommodate their thinking to the world around them. There is sage motherly advice in the words "choose your friends wisely" because, given time, we will begin to think like them. Accommodation will produce dramatically different results depending on whether a teenager's primary social group is the youth group at church or the gang on the street.

The classroom is a learning world. Teachers have the power to create a learning world that is safe and open yet challenging, a learning world where students can ask any question without fear of humiliation. Where teachers listen as well as talk. Where ideas can be challenged, defended, or refuted without harsh words or flaring tempers. Where misconceptions can be aired without condemnation. Where teacher and learner interact, sharing together questions and answers drawn from the material but anchored in real-life issues.

Establishing a safe learning world takes time. Learners carry negative learning baggage from past bad experiences. They have preconceptions of who we are as "teacher," as "American," as "foreigner." If we are too harsh, will we be rejected? If we are too soft, will we be bullied? I have found that "love covers a multitude of sins" (1 Pet. 4:8). As I engage the minds of learners for their sake, as I show compassion for them as human beings (see chapter 5), as I listen, and as I speak in terms they can understand within their own context, they come to see me as helper rather than hurter. As they learn that no student will be humiliated for asking a question, and, further, that they can actually get meaningful answers to their questions, a loving, rational environment develops in which real-life transformation can occur.

9. The Holy Spirit as Teacher. (This section restates chapter 2 from another perspective.) I freely admit that the biological mechanisms of equilibration and adaptation *are inadequate* to produce biblical results when teaching *spiritual* truths. Such mechanisms may help us accommodate to a particular religion or allow us to become experts on ancient Middle East culture or categorize the books of the Bible or learn the major events, people, and places of Scripture. But until our learners' thinking interacts with the Lord himself, we produce nothing more than a biblical intellectualism. The circle of the Disciplers' Model emphasizes the role of the Holy Spirit as teacher. Jesus promised us spiritual help by means of the Holy Spirit. "If you love me, you will obey what I command. And I will ask the Father, and he will give you another Counselor to be with you forever—the Spirit of truth. The world cannot accept him, because it neither sees him nor knows him. But you know him, for he lives with you and will be in you" (John 14:15–17).

The primary work of the Holy Spirit is to teach spiritual truths. Jesus explained, "But the Counselor, the Holy Spirit, whom the Father will send in my name, will teach you all things and will remind you of everything I have said to you" (John 14:26).

The Holy Spirit provides a spiritual context by which we may accommodate our thinking to the teachings of Jesus and grow spiritually. And who is this Counselor, this Holy Spirit? Jesus identifies himself with the Holy Spirit, his divine personal presence in the lives of his disciples. "I will not leave you as orphans; I will come to you" (John 14:18). This may explain why Peter and Paul use the terms "Spirit of Christ" or "Spirit of Jesus" and "Holy Spirit" interchangeably.[8]

However we handle the difficulties of the trinitarian nature of God, the point is clear. Spiritual understanding requires a spiritual teacher. No purely biological process can explain spiritual understanding to the satisfaction of the one who made us to be like him.

The Holy Spirit, the Spirit of Christ, is part of the immaterial environment in which we operate. Interaction with him injects a spiritual underpinning to biblical studies, which leads to biblical thinking, which leads to a biblical lifestyle, which is defined as "walking with the Lord."

Jesus taught his disciples for three years. They lived together, ate together, shared ministry and miracles together. And yet, when the soldiers came to the garden of Gethsemane, they ran away. They understood a great deal from their experiences with Jesus. After all, Jesus was the greatest teacher who ever lived. But it wasn't until after the resurrection, when Jesus appeared to them, and after Pentecost, when they were filled and empowered by the Holy Spirit, that they truly understood what had happened. Then they became courageous concerning the truths of the kingdom and by his power turned the world upside-down (Acts 17:6).

When we teach in a mission context—preaching, Bible studies, discipleship classes, leadership conferences—we may teach for a long time without visible results. Then, without any apparent reason, we see lives transformed, attitudes changed, behaviors improved. This is the work of the Spirit of the Lord, who moves not in the constrained forces of

---

8 For examples of Paul's uses of the terms, see Romans 8:9 and Philippians 1:19; then Romans 9:1, 1 Corinthians 6:19, 2 Corinthians 6:6. For Peter's, see 1 Peter 1:11 and 4:14.

biological processes but freely like the wind: "The wind blows wherever it pleases. You hear its sound, but you cannot tell where it comes from or where it is going. So it is with everyone born of the Spirit" (John 3:8).

When our content is spiritual truth, we must do all we can to embrace the principles discussed here. Develop concepts, relate materials to the thinking abilities of your learners, use small groups and interaction. Then pray for the Holy Spirit to infuse the concepts of those who know him with his own power, his own teaching, in order to transform their understanding into spiritual growth. Our dependence on the Holy Spirit to teach spiritual things undergirds our best efforts in explanation, illustration, questioning, and problem-solving. It is not an excuse for poor methodology or faulty teaching procedures.

Strong Tea, Tapioca, and Breadcrumbs Revisited

What I thought was tea in a pitcher in a Ukrainian dining room turned out to be *zavarka*, a concentrated tea liquid that is mixed to taste with boiling water drawn from a *samovar* electric water heater. A principal of a deaf school considered dislike of tapioca pudding a characteristic of deafness. In fact, the pudding was inedible. He further interpreted the hand movements of the students as "brushing crumbs on us." In fact, the students were politely saying, "Excuse me," as they passed the principal and his guest.

While these are humorous examples, misconceptions can have serious implications. What we in the West consider cheating (stealing), even Christian students in other cultures may well view as "helping a brother (sister) in need." Copying answers off a neighbor's paper is a violation of honesty in a highly individualistic culture but can be a measure of koinonia in communal ones. It can also be irresponsible behavior! Regardless, this cultural acceptance of "sharing" has a negative impact on learning. Students may divide up the test for study (each of four groups studying one-fourth of the material) and then sharing answers with one another ("After all, why should every person memorize the same material?"). Or students may distribute the responsibility to take notes in class. Then they share the notes with one another ("After all, why should we all take notes at the same time?").

Rather than chastising students for stealing or dishonesty, help them see the importance of each student's earning his own grade as a matter of honor. Emphasize small-group projects, which allow students to work together on a common task. Create two or three parallel forms of an exam which present the same questions in different orders, and then distribute the tests so that students cannot easily copy the answers of neighbors. I have done this for the last three years; and, out of over 150 students in my classes, I have had only one student ask why his test was not the same as his neighbor. ("How do you know?" I asked. He stammered a little, smiled sheepishly, and went back to his test.) Yes, he was trying to cheat.

Beyond educational ethics, is it acceptable for Christians to refer to God as "Allah" in Muslim areas? Do we insist on keeping time schedules in event-oriented cultures? These and hundreds of other issues will rock our mental boats as we interact in cultures different from our own. Piaget's observations help us analyze these sources of disequilibrium and, while they will not prevent culture shock, help us understand what is happening to us.

We close this chapter with a quote from Jean Piaget. It describes his goals for the educational process.

> The principle goal of education is to create men who are capable of doing new things, not simply of repeating what other generations have done—men who are creative, inventive, and discoverers. The second goal of education is to form minds which can be critical, can verify, and not accept everything they are offered. The great danger today is of slogans, collective opinions, ready-made trends of thoughts. We have to be able to resist, individually, to criticize, to distinguish between what is proven and what is not. So we need pupils who are active, who learn early to find out by themselves, partly by their own spontaneous activity and partly through material we set up for them; who learn early to tell what is verifiable and what is simply the first idea to come to them.[9]

Piaget's language rocks the boats of some Christians because it is so open-ended, so man centered, so oblivious to Scripture's absolutes, even rebellious to the established order.

All I need do in reply is to think of the Lord who authored Scripture and who was best known on earth as Teacher. The Lord loved people and

---

9 From *Piaget Rediscovered*, p. 5, as quoted by Herbert Ginsburg and Sylvia Opper, *Piaget's Theory of Intellectual Development: An Introduction* (Englewood Cliffs, N.J.: Prentice-Hall, 1969), 231–32.

met their needs. He began with concrete experiences of their day and led them to consider the spiritual reality of the kingdom. He asked questions and posed problems. He used concrete demonstrations, parables, and stories. He sent the disciples on mission trips for hands-on ministry experience. He demonstrated repeatedly that the religious establishment had missed God's truth and had pursued their own rituals.

Or I think of the apostle Paul, who, as a Pharisee's Pharisee (Acts 23:6), assimilated the idea of "The Way" by condemning its early followers, hunting them down and putting them in prison. Then he met the Lord and accommodated his thinking to the reality of the resurrection. As a missionary teacher he reinterpreted the Old Testament in light of the cross and the empty tomb. He understood the Pharisees in particular and the Jews in general, as well as the Greeks and the Romans. He taught in a variety of ways so each could understand and come to faith in the risen Lord.

Jesus established the church as the base for teaching ministry (Matt. 28:19–20). Paul believed in the church as a learning environment in which the lost could find salvation and the saved grow in the Lord. The Great Commission of reaching people where they are and teaching them all things after they're reached requires the flexibility of thinking, the open-mindedness, and the problem-solving skills Piaget so ably suggested.

May God bless us as we give our minds to him to be elevated above old established schemes, to be opened to new ways of seeing him, and to be transformed by his own teaching. May we reach across cultural divides to engage different perspectives, and "take captive every thought to make it obedient to Christ" (2 Cor. 10:5), as we disciple and equip others in Jesus' name.

Mike's Reaction

This chapter is powerful because it pinpoints a huge challenge for missionaries, that is, misunderstandings brought about by cultural clashes between cognitive realities—beliefs, knowledge, worldview. Here we find practical help for preventing and/or dealing with these misunderstandings. There is an infamous story of the tribe who observed foreigners eating food from cans with pictures on them. When they saw a jar of baby food with the Gerber baby on the label, they misunderstood what was inside! It seems to me that cross-cultural disciplers need to be aware of their own cognitive development (or lack thereof) as well as that of the locals.

I understand that the whole subject of contextualization will arise during this discussion. How far should we accommodate a foreign, pagan culture? How creative can we be when we communicate the gospel? Cross-cultural dilemmas arise for which there may not be obvious answers. Can we establish "Jesus mosques" rather than churches? Should we use the term *Allah* for *God,* or not? Do we really believe that our methods (church planting movements, house churches, multiple leaders, and so on) work the same way in every culture? A solid rational character, anchored in God's Word, will be the key.

What Rick discusses here has great implications for me as a teacher/discipler. We must learn to teach others to learn from the Bible rather than from us. We must teach (that is, model) how to depend on the Holy Spirit. Our role as disciplers and equippers is to facilitate and affirm rather than to indoctrinate or prescribe for them what must be believed and done. We serve as coaches on how to reproduce disciples and disciplers within their own cultural context.

Of all the practical suggestions Rick gives to cross-cultural disciplers, I see mastering the art of asking questions and listening as the best practice. In general, as I read his practical suggestions, I thought that these tactics are most needed but seldom applied. I might be bold in saying, "When they are applied, God blesses, and they work!"

Having read Rick's other books, I know he cut back in this chapter on pure psychological theory in order to focus more on the practical dimensions of our work of discipling and equipping. *Created to Learn* and *Called to Teach* can provide this theoretical basis for those who wish to go deeper.

The Compassionate Character
of cross-cultural
Disciplers

Disciplers' Model

5

Developing a Compassionate Character
Mike Barnett

When he saw the crowds, he had compassion on them,
because they were harassed and helpless, like sheep without a shepherd.
Matthew 9:36

The discipler develops a compassionate character, a perspective devoted to caring for and meeting the needs of others, and is better able to connect with learner-leaders than those who do not. Chapter 5 addresses the question of where the needs of learner-leaders fit into the discipling process. We then describe how we develop a compassionate character as a solid foundation for discipling across cultures.

The Toxic Flip Side

Focusing on our tasks, ignoring needs of learner-leaders

An Unexpected Visitor

He was a young business owner in the fast lane of boomtown Houston, Texas, in the 1970s. Life was good. The new business was going well. Of course there was much to do, leading and managing a company of twenty-five employees. He and his partner were always working, six days a week, long days, but this was what it was all about, wasn't it? With increased sales, inventories, and new customers, it was time to focus on the business—nothing was more important!

It was after 6:00 PM that Wednesday evening, and he was going over the monthly sales reports when he suddenly felt the presence of someone in the room. He looked up from his desk and there she was, an old bedraggled lady apparently off the streets. Her face revealed many years of hardship and rough living. How had she gotten into his office at this hour? Everyone was gone except him, and he always locked the front door to the office after hours?

"Can I help you?" he asked impatiently.

"Could you spare some money for food and milk for my grandbaby?" the old lady pleaded.

"I'm afraid not," he replied as he rose to escort her out of the office and back onto the streets. "But if you go three blocks further down the street, there is a good church, and I'm sure they can help you." He opened the door for her as she politely thanked him and left his office building.

The young businessman made sure he locked the door this time, and he quickly returned to his office and work. *Strange how she got into the office,* he thought. *You know it's not really that safe in this industrial neighborhood. I'll have to be more careful next time.* And then it hit him—a terrible feeling. A sensation, no, not of guilt but of a lost opportunity. After all, she obviously wasn't a con artist. She was really a lady in need. Why hadn't he helped her? Why didn't he share the love of Jesus with this lady?

He of all people. A committed follower of Jesus. In fact, he was headed to church choir practice that evening. And one who had been blessed with more than enough money—why, he was an over-and-above tither! And yet he kicked that poor, needy lady out of his office and gave her nothing, not a penny! Why, just last week he taught the youth group that Bible study lesson on helping the poor. What was the text—Matthew 6:3–4? "But when you give to the needy, do not let your left hand know what your right hand is doing, so that your giving may be in secret. Then your Father, who sees what is done in secret, will reward you." Yes, the Father sees, and the Holy Spirit convicts. The young businessman knew he missed a chance to give to the needy in secret. He failed to obey the command of Jesus. Even worse, he ignored the leading of the Holy Spirit. And now the Spirit was convicting him. He had to fix it! He had to make it right. He rushed to the front of the office and out into the parking lot to look for the old lady. . . .

The Right Foundation Stone: The Needs of People

The right foundation stone in the model represents the needs of those we teach. The Bible was written by men who were inspired by God, who hungered for him, whose deepest needs were met, and whose lives were filled by a loving God. Learners discover these riches by applying biblical teachings and experiences to their own needs.

Jesus Focused on Needs

Jesus taught people Scripture by focusing it at their point of personal need. Zacchaeus was lonely. Jesus asked to have dinner with him (Luke 19:10). Jairus grieved at the death of his daughter. Jesus raised her to life (Mark 5:21ff). Nicodemus the Pharisee sought Jesus' words on the kingdom of God. Jesus gave him specific instructions (John 3). Jesus reached across deep cultural divides when he healed the servant of the Roman centurion (Matt. 8) and healed the daughter of a Canaanite woman (Matt. 15).

Disciplers' Model

Jesus did not dine with everyone or raise all the dead people or give special instructions to all. *He met needs in the lives of people and in doing so taught us about our Father and his kingdom.* Jesus pointed to soils and light and salt and sheep, basic things that were familiar to those who pressed close to hear him teach. He had no use for sideshow gimmicks. He spoke the words of life everyone hungers for! He shared with his learners a caring Father who wants only the best for them. The eternal truth of Scripture became real to the persons he touched because he first touched them at their point of need.

Our Learners Have Needs

Our learners, regardless of culture, have the same basic, personal needs that Jesus found in the people of his day. We need to follow the Master's example in order to connect with others as he did. We do this by loving our learners and teaching so they can understand Scripture as it relates to the nitty-gritty concerns in their world. What the Bible says is unchanging, but how we explain it varies with those we teach. Learners have differing needs, both general and specific.

General Needs. What are the general needs of those we teach? How do they differ from our own? *What we see as needs may not be an issue for those from a different culture.* As we teach, the spotlight must be on the felt needs of those we teach. We must relate to their needs, not ours. We must focus on communicating the gospel across cultural barriers in a way that meets their felt needs, not ours.

As Westerners our first thoughts are often of physical needs—food, shelter, health care, education, jobs, and so on. But there is another, larger area of general need: the need to know the Lord personally, to grow in the Lord, to use one's gifts from the Lord in a place of service to others. Every believer needs to worship God. Every believer needs to read and understand God's Word. Every believer needs to pray. Every believer needs fellowship with other believers. Every believer needs to share the gospel with others. These general areas of need guide us as we prepare to teach. Meeting these needs will ultimately result in the maturational character of the discipler or learner-leader—the capstone of the Disciplers' Model (see chapter 8).

Specific Needs. Perhaps the first way to connect with the learner-leader is to relate to their specific needs. These are the physical needs mentioned above and the emotional needs of oppressed and persecuted peoples. These often include the need to deal with personal failures, past tragedies, present struggles, family influences (and, perhaps, rejection), and areas of spiritual drought.

There is much pain in life. Until an atmosphere of trust is established with learners, a connection made, these areas of need remain hidden. So we give ourselves to knowing our learners as persons, as individuals. We rejoice with them when they celebrate and empathize with them when they hurt. We accept their invitations and put our feet under their tables. We drink tea and eat their food with grace and gratitude. We listen for the areas of need and hurt in their lives and then minister to them as we are able in the Lord. When learners discover we care for them, that we want them to succeed and grow and share their lives with us, they are more likely to trust the message and model for life and work that we share and teach. They not only listen better, but they take it in, absorb it, treasure it. They learn with their hearts as well as their heads.

Compassion—the Real Meaning?

An effective cross-cultural discipler must have a compassionate character. Sounds simple enough. But what exactly do we mean by *compassion?* We say that people with compassion feel sorry for the misfortune of others. They like to help others; they meet their needs. They are advocates for those who suffer. They give their money, influence, and prayers on behalf of others. That is all true enough. But let's see if we can sharpen our understanding of this characteristic of the cross-cultural discipler.

> Compassionate character goes beyond impersonal sympathy. Disciplers are sometimes called to *suffer with* the leader-learner and his family, tribe, or nation!

The word *compassion* is defined in the Collins dictionary as "a feeling of distress and pity for the suffering or misfortune of another." This is how many use the term today. But the Latin root is *compatī. Com* means "with" and *patī* is from the verb "to bear" or "to suffer." So the root idea of compassion is "to suffer with" another. Compassionate character goes beyond impersonal sympathy. It involves more than feeling sorry and having pity from a distance. Effective cross-cultural disciplers are sometimes called to *suffer with* the leader-learner and his family, tribe, or nation!

Compassionate Disciplers

We have many examples of the compassionate character of cross-cultural disciplers. One of the best-known missionaries of the 1800s was Charlotte Digges Moon, known as Lottie Moon. Lottie was one of the first Southern Baptist single women missionaries. She spent almost forty years teaching and discipling people in China. Lottie was known for her aggressive advocacy of the gospel for the Chinese peoples. She provided personal funds for ministry when the mission at home had none. She led others to pray for the lost peoples of East Asia, and she used her personal influence as a veteran missionary to promote the mobilization of human, financial, and prayer resources on behalf of the peoples of China. Today the annual international missions offering of Southern Baptists is still called the "Lottie Moon Christmas Offering." Yet her most lasting legacy is undoubtedly the compassionate way she lived and died among the unreached peoples of China.

Lottie invested her life with the suffering masses of China. She knew the only way to build trust and confidence with her Bible students was to *suffer with* them. She called on workers from North America to prepare to sacrifice for the sake of witness among the Chinese. This was serious business—God's business. In her recruitment letters to home, Lottie clarified the costs by invoking the model of the Suffering Servant himself.

They [new missionaries to China] must be men and women of absolute self-consecration, ready to come down and live among the natives, to wear Chinese dress and live in Chinese houses, rejoicing in the footsteps of Him who "though he was rich, yet for our sakes became poor, that we, through his poverty, might be made rich." We do not ask people to come out to live in costly foreign style . . . barely touching the heathen world with the tips of their fingers, but we ask them to come prepared to cast in their lot with the natives.[1]

Indeed, many of our missionary heroes seem to *suffer with* the nationals to the point that their lives are transformed along with those of their learner-leaders. It makes sense, doesn't it? As we serve those we teach, God teaches us, and our lives are changed forever. After years of suffering with the Chinese people, Lottie Moon evidenced this transformation. "She was no longer an aloof emissary who arrived to give the heathen glad tidings. She could no longer divide people into 'us' and 'them.' The Chinese people and Lottie Moon were one. She took on their struggles one by one as they appeared at her door. The 'school' of women was now a hostel for beggars. She not only doled out pittances to those who asked, but she took them into her home."[2]

Lottie wasn't the only missionary with true compassionate character. Her English peer and coworker, J. Hudson Taylor, became so frustrated with his missionary colleagues, who were satisfied to remain in the comfort and security of Shanghai, that he broke away from them and established the China Inland Mission. Taylor led the charge into the inland regions of China. He suffered with the Chinese as he taught and discipled them in the name of Jesus Christ.

William Carey never once returned to England during his forty-one years of work and ministry in India (1793–1834). The price that he and especially his first wife Dorothy paid was sometimes seen as "over the

---

1 Catherine B. Allen, *The New Lottie Moon Story* (Nashville: Broadman Press, 1980), 174.
2 Ibid., 273.

Was Jesus a Cross-Cultural Discipler?

Without a doubt Jesus modeled cross-cultural discipleship. The incarnation itself is the ultimate expression of crossing culture with compassion. Jesus, "being in very nature God," knew that his learner-leaders would never comprehend who he was by looking through human lenses. People would not be able to grasp God unless he "made himself nothing, taking the very nature of a servant, being made in human likeness" (Phil. 2:6–7). So Jesus modeled for us that we must become like those we teach to the point of understanding how effectively to communicate Christ and model the life of discipleship among them.

Jesus also models the cross-cultural aspect of discipleship in that, though he focused his ministry on twelve Jewish Galileans from his same earthly culture, he taught a gospel of international significance. He laid a biblical foundation that would spread to all nations. He was a master at communicating the message to Jews and Gentiles. He could influence all strata of society—from religious and political leaders to rich young rulers, and the common masses themselves. Yes, Jesus was a cross-cultural discipler.

---

top" by those who remained at home.[3] But this kind of suffering with the nationals is a common characteristic of those we consider our best cross-cultural disciplers. Like Lottie Moon, they have compassionate character.

But you don't have to be an international missionary to be an effective cross-cultural discipler. Almost every church in North America has their unsung heroes of compassion. My wife works at a local church. She frequently talks about Bill Windham, the coordinator of a ministry called Mission Columbia. Bill coordinates this ministry arm of Northside Baptist Church to help those in need.

Bill doesn't think much about it, doesn't dwell on it. He simply responds to God's call on his life to help those who are suffering. He has a humble spirit about this ministry. But Bill does in fact *suffer with* the people he assists. He takes his time and invests his life in meeting the needs of those in his community. You may well ask, "Where is the cross-cultural aspect of Bill's suffering with others?" The people Bill assists are seldom from his middle-class world. They are the disinherited

---

3 Timothy George, *Faithful Witness: The Life and Mission of William Carey* (Birmingham: Christian History Institute in Association with Samford University, 1998).

slice of South Carolina society. They include immigrants from around the world. They are indigent peoples alienated from the mainstream—under-employed, dependent on chemical substances, chronically ill, and often homeless. Bill has compassion for these displaced people. He recognizes their general need for Jesus Christ, and he shares the gospel with them in a culturally sensitive way. He also meets their specific physical and/or emotional needs. He is a cross-cultural discipler with compassionate character. Do you know any Bills?

Compassionate character embraces suffering alongside those who are, themselves, suffering. It is up close and personal, down and dirty, front-line work. Compassion enables us to connect with our learner-leaders at *their point of need.* Such character follows the pattern modeled by Jesus Christ himself, the ultimate cross-cultural Discipler, who reflected this kind of compassionate character.

The Compassionate Character of Jesus

One undeniable aspect of the three-year ministry of Jesus is that he was continually meeting the needs of others. We see him "teaching in their synagogues [and] preaching the good news of the kingdom," meeting the *general needs* of the people. We also see him "healing every disease and sickness" (Matt. 9:35)—meeting the *specific needs* of the people. Our task as cross-cultural disciplers is a both-and proposition.

In fact, it seems that Jesus' compassion for people's needs often precedes and initiates his ministry of the gospel. "When he saw the crowds, [Jesus] had compassion on them" (Matt. 9:36) and was compelled to send out the disciples with his authority to preach and heal "every disease and sickness" (Matt. 10:1). He instructed them, "As you go, preach this message: 'The kingdom of heaven is near.' Heal the sick, raise the dead, cleanse those who have leprosy, drive out demons" (Matt. 10:7–8). Later in his Galilean ministry, Jesus "had compassion" on the crowds, and he led the disciples in the feeding of the five thousand (Matt. 14:14). Along the roadside between Jericho and Jerusalem, once again Jesus "had compassion" on two blind men. He "touched their eyes" and "immediately they received their sight and followed him" (Matt. 20:34). Once again we see the *both-and* style of Jesus. The Master Discipler taught spiritual truth as he ministered to the specific needs of those who followed him. The gospel message is accompanied by the ministry of compassion and vice versa. This is the compassionate character of a cross-cultural discipler!

Another interesting account of the compassion of Christ takes place in Galilee. After days of teaching and ministering to the needs of those near Capernaum, the home base of his ministry, Jesus had become somewhat of a celebrity. His reputation in the region was becoming a concern among religious authorities. Indeed, later in his ministry the Pharisees began to plot to kill Jesus (Mark 3:6) in order to remove him as a threat to the status quo of their religion. Not only that, the pressing needs of the crowds were overwhelming. Time for physical refreshment, prayer, and private contact with the twelve was becoming scarce. The disciples regularly tried to guard Jesus' schedule. Jesus had a big security problem.

In the midst of this volatile situation, Mark's Gospel (Mark 1:40–45) says that "a man with leprosy came to him and begged [Jesus] on his knees" to heal his disease. The Bible says Jesus was "filled with compassion" as he reached out his hand and healed the man. In this case, for security reasons Jesus warned the healed leper not to tell his story to the crowds but to find a priest and let his new sacrifices to God according to the teachings of Moses serve as his testimony. But the man could not help himself. "He went out and began to talk freely, spreading the news . . . [so that] Jesus could no longer enter a town openly but stayed outside in lonely places" (Mark 1:45).

What an example of compassion! Jesus risked his own time, ministry, comfort, and even his life in order to heal the leper. Time and time again Jesus models for us how the compassionate character of a cross-cultural discipler is absolutely necessary. Of course, Jesus later paid the ultimate price in order to *suffer with* his followers, but we don't want to get ahead of ourselves—the passion of Christ is for the next chapter.

Rebekah Naylor, "A Discipler of Compassion"

I first met her in the spring of 2001. Of course I knew who she was— Dr. Rebekah Naylor, the medical missionary to Bangalore, India, and daughter of a past-president of a seminary, Robert Naylor. But I'd never met her face-to-face. My dean suggested that I meet with Dr. Naylor and discuss the possibility of her teaching a missions course at the seminary during her indefinite time in the States.

It was an interesting meeting. I quickly learned that Rebekah had returned to the States after thirty years of service in India in order to assist her elderly mother. I would soon learn that this woman's concern for her mother was a reflection of a driving need to help others. Don't get me wrong, Dr. Naylor is not a person of "warm and fuzzy" emotionalism. As

a surgeon, medical administrator and teacher, veteran missionary, and seminary professor, Rebekah is rigorous and task oriented. I will never forget her amazement when we reviewed the syllabus for our introduction to missiology class. "Is this all they have to read?" she inquired. But beneath the skin of this hard-driving professional was the mind of a lifelong learner and the heart of a compassionate cross-cultural discipler.

Through her years in Bangalore, Rebekah and her colleagues served those in need over and above the normal medical requirements. Naylor acknowledged that hospital patients came expecting "the foreign doctors . . . to know something more than others, so they came hoping that they would find excellent care. They did find excellent care, but they also found people who really cared about them."[4] When asked what she misses most about India, the answer is always the same. It's the people. Relationships built over three decades. Indian medical colleagues, patients, pastors, and church planters—these are the fruit of her ministry. Her eyes often well up as she tells stories of her days of doctoring and discipling in Bangalore.

Today the Bangalore Baptist Hospital delivers fifteen hundred babies and sees more than 100,000 patients each year. The hospital staff is almost completely made up of Indian nationals. But the legacy of the discipling ministries of Dr. Naylor and her missionary colleagues lives on through the lives and ministries of learner-leaders scattered throughout the state of Karnataka, India. As dozens of local church planters sent from hundreds of churches carry the gospel of Christ to some thirty thousand villages through three hundred different languages, you can rest assured they will serve the needs of others with compassion.[5]

By the way, Rebekah is far from finished in her profession and ministry. Her role has matured into that of an encourager, a coach, and a role model. She teaches at a medical school in North America along with her role as an adjunct professor at a seminary. She returns regularly to India and speaks around the world working from her stateside base as she con-

4 http://www.tconline.org/stories/1029751.html, accessed 25 February 2005.
5 Ibid.

tinues to care for her mother. Don't be surprised if you bump into her on the fields of the harvest—Dr. Rebekah Naylor, a discipler of compassion.

How to Develop and Maintain Compassionate Character

By now we can see a complementary pattern that characterizes effective cross-cultural disciplers. They surrender to the leadership of the Holy Spirit (spiritual character). They live out the principles, teachings, and models of the Bible (biblical character). Cross-cultural disciplers understand the perspective of nationals as they lead them to think biblically in ways that make sense in their own culture (rational character). And they care for and meet the needs of others, even to the point of *suffering with* those they serve (compassionate character).

How do we develop and maintain compassionate character? Because compassion is bound with a spirit of selflessness, I like to think of it as an act of worship—a recognition of worth, an offering. We develop compassionate character by *offering ourselves, our services, and our witness* to God in behalf of those in need.

First, We Decide to Offer Ourselves

Some people seem to be born with compassionate hearts. Since her earliest years, my daughter reflected a heart for helping those in need. Even as a little girl, she always rescued those with special needs—babies, elderly, the ill, the poor. She would be concerned for those homeless people on the side of the road with their signs asking for food or money. And she always questioned why I didn't stop to assist them. As a teenager, after a trip to the Bible lands, she mobilized her British secondary school class to raise funds to support refugees in Palestine. In college she worked as a nurse's assistant at a mental hospital. And now she is doing graduate studies in counseling in order to serve those in desperate mental and emotional need. She is not motivated by money, fame, or fortune. She loves to help others. Wouldn't it be easy if God made all of us like her? If we all had tender hearts of compassion, if we all readily offered ourselves to serve others at their greatest point of need?

But it doesn't work like that for most of us. We have to work at developing compassionate character. And it begins by deciding. Deciding to be compassionate. Of course, it is easy to say we will be compassionate, but it takes hard work and discipline. We need a plan, a strategy, for developing compassionate character. The first step in developing compassionate character is deciding to serve and help others. The following steps should help us begin.

1. *Talk and listen to God* about your level of compassionate character. Admit to him that this is a critical aspect of effective cross-cultural discipling. Agree with him to look for opportunities to serve others at their point of need. Journal your ongoing conversation with God about compassionate character. Talk and listen on a regular basis.

2. *Find an accountability partner.* Agree with a like-minded brother or sister in Christ to hold each other accountable regarding your development of compassionate character. Communicate on a regular basis.

3. *Do an honest self-assessment* of your capacity for compassion. Is it a strength or weakness for you? Are you committed to offering compassion to those in need? Where do you struggle with this aspect of character. Share your assessment with your accountability partner. Self-assess on a regular basis.

4. *Follow biblical principles, teachings, and models of compassionate character.* Share with others every time you read a biblical example of Christlike compassion. Share in church, through your newsletter, in small groups, with those you disciple. Share your struggles and celebrate your progress as God grows compassionate character in you.[6]

If you already have a system of self-assessment and evaluation, simply build this character aspect into your current practice. The main thing, the first thing, is to *decide to offer* compassion to others.

We Offer Ourselves

The next step in developing compassionate character is intentionally making ourselves available to others. Easier said than done! Especially if we come from a fast-paced, self-focused, individualistic, and impersonal culture.

Perhaps you have heard the testimonies of international cross-cultural disciplers (missionaries) who live and work "in the bush" in some remote

---

6 It helps us to set aside some time each week to evaluate our lives—maybe one lunch hour or a predictably slow time of the week. For me it is Friday afternoons. During this time I will stop, offer my time and my life to the Lord, and listen to his words and guidance about my life. I do not have a set format for this time, but whenever I do it, the Lord reveals himself to me. God will always work in our lives if we wholeheartedly give ourselves to him. AL

land. They live in a tribal culture where everyone cares for one another. They are far removed from the fast pace of the high-tech, globalized urban world. It's as though they live back in the nineteenth century. And, yes, they do spend time drinking tea and talking about Jesus! Wouldn't it be great to have time just to sip tea and serve the needs of others?

But wait a minute! Did Jesus have a laid-back, low-paced, rural assignment? I don't think so. Jesus was living and working in the fast lane; people were pulling at every part of him. Though the Galilee region was hardly urban by modern-day standards, it was a center of commerce along the trade routes from Jerusalem to Damascus. More than once Jesus had to separate himself from the pace of ministry and retreat to "a mountainside by himself to pray" (Matt. 14:23). Granted he was caught up in the frantic pace of preaching and healing ministries, but the point is that even Jesus had to consciously offer himself in behalf of others. Likewise, compassionate cross-cultural disciplers must intentionally offer themselves to others in need.

1. *Offer your time.* For many of us, this is the toughest thing about compassionate character. It costs the most precious thing for many of us—our time. How much of your time is spent serving the needs of those who are hurting? Don't let yourself become insulated from this frontline aspect of suffering with others. Build this time commitment into your life and work. Put it in your personal ministry plan. Include it in your time budget. Jesus did!

2. *Offer your possessions.* This one can be deceptive. In my case it usually becomes a matter of giving money. Cindy and I have become so systematic in tithing and planning for certain special offerings that giving our possessions has become somewhat routine and painless. We need to give freely what we have to someone in need. Let it become more than a tax-deductible transaction. The times we give spontaneously and over and above our planned giving are the best times of offering in our lives—times of developing compassionate character.

3. *Offer your attention.* In fact, this may be the most valuable offering we have for those in need—our attention. Be there for others. Listen to what they have to say. Empathize with them. Encourage them. Don't ignore them. What a contrast Jesus was to the religious leaders of his day. He gave his attention to the masses and undesirables. He invested in the lives of those in desperate need, and God transformed lives and launched his kingdom.

4. *Evaluate your offerings.* Schedule a regular time (at least annually) for honest evaluation of your offerings to those in need. Have you kept to your time budget for others? Did you give freely of your possessions, your material resources? Have you really given your attention, or is your agenda constantly driving your service of others? Evaluate your progress. Share with your accountability partner your losses and wins in this area of compassion building.

We Offer Our Witness

Woe unto us if we fail to testify to the life-changing power of the gospel of Jesus Christ! How can we possibly have compassion for—*suffer with*—others and not offer our witness? I believe that as the Holy Spirit nurtures compassionate character in our lives we become better witnesses. It makes sense, doesn't it? If you suffer alongside those in need, then the inhibitions that block us from sharing our faith in Jesus seem silly. It's really not that difficult. The Manual gives us at least two consistent models for offering our witness to those in need.

1. *Share your testimony.* Tell those you are suffering with how Christ changed your life. Be vulnerable and transparent. Where did we get the impression and practice of never sharing our personal struggles with those to whom we are ministering? Admit your humility and dependence on the one with ultimate compassionate character—the Suffering Servant himself (Ps. 53; Phil. 2:6–11). Share what Christ has done in your life. This is what the Samaritan woman at the well did. She told her story, "Come, see a man who told me everything I ever did. Could this be the Christ?" (John 4:29). This is what the blind man did: "One thing I do know. I was blind but now I see!" (John 9:25). Tell them your story.

2. *Tell his story.* Tell those you are serving "the story of his glory."[7] Throughout Scripture this seems to be the most-used approach in communicating the gospel to those in need. This is what Moses and Miriam did after the exodus from Egypt (Exod. 15). This is what Joshua did as he bade farewell to his leaders (Josh. 23). This is the song Zechariah sang when he celebrated the birth

---

7 Steven C. Hawthorne, "The Story of His Glory" in *Perspectives on the World Christian Movement*, 3rd ed., ed. Ralph D. Winters and Stephen C. Hawthorne (Pasadena, Calif.: William Carey Library, 1999), 34–48.

of his son, John the Baptist (Luke 1:67–79). This is the good news—gospel—that Peter preached on the first Pentecost for the church in Jerusalem (Acts 2). This is the defense of Stephen to the religious leaders of his day—the story of God's glory—that resulted in his stoning and martyrdom (Acts 7). This is the story of faith that the author of Hebrews celebrates (Heb. 11). Tell his story to those with whom you suffer. Compassionate character demands it!

Lest we get too wrapped up in what *we* can do to develop compassionate character, remember that this is God's business—his mission. If we depend on the Holy Spirit to lead us and the teachings of the Bible to instruct us, God can grow compassion in us. If we offer our time, our possessions, and our witness, we can develop and maintain compassionate character.

> On the same day they rolled back the stone and found the empty tomb, the resurrected Jesus met two of his disciples along the road to Emmaus. They were confused about the events of the day and did not recognize him. He responded to their question, "Are you only a visitor to Jerusalem and do not know the things that have happened there in these days . . . about Jesus of Nazareth?" Jesus responded by reminding them, "Did not the Christ have to suffer these things and then enter his glory?" And the Gospel says, "Beginning with Moses and all the Prophets, he explained to them what was said in all the Scriptures concerning himself." Jesus told his story and so should we. This is a part of compassionate character (Luke 24:13–27).

Compassionate Character and the Teachers' Triad

The apostle Paul is a classic case study on compassionate character applied through all three aspects of the Teachers' Triad. Indeed, Paul was a master teacher, an effective cross-cultural discipler. He must have understood that people learn in different ways. He used different approaches. As he put it, he became "all things to all men" in order to communicate effectively the gospel for their salvation (1 Cor. 9:22). Paul understood the triad.

That Paul communicated effectively with the *rational thinkers* of his day is a given. To this day we use his letters as the foundation for much of what we call systematic theology.

Paul was a thinker. Surely he was a cross-cultural discipler with rational character. But his compassionate character lay beneath the rational. In Athens we find an extraordinary example of Paul's compassionate character serving the needs of the greatest thinkers of his day.

> While Paul was waiting for them in Athens, he was greatly distressed to see that the city was full of idols. So he reasoned in the synagogue with the Jews and the God-fearing Greeks, as well as in the marketplace day by day with those who happened to be there. A group of Epicurean and Stoic philosophers began to dispute with him . . . where they said to him, "May we know what this new teaching is that you are presenting?" . . .
> Paul then stood up in the meeting of the Areopagus and said, "Men of Athens! I see that in every way you are very religious. For as I walked around and looked carefully at your objects of worship, I even found an altar with this inscription: TO AN UNKNOWN GOD. Now what you worship as something unknown I am going to proclaim to you (Acts 17:16–19, 22–23).

Paul was distressed. He felt compassion for this great city chasing after false gods and idols. He spent his days in Athens gaining respect that eventually earned him an invitation to speak in the greatest speaking hall of the empire. And then Paul appealed to the philosophers with his rational presentation of the gospel. He met them at their point of need even as he offered his witness of the Christ.

Paul was also a discipler who connected with *affective feelers.* Read his farewell address to the Ephesian elders in Acts 20:18–38. This is an emotional, tearful good-bye from the compassionate Paul, who had *suffered with* the Ephesian church for more than two years. Bound for Jerusalem he bypassed Ephesus so as not to be delayed. One wonders if he feared he would lose his resolve to continue his journey if he returned to Ephesus among the people he loved so deeply. So the elders came to Miletus to meet with him. Twice he mentioned his humble work among them in the midst of great testing, suffering, and "with tears" (19, 31). Paul's compassion flowed from his heart as he warned them to "keep watch over yourselves and all the flock" when "savage wolves"—false teachers—rise up and seek to destroy them (28–29). Perhaps the clearest evidence of the affective nature of Paul's compassion lies in the final farewell. Luke writes, "When he had said this, he knelt down with all of them and prayed. They all wept as they embraced him and kissed him. What grieved them most was his statement that they would never see his face again. Then they accompanied him to the ship" (36–37). Paul the theologian, the man of action, the church-planting strategist, was also the compassionate Paul—the one who suffered with those he served.

Finally, Paul was a cross-cultural discipler who inspired the *behavioral doers*. We could turn to many examples, but this same farewell to the elders of Ephesus reveals the way that Paul modeled discipleship by his actions. "You yourselves know that these hands of mine supplied my own needs and the needs of my companions. In everything I did, I showed you that by this kind of hard work we must help the weak, remembering the words the Lord Jesus himself said, 'It is more blessed to give than to receive'" (34–35). In a day and age when followers of religious sects were notorious leeches on society, Paul modeled through his own work the life of a responsible follower of Christ. He inspired the doers.

What a classic case study in compassionate character applied through the learner's triad. I think Paul was primarily a doer, but he didn't focus so much on tasks that he ignored the needs of the learner-leaders he served (toxic flip side). Paul connected with thinkers, feelers, and doers as he led them to a life of discipleship. He knew how to serve the needs of all three learner types. Most important, Paul was a cross-cultural discipler with compassionate character.

An Unexpected Visitor

Whatever happened to that young business owner in Houston, Texas? We left him running out of his office to catch the old lady and offer her some grocery money for her and her grandbaby. When he got into the open parking lot, she was nowhere to be found! He looked both ways down the street—nothing. There had been no car; she was on foot. He ran to the sides of his property, and no one was there. Just a few seconds had passed from the time he escorted her outside his office to the time he ran into the parking lot. He locked the office, rushed to his car, and began to drive through the area in search of this unexpected visitor. She had simply disappeared!

That night at church choir practice, the young businessman shared his story with his fellow choir and church members. He and his friends speculated. Maybe this lady was an angel sent from God with a message. The young businessman wasn't too familiar with angels, but one thing was sure: the Holy Spirit had his attention. He received the message. He needed to pay attention—no, he needed to suffer with those in need.

That day was the beginning of a life-changing new direction for the young businessman. It was one of several events in his life that shifted his focus from himself to the needs of others. Some twenty-five years later he still struggles with maintaining a sense of compassion for those he teaches and serves.

Today he has former students and colleagues in ministry and the marketplace literally around the world who confide in him about their challenges as cross-cultural disciplers. No, he is not recognized as the most compassionate saint on earth, but God isn't finished with him yet. He travels the world and is involved with numerous human aid and community development organizations. He learns more every day about the needs of others and the importance of compassionate character in the lives of cross-cultural disciplers. And he seldom ignores unexpected visitors!

No matter how hard we try, we cannot escape the fact that effective discipleship involves authentic compassion. We must meet the felt needs of those we teach and lead. Jesus modeled this throughout his life and work on earth. Paul and others exemplified this disciplers' character trait. Compassion is more than feeling sorry from a distance; it involves *suffering with* the learner-leaders we serve. Some disciplers are gifted with a compassionate spirit. Others are not. But all cross-cultural disciplers must seek to develop and maintain compassionate character. God's grace is the ultimate source of compassion, but we can take the initial steps. It begins as an offering. First we *decide* to offer; we commit ourselves to this character development. Then we offer ourselves—time, possessions, attention. We continuously assess our level of compassionate character. We evaluate how we are doing. Finally we offer our witness. We tell our story about our encounter with Jesus. And we tell his story—the simple yet powerful gospel. That is what compassionate character is all about.

Rick's Reaction

Mike shares openly about his struggle as a doer to develop and maintain compassionate character. I confess the same struggle as a thinker. This chapter touched me deeply, calling me yet again to move beyond knowledge, concepts, and principles to the real needs of real people.

While I am naturally drawn to the rational—illustrating, explaining, clarifying—I am reminded here that the greatest experiences of spiritual growth have come through (moments of) selfless devotion to the needs of others. How thankful I am that God trained me early to live and work among deaf people, focusing on *their needs,* before I ever entered seminary.

The following parts of the chapter specifically caught my attention:

Compassionate character goes beyond impersonal sympathy. It involves more than feeling sorry and having pity from a distance. Effective cross-cultural disciplers are sometimes called to suffer with the leader-learner and his family, tribe, or nation! The call to *suffer with* is hard to hear in a culture of convenience and self-service. But those who filter the noise of self and give themselves to others in Jesus' name find the deepest riches of purpose and contentment.

We do not ask people to come out to live in costly foreign style . . . barely touching the heathen world with the tips of their fingers, but we ask them to come prepared to cast in their lot with the natives [Lottie Moon].

J. Hudson Taylor became so frustrated with his missionary colleagues—who were satisfied to remain in the comfort and security of Shanghai—that he broke away from them and established the China Inland Mission. Taylor led the charge into the inland regions of China.

One of the great personal battles of missionaries with families is the degree to which they live inside the culture: the type and size of apartment, the school the children attend, where they buy their groceries. "After all, we have 'given up everything' to move to this place and minister. It is important to keep a sense of 'home' [read, an American lifestyle] for the children." I cannot criticize such an attitude, having never walked in this particular set of moccasins myself; yet I resonate with Lottie Moon's sentiments. I know from firsthand experience that missionaries who live in the culture—native residences, native markets—have far more connection to the people than those who "live in costly foreign style." Have they really "given up everything"?[8]

Many of our missionary heroes seem to suffer with the nationals to the point that their lives are transformed along with those of their learner-leaders.

---

8 As missionaries, we are called to love people into the kingdom. We are not called to a comfortable or secure life. Our call should always be set before our comfort, lifestyle, preferences, or methods. Being "called to reach" means that, despite discomforts, we continue to fulfill our call to reach people for the kingdom. AL

This suffering may well be what develops their characters—"their lives are transformed"—to heroic proportions! If I desire to be transformed by God's presence and provision, mustn't I also embrace the inevitable suffering which comes from connection with those who are suffering?

She could no longer divide people into "us" and "them." The Chinese people and Lottie Moon were one.

The beginning point for this was her *desire* to be one with the Chinese. She put off her American ways and adopted others' ways. The result of this compassionate approach to the Chinese was the simultaneous development of a relational character, the ability to build bridges of relationship for ministry (see chapter 7).

I think Paul was primarily a doer, but he didn't focus so much on tasks that he ignored the needs of the learner-leaders he served (toxic flip side).

I suspect Mike makes this connection because of his own strong task orientation. We tend to see ourselves in others. I naturally see Paul as more "thinker" than anything else. His theological explanations, which even Peter found difficult to understand, point to solid academic preparation and a keen mind. It seems to me that we're both wrong in this identification. Paul is considered the most powerful cross-cultural discipler in history specifically because he was so balanced—rational and creative, emotionally mature, a skilled practioner, a spiritual man. He is indeed an excellent example to emulate, second only to the Master.

Some disciplers are gifted with a compassionate spirit. Others are not. But all cross-cultural disciplers must seek to develop and maintain compassionate character.

The excuse "that's not my gift" has no place in the hearts of cross-cultural disciplers. There is a gift of giving, and yet we are all called to give. There is a gift of administration, but we are all called to be organized. There is a gift of evangelism, but we are all called to witness. There is a gift of teaching, but we are all called to teach others what we've experienced. *The spiritual gifts are teaching, discipling, equipping gifts, given to specific ones by the Lord to enable them to teach the body how to grow into these disciplines.* Mike's daughter, carrying within her the gift of compassion, teaches others how to be compassionate. Paul tells all of the rest of us to "put on . . . compassion" (Col. 3:12 NASB). And in this chapter Mike has helped us discover how.

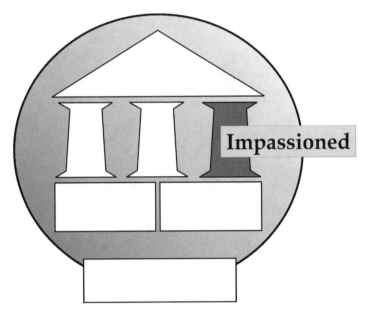

The Impassioned Character
of cross-cultural
Disciplers

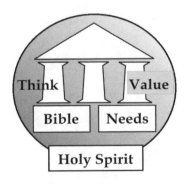

Disciplers' Model

6

Developing an Impassioned Character
Mike Barnett

Jesus wept.
John 11:35

He overturned the tables of the money changers
and the benches of those selling doves,
and would not allow anyone to carry merchandise through the temple courts.
And as he taught them, he said, "Is it not written:
'My house will be called a house of prayer for all nations'?
But you have made it 'a den of robbers.'"
Mark 11:15b–17

"Abba, Father," he said, "everything is possible for you.
Take this cup from me.
Yet not what I will, but what you will."
Mark 14:36

Disciplers who develop an impassioned character, one personally and energetically devoted to engaging the nations and following Christ whatever the costs, are better able to connect with learner-leaders than those who do not. Chapter 6 separates conceptions of *popular* and *personal* human passion and then defines *biblical passion* in terms of suffering. Finally, we identify and develop the role of impassioned discipleship that energizes discipleship across cultural divides.

The Toxic Flip Side

Seeking first our own convenience and welfare in ministry.
Wearing religious masks, working at religious tasks and programs,
hiding our hearts.

A Missionary Dilemma

It was my first trip into East Asia as a rookie representative of the mission board. I'd crossed cultures before in the international business world; but this three-week trip through Hong Kong, China, and now

Japan was an eye-opening, formative moment in my young missions career. I was excited. New experiences, new ideas, opportunities to build relationships that would last a lifetime. A chance to interact with peoples and cultures that God created and that would be represented at the foot of the throne in the last days. Oh, and don't forget! This was my first real chance to walk alongside real career missionaries. Heroes of the faith. I could hardly believe it!

That first evening the veteran missionary couple picked me up at the guest house. We drove through a matrix of villages within the megacity of Tokyo to a pleasant, almost quaint section of town. In the shadow of skyscrapers, we walked a couple of blocks to a small restaurant and sat down for our evening meal and my briefing before the next day's work. The couple had served in Tokyo for almost ten years. They had key responsibilities in providing support services for the international missionaries and local church leaders and believers. They were called to serve in Japan. They'd paid their dues, learned the language, experienced the culture, and made many personal sacrifices. They should have been in the prime of their missionary careers.

But something wasn't right with this couple. I couldn't put my finger on it at first, as they described the culture, customs, and worldview of 1990s Japan. The longer they talked, the clearer it became. And then I realized it. They hated the Japanese people! No, I'm not exaggerating. These two precious people, servants of God, passionately committed to his mission to disciple all peoples on earth, could not stand to live and work among the Japanese people. It was as though I were talking to two modern-day Jonahs who were sick of the thought that God could or would save this people he had called them to serve. On and on they went, for over two hours. One example after another. Frustrations, misunderstandings, hurt feelings, confusions, disgusts, fears—all piled up on that dinner table that night in Tokyo. How could this be? What could have happened for this hatred to develop? Were they even aware of their own feelings and bitterness? With such emotional baggage, how could they possibly serve the Japanese people with the gospel of Jesus Christ?

Even as a rookie missions worker, I remember asking them if they'd considered leaving the field so they could reassess where they fit in God's mission for the future. In fact, in the months ahead they were reassigned. I don't know how they made the transition, but I hope our brief encounter on that single night in Tokyo was one of the sparks that led them to connect with their own emotions—their passions. I pray that today they are serving God from a fresh and full foundation of impassioned character—emotionally honest with themselves, God, and those they serve.

The Right Pillar: Helping People Be Real

The right pillar in the model symbolizes the subjective focus in teaching. It addresses the emotional aspects of Christian growth and maturity, the values we place on our beliefs, the passion we have for Christ and his cause. Spiritual growth results in an emotional life that is both balanced and controlled yet drives us outward to others.

Life's irritations and problems can test our patience. Strained emotions cause fusses and fights, improper actions and overreactions. With anger within but a "Christian image" to display, we can opt to replace God's presence and true joy with a smiley-face mask.

Disciplers' Model

We see this here at home in our churches. Teenager has a drug problem, but Mom and Dad are afraid to share their anguish with their brothers and sisters in Christ. "What would people think?" So smiley-face masks replace joy and integrity. A young married couple in seminary have an infant who requires a special formula that takes most of their food budget. They're literally starving but don't tell anyone because "God will take care of them." Behind their smiley-face masks lurk hunger and fear. Or an unemployed Christian can't find a job, but he keeps this to himself because someone might think him a failure.

We see it on the mission field. Missionaries struggle to learn a new language but refuse to ask nationals for help, or worse, reject help when it is freely offered. Perhaps it is pride ("I don't need their help"), or fear ("Will they think less of me?"). I have known interpreters for the deaf who will not allow deaf people to teach them their language. One actually told me why: "I'm the interpreter. What can deaf people teach me about interpreting?" Emotional masks. Hidden hearts. Real problems. The best resource I had as I developed fluency in sign language was the help of my deaf friends and students. But beyond language skills, I was better able to connect heart to heart with the deaf because "I humbled myself" to learn from them. And because I used "their language," I was better able to connect with all deaf people.

Jesus was *real* in the way he reacted emotionally to life. He wore no smiley-face mask. He was not a dark-hearted prophet of doom or a lighthearted Pollyanna. He dealt with the world realistically, meeting life as it was and responding appropriately to events as they came. When his good friend Lazarus died, Jesus didn't grin and shout, "Praise the Lord anyway!" He wept (John 11:35). When his disciples were exhausted by the press of the crowds and their ministry, Jesus didn't try to pump them up with false enthusiasm. He led them to a place of rest and recuperation (Mark 6:31). Even when dying on the cross, he arranged for his mother to be cared for (John 19:26).

Jesus wore no pious mask to hide his inner feelings. Nor did he gush frothy feelings for all to see. He was not controlled by his emotions, nor did he repress them. He owned them and used them to manage life's circumstances. He directed them into tangible expressions of love and concern for others. His passion for the Father, and for the Father's mission, overcame his human fears and drove him to death on the cross. Emotions properly engaged by the Lord lead to vibrant ministry: "Deny [yourself] and take up [your] cross and follow me" (Matt. 16:24).

Emotional Freedom

Emotional development does not come by means of knowledge or understanding. It comes as we remove masks and face life experiences as they are. We help learner-leaders remove their own masks as we develop rapport with them, promoting a personal willingness to share and a general sense of openness.

Jesus met the woman at the well and changed her life forever. But before he could teach her, he needed to "connect" with her. Respectable Jewish men did not talk with women in public and especially not Samaritan women! How did he reach across a hostile cultural divide to bring true life, Living Water, to this sinful woman? First, he accepted her as a *person,* not a female person or a Samaritan person. His message of hope and life was as available to her as to anyone because "God is no respecter of persons" (Acts 10:34 KJV). Second, he did not present himself as a

Jewish man but as Lord of all. Third, he bridged the cultural gap between Jews and Samaritans with *her interest*—water—so that he could teach her.

In response, she opened herself to *his words*. She listened to the Messiah of Israel, the Lord of the universe, the Thirst Quencher, who told her everything she'd done and how to have Living Water. She opened herself to *him* and accepted his message. Her life was changed from sinner to saint, and her first action was to go as his missionary back to her own people. We develop openness in learners by being open to learners, by engaging them where they are, listening, and sharing the message of faith as they become willing to listen.

Removing Emotional Barriers

Our ministry cannot succeed until emotional barriers are dismantled. These barriers are built from cultural hostility, differing agendas, lack of language proficiency, and hurtful personal experiences. The subjective side of the model will touch them—not doctrine, logic, or words. Emotional barriers of distrust and suspicion are removed by the gentle touch of caring, of listening, of loving, of self-sacrificing.

Emotional Growth

The majority of problems in ministry relationships, whether with colleagues or with national learner-leaders, come not from ministry practice, or doctrine, or worship style but from some symptom of emotional immaturity: rash comments, fickle conduct, irritability, fear, anxiety, short temper, ambition, self-interest. The subjective focus of the model reduces the effects of these destructive traits as learners develop love for and trust in one another.[1]

Further, subjective teaching strengthens positive emotional traits as learners accept themselves and others more honestly. These positive traits include such things as working well with other learners, managing temperamental impulses, expressing good feelings without embarrassment, refraining from worry, and accepting constructive criticism. Jesus brought unity to the fragmented personality of the Gadarene demoniac

---

1 Emotional growth is learning to own our emotions and using our emotions appropriately to manage life's circumstances. Learning to desire the right things is the key to emotional growth in a cross-cultural environment. Until we accept responsibility for our emotions, good and bad, and then manage them, they will manage us. AL

(Mark 5:1–20). He can also bring emotional coherence out of the chaos of uncontrolled feelings.

Finally, learning to open ourselves to the Lord—surrendering our own agendas for his—leads to a filling of his Spirit (chapter 2), resulting in a passion for his mission throughout the whole world: to open peoples of all nations and cultures to salvation, healing, and the leading of the Lord.

Passion and Impassioned Character

Before we venture into a discussion of impassionment, we need to make sure we are on the same page regarding passion itself. What do we really mean when we say the word *passion?*

It Had Been a Good Day

It had been a good day—March 15, 2004. David and Carrie McDonnall, Larry and Jean Elliott, and Karen Watson were a team of five experienced, culturally savvy, humanitarian workers in the midst of war-torn Iraq. They were doing a survey of humanitarian needs—especially water resource development—in the predominately Sunni Muslim city of Mosul. Later Carrie recalled how receptive the Iraqis were to their inquiries. "We had a great day with them. . . . They were so eager for our help."[2] It looked promising. A real chance to provide vital assistance for those in desperate physical and spiritual need.

I never met the Elliotts or Karen, but I knew David and Carrie. David was a student of mine at Southwestern Seminary. He and Carrie served on the leadership team of a practicum project of eighteen students who worked in Iraq in the summer of 2003. The team often met in our home during the spring semester. Like many of my students, David and Carrie

---

2 A complete account of this event and others like it may be found in Erich Bridges and Jerry Rankin, *Lives Given, Not Taken: 21st-Century Southern Baptist Martyrs* (Richmond, Va.: International Mission Board, 2005).

were passionate about serving God among Muslims. They had both lived and worked in Arabic-speaking lands before they met and had since married and were preparing for long-term service in the Arab world. There was nothing superficial about their commitment to serve the Lord. This went far deeper than just wearing a religious mask. It wasn't about career paths or resumé building. And it was not for the sake of adventure. This was about passion. This was about a willingness to do whatever it takes to follow the mandate and call of Jesus Christ to disciple all nations. This was about taking up the cross of Christ no matter what the cost.

The two returned to Iraq in November 2003 and joined the ranks of NGO workers in the wake of the war. The survey trip into the heartland of Saddam Hussein's regime held much promise. The strategic importance of Sunni cities like Mosul was vital for the reconstruction of physical and political infrastructures in a new and free Iraq. More importantly for David and Carrie, the opportunity for building new bridges of spiritual infrastructure that would last an eternity was the chance of a lifetime.

It was a good start. The locals were receptive to these outsiders. There was great need for restoration of clean water delivery, sanitation services, reconstruction of schools, and education projects. It had been a good day . . . so far.

Three Kinds of Passion?

Let's look at three kinds of passion and see how they relate to one another in the lives of effective cross-cultural disciplers.

Popular Passion. I remember when the term *passion* became a part of the pop culture of America. It was in the 1990s. Our family lived in the United Kingdom, and though the British culture had an obvious fascination with American pop culture, the trans-Atlantic influences often took a while to flow across the waters. So we were somewhat out of touch with the most avant-garde concepts and lingo of the American scene when we returned to live in the States in the summer of 2000.

I remember those first days watching television in America and wondering, *Where did all of this talk about passion come from?* Everything was about passion. Do you have enough passion for a BMW? Is the Tag Heuer watch you wear a sign of passion? Do you have a financial program that reflects your passion for life? And, by the way, are you wearing a fragrance with passion? There was even one called Passion! The other 1990s word which firmly stuck in the vocabulary of America in the nineties (and still today) was *absolutely*. Makes sense. In order to be really passionate, you *absolutely* need to be committed to the object of your desires. Don't you agree? Absolutely!

And that is the core of the popular definition of *passion*. This pop passion of extremes is about whatever it takes to get what *you* desire—a car, a watch, a guy, a girl, blah, blah, blah. The problem with this self-focused passion is that it watered down the true concept of passion. It trivialized passion. Passion became too easy, too obtainable. No need to count the costs. Like NIKE says, "Just do it!" Of course, we cannot ignore pop passion, but we need to take it for what it is—a superficial, often self-serving, and sometimes sinful preoccupation with our own agenda, not God's.

Personal Passion. On the other hand, we cannot disregard the fact that we are created as emotional humans. We all are influenced, even driven, by personal passions—loves, hates, angers, sorrows, frustrations, ambitions, joys, fears—that play a part in who we are—our character. Personal passion can be one of the greatest assets of an effective cross-cultural discipler. But it can also get us into trouble. Look back at passionate teacher-leaders in the history of God's mission, and you can find the trouble excessive passion caused them.

- The young Joseph displayed a bit too much personal passion when he shared his dreams of greatness with his family (Gen. 37).
- King David's ego and lack of discipline in the wake of military victories led to his moral failure with Bathsheba (2 Sam. 12).
- Simon Peter's impulsiveness repeatedly got him into trouble. His stubborn vision of King Jesus and his earthly rule caused Christ to admonish him, "Get behind me, Satan!" (Matt. 16:23). In the garden of Gethsemane, his natural courage and perhaps rage required a miraculous restorative act by Jesus—replacing the ear of the high priest's servant (Matt. 26:51).
- The apostle Paul was a passionate fighter, focused on the task at hand, to preach the gospel to the Gentiles. I wonder what role his personal passions, his emotions, played in his being thrown into jail time and again?
- What kind of passion did it take in the fifth century for Patrick of Ireland to return as a missionary to the land of his childhood of slavery?
- Francis of Assisi connected at a heart level with those he served and led like none other than Jesus himself.

- Hudson Taylor and his wife Maria were so burdened for the Chinese people to hear the gospel that they went against the council and support of colleagues and established a radical new missions agency called the China Inland Mission (OMF today).

God gives us personal passions. When we commit them to his will, he uses them for his glory. That's one big reason the life of an effective cross-cultural discipler is seldom boring! Of course, we have to learn how to harness that God-given passion, but I'm getting ahead of myself. First, the third kind of passion.

Biblical Passion. The ultimate kind of passion is the kind that Jesus lived. I call it biblical passion. It comes from the root meaning of the word in Latin *patō,* to suffer, or *passiō,* suffering. This is Christlike passion. This is where we get the Easter "passion" week. The picture painted by this kind of passion is Christ's life during that final week in Jerusalem. In fact, his entire life and ministry focused on his passion, his suffering for our sakes and the Father's glory.

Biblical passion is not about what we are willing to live for—even good things like helping others, serving Jesus, giving money to good causes. It is about what we are willing to die for! If we say that *com*passionate character calls us to *suffer with* others (chapter 5), then *im*passioned character compels us to *suffer for* the Lord Jesus Christ.

> **Com**passionate character calls us to **suffer with** others (chapter 5). **Im**passioned character compels us to **suffer for** the Lord Jesus Christ.

Biblical passion is the call and cause of Jesus. Jesus said, "If anyone would come after me, he must deny himself and take up his cross and follow me. For whoever wants to save his life will lose it, but whoever loses his life for me will find it" (Matt. 16:24–25).

This is biblical passion. To take up our cross. To follow him every day. To tell his story. To share his love. To free those in spiritual bondage. To introduce them to a life of meaning today and an eternity with God. To connect with the learner-leaders of tomorrow. To enable them to fulfill God's mission among all peoples. Listen to the voice of the martyrs. Theirs is a testimony of biblical passion.

How Do We Manage Our Passions?

We are all emotional, passionate beings. We are all influenced by the full range of passions in life, from pop to personal and even biblical passion. If we are to be effective cross-cultural disciplers, then we need to be able to manage, to direct, to capitalize on our passions. How do we do that?

Be honest with ourselves. The first step is for us to be honest with ourselves. I wonder how long it took—how many years—before the missionary couple to Japan, mentioned above, admitted to each other that they had a problem with the Japanese people and culture? When was the first time they admitted to each other that the experiences of crossing culture, learning language, and living and working in a strange place had grown into bitterness. Better yet, how long had they ignored the signs, suppressed the feelings, denied the resentment to themselves as individuals. Emotions are tricky. They can lock us into an internal denial that keeps us shut off from what is true and good and what can refresh and restore healthy, impassioned emotional character. Emotions can even coerce us from openly sharing with our most trusted friend, our family, our spouse, our colleague.

We must consciously face ourselves. We must look into that daily mirror and know who we are. We must have those internal conversations with ourselves that ask the hard questions about who we are and who we want to be. It starts within us. As believers, the Holy Spirit is in us and with us throughout these moments of total personal intimacy. There is no one to fool, no one to convince, nothing to hide. It is a time of total honesty with ourselves.

In my life it helps to have trusted, intimate, spiritually accountable friends. Some call them "co-mentors."[3] I like that. Others refer to them as accountability partners. We give them permission to "speak into our lives." I need these friends. I've had many throughout my life. My wife is my main co-mentor, my best friend in life. But God has graciously provided numerous others that I know I can trust with my most precious and fragile emotions. You know who you are. Is it biblical? David and Jonathan, Jesus and John, Barnabas and Paul, Paul and Timothy/Titus—the list goes on. Is it easy? Little in life that is worthy is easy. I think it becomes easier with practice. Is it necessary? For me it is. I'm not sure how honest I would be with myself without my co-mentors.

---

3 Paul D. Stanley and Robert Clinton, *Connecting: The Mentoring Relationships You Need to Succeed in Life* (Colorado Springs, Co.: NavPress, 1992).

Though small groups are often misunderstood and misused, "real teams" can serve as safe communities for self-disclosure and honesty that result in impassioned character. I teach a seminary course on building and leading effective ministry teams. It is probably my most popular course. We use Henry and Richard Blackaby's definition of *spiritual leadership*—"moving people on to God's agenda"—as our primer on leadership.[4] Once we biblically align our thinking on leadership, students are put into work groups and challenged week after week in a way that invites them to be honest with themselves and one another about their call, their strengths and weaknesses, their personality attributes, and their emotions—their impassioned character. My experience has been that once they understand that leadership is about serving others, not ourselves—for example, Jesus washing the feet of the disciples—and after they work alongside one another for a common purpose that glorifies God, the chances increase for an honest, trustworthy, mutually beneficial community of coworkers. It's a great way to be honest with yourself about you, working well with others.

Regardless of our approach, whether it is through co-mentors, longtime confidants, your lifelong spouse, or a ministry team, we need to start by being honest with ourselves about our emotions, our passions.

Be honest with God. You might ask why I didn't put honesty with God before honesty with self. I guess it's because I've actually seen people who try to be honest with God but cannot because they have deceived themselves. As we become honest with ourselves, we are better able to be honest with God. Of course, God knows us totally. We cannot hide anything from him. But if he is going to grow our character, we must talk and listen honestly with him about us.

What does being honest with God involve? It involves being honest about our sin and the sins against us. You knew it was coming. We cannot escape being honest with God about sin. In the book *TrueFaced,* a missionary explains the problem of hidden sin.

> Before I came to Jesus, I felt discounted in relationship after relationship. My own mother disowned me. My deep hurt caused me to believe that no matter how hard I tried, I would still be worthless—and I continued to believe this as a Christian. My own sin and the sin of

---

4 Henry and Richard Blackaby, *Spiritual Leadership: Moving People on to God's Agenda* (Nashville: Broadman & Holman Publishers, 2001).

others against me prevented me from even understanding what it really meant that I had a new identify—but I was sure trying to get one.

In my fervor, I could trust God for cities, countries, nations, for thousands to accept Christ, but I could not trust God with me. I did not see myself as godly. I was ready for martyrdom, to live among any tribe, but I could not live with who I was. I was a failure, doing my best to break out of my junk and hiddenness.[5]

If we are to be effective cross-cultural disciplers. *If* we are to effectively communicate the gospel in a way that draws others to Christ. *If* we are to model our lives in a way that encourages others to become Christlike. *If* we are to teach leader-learners in a way that results in the multiplication of disciplers with mature, godly character, *then* we must be honest with God about ourselves.

Be honest with those we serve. Most of my years as a cross-cultural discipler focused on coaching those who work among the least reached people on earth—that is, peoples who haven't known many missionaries. But during a three-year assignment I spent considerable time working with national or local Christian groups in several nonwestern countries who had been influenced by generations of Western missionaries. These were the new national church bodies of the twentieth century. I learned a lot from these faithful brothers and sisters. Some of what I learned surprised me.

Impassioned adj. filled with passion; fiery; inflamed (*Collins English Dictionary,* 1995)

I will never forget the first time I realized that the heroes of these national church bodies often were the old and gone missionaries! In many of the older nonwestern mission fields, there is a longing for the "good old days" of the past. There are fond memories of those first pioneers who came and brought the gospel, converted believers, developed churches and Christian institutions that provided Bibles, literature, education, and jobs for locals and their families. I was not so surprised to learn about the perceived "good old days." After all, they were great days of breaking forth God's truth and establishing first footholds for the gospel. What surprised me was the reputations of the dead-and-gone missionaries. The "good ole" missionaries were all remembered as sinless saints! Maybe this was a natural product of memorializing our heroes, but I don't think it was a

---

5 Bill Thrall, Bruce McNicol, and John Lynch, *TrueFaced: Trust God and Others with Who You Really Are* (Colorado Springs, Co.: NavPress, 2004), 59.

healthy memory. Basically there were two kinds of missionaries. Those dead-and-gone sinless saints. And those who remained and could not live up to the standards of the dead-and-gone sinless saints.

My point is this. As cross-cultural disciplers (and even same-culture equipping ministers), we *must be honest with those we serve.* We must not leave them with the impression that disciplers are sinless. We must not hide ourselves from those we serve. Paul openly revealed and discussed his frailty in order to point believers to the only sinless saint, Jesus Christ. We must honestly share our emotions, our passions, with those we serve.[6] They must know that we too have to work at being honest with ourselves, our God, and those we serve. Only then can we demonstrate and indeed replicate impassioned character. Let us be real, true faced, and honest with those we serve.

Developing and Maintaining Impassioned Character

Now we move beyond managing passions to developing an impassioned character. We defined *passion* as more than a pop culture, more than a self-serving collection of desires—things we are willing to live for. We discussed aspects of personal passion that are part of who we are. We talked about how these aspects play into our discipling abilities and practices. And we defined biblical passion as the ultimate sacrifice of our entire lives, modeled after the passion of Christ himself—who we are willing to die for. Why don't we call this characteristic of effective cross-cultural discipling "impassioned" rather than "passionate" character. This distinction hints at how we get it and how we keep it.

The word *impassioned* describes one who has been filled or fired with passion. How are we filled or fired with that commitment, that desire to give our all, our lives, for the cause of Christ? You are ahead of me already, aren't you? Think back to our Disciplers' Model and the other characteristics we have discussed. Biblical character informs our impassionment; it defines it. The Bible presents example after example of impassioned disciplers, Old Testament to New. It leaves us with the ultimate model and mandate from Jesus Christ, to be impassioned disciplers. Spiritual character fills and fires our impassionment; it requires it. Finally, the body of Christ itself, through the blood of the martyrs,

---

6 Jesus told his disciples to follow him, to be with him. Literally Jesus meant for his disciples to live with him. Honesty is hard to hide when you live with someone. Involve your disciples in your life and find ways to be a part of their lives. Be with them and honesty will result. The reverse is also true: if you are not with your disciples, you will never become truly honest with them. AL

motivates our impassionment; it inspires it. You might say that the biblical definition, the model and mandate of Jesus, the power and presence of the Holy Spirit, and the witness and example of the martyrs, together, impassion us.

The Bible Defines It

A discipler with biblical character is one who puts into practice the principles, teachings, and models of the Bible as demonstrated through the life of Jesus Christ (chapter 3). Such a discipler is continually reminded, vividly aware, of the reality *that suffering is a part of discipleship.* By reading, discussing, and meditating upon biblical examples of impassioned disciplers of the Lord, we understand what *biblical passion* is. If we are already living the life of a biblical discipler, "walking the walk," we are less likely to slide into the pop passion culture of our day. Less likely to hide our struggles, doubts, and fears. More likely to stand firm and faithful when life gets tough, in the face of suffering.

Our biblical character defines for us what it means to follow and *suffer for* Christ. When hardship hits us, we know what it is, and we are better able to handle it. We are intimately familiar with the "great cloud of witnesses" that have gone before us (Heb. 12:1). We remember their examples. How they dealt with suffering. How their faith grew through persecution. How God was glorified as a result of their impassioned character.

The effective discipler still suffers. In fact, some say they may be called to suffer more for the sake of God's name, but they are better prepared to handle their suffering. When they find themselves face-to-face with evil and suffering, they are less likely just to put on a religious mask and ignore the challenge and the consequences. They are more likely to deal openly with the crisis in a way that glorifies God. They are not caught off guard. They know what suffering is. Their biblical character defines it for them.

The mandate and model to *suffer for* the Lord comes from Jesus himself. I freely unpack the Matthew 28:18–20 mandate like this: Jesus told his followers (that's us) to disciple all nations—every people, every culture on earth—by introducing them to and baptizing them in the name of the Father, Son, and Holy Spirit. But don't stop there! We must also teach them to live out all that Jesus taught us. Teach like he taught, through his words and life. And know that *we will suffer along the way,* as he did, maybe even unto death. That is why he assures us that he will be there with us, to walk us through the trials, always and forever.

Jesus commands us to take on a mission that requires biblical impassionment. But he also models for us how to be effective, through life, work, and even death.

How do we develop and maintain impassioned character? We make sure that our biblical character is healthy. We read and study the story of how God has called his followers to face evil and suffering. We live out this character. We develop a track record with God that we can fall back on when the going gets tough. We learn to expect to *suffer for* him. We depend on the Bible to define our impassionment. And all along the way, our leader-learners watch us as we model for them a life of impassioned character for Christ.

The Holy Spirit Requires It

When Paul was struck by a light from heaven on the road to Damascus, the Lord directed Ananias to disciple him. Who could imagine that this man, notorious executioner of Christ followers and most unlikely convert to the Way of Jesus Christ, would become the prototype international missionary! The Lord told Ananias, "Go to the house of Judas on Straight Street and ask for a man from Tarsus named Saul, for he is praying . . . Go! This man is my chosen instrument to carry my name before the Gentiles and their kings and before the people of Israel. I will show him how much he must *suffer for* my name" (Acts 9:11, 15–16, italics added). And Luke reported that Ananias found Saul and proclaimed, "Brother Saul, the Lord—Jesus . . . sent me so that you may see again and be filled with the Holy Spirit" (Acts 9:17).

It is an amazing text. First, Paul is called not just to be a "Brother," as Ananias put it, not just to be able to see, but indeed *"to suffer for"* the name of the Lord! What else did this filling and firing of the Holy Spirit do for Paul and others as they suffered for the name of Jesus? The Holy Spirit impassioned Paul and others by:

- Calling them out as effective cross-cultural disciplers (Acts 13:2).
- Empowering them to be witnesses to all peoples (Acts 1:8).
- Giving them words to speak in the midst of persecution (Mark 13:11; Luke 12:12).
- Enabling them to speak the gospel and be heard (Acts 2:4).
- Inspiring them to proclaim boldly God's Word (Acts 4:31).

- Strengthening and encouraging them to celebrate God's victories (Acts 9:31).
- Warning them that persecution and suffering will come (Acts 20:23).
- Redirecting them according to God's plan (Acts 16:6).

The list goes on. The Holy Spirit fills and fires us to be effective cross-cultural disciplers. He carries us through the challenges. He is our number one coach, counselor, and cohort as we suffer for the sake of the name of Jesus Christ. He expects, requires, that we live lives of impassioned character.

How do we develop and maintain impassioned character? We make sure that our spiritual character is healthy. We devote ourselves to ongoing surrender to the Holy Spirit's leadership in our lives (chapter 2). We depend on him in the midst of suffering. "And surely [He is] with [us] always, to the very end of the age" (Matt. 28:20).

The Body of Christ Inspires It

The third-century church father from North Africa, Tertullian, pronounced, "The blood of the martyrs is the seed of Christianity." Indeed, the martyrs, the "witnesses" who have gone before us, inspire us.

I teach a course in the history of missions to graduate-level students in a day and age when historical studies are not supposed to be popular. Have I got news for us! Once we throw the traditional lecture in the bin, the history of disciplers of Jesus Christ comes alive. Our postmodern generation, void of metanarrative and historical understanding, really tunes into the truth of the gospel when they meet the martyrs of the faith. What better way to grasp the seriousness of a faith that says it requires our all than to study the real lives and work of those who gave their lives? Of the many courses in intercultural studies and missions that I teach, the one that hits students in the heart is the history of missions. The stories of those who suffered with others for the name of Christ, and who even died—martyrs of the faith—truly inspire my students.

It Had Been a Good Day

The team of five NGO workers had already accomplished more than expected that day in Mosul. They must have been thinking of the possibilities for the future. And then it happened. While driving through the city, a random vehicle pulled alongside and unexpectedly opened fire, strafing their vehicle with automatic weapons. The Elliotts and Karen died at the scene. David and Carrie, both severely wounded, were rushed in a taxi to a local hospital. Today Carrie recalls how "David's thoughts and actions were focused on [her]" more than himself.[7] Carrie survived the attack with multiple wounds and months of rehabilitation. David did not. He died within hours of the attack. He joined his three colleagues and untold scores of others—martyrs of the faith.

Looking back, we know this was the beginning of the now infamous insurgency movement in Iraq. In the weeks that followed, similar attacks on innocent, nonmilitary personnel and Iraqi citizens became routine. But on that day—March 15, 2004—it came as a surprise to many. And though the five victims of this brutal assault were attacked without warning, they were ready. They knew what they were getting into. They counted the costs. The five understood the price they might have to pay. They were prepared spiritually. They were impassioned—filled with passion—cross-cultural disciplers.

The ultimate picture of biblical passion is Jesus on the cross. He is the most inspirational martyr in the history of God's mission to redeem and be worshipped by all peoples. Mel Gibson's film *The Passion of the Christ* vividly tells the biblical account of the crucifixion of Jesus Christ. The climax is his guiltless suffering on the cross: the sacrifice of his life for those he served and loved according to the call and plan of God the Father. The film impacted believers and nonbelievers alike. Every spring around the world, Christians remember the passion of Christ. Some are inspired to *suffer for* him. We need to remember the passion of Christ.

God impassions us through his Word, his Spirit, and his church. The Bible displays time and again what true passion for Christ involves. The Holy Spirit keeps the imperative before us. He requires us to live and be willing to die for the cause of Christ. And the body of Christ, the church, inspires us with its historical and modern-day examples of impassioned character among cross-cultural disciplers. How do we keep ourselves available for his impassioning? Read God's Word, listen to his Spirit, and watch and walk alongside his church.

---

7 Bridges and Rankin, *Lives Given, Not Taken*, 153.

Impassioned Character and the Teachers' Triad

How does impassioned character relate to the Teachers' Triad? The answer is found in the way we deal with our personal passions. How we manage our feelings as we relate to others. How we passionately serve and *suffer for* the Lord. All of these are vital aspects of our witness and discipling relationships with leader-learners. They look to us as examples and models of impassioned character. They listen to the ways we define our passions. They watch as we manage our feelings. Are we being honest with ourselves, with God, and with them? They learn as we work alongside them and effectively deal with and capitalize on our passions.

Daniel lived a life of impassioned character. From his earliest years of service to the court of King Nebuchadnezzar, Daniel seemed to be in touch with himself and God. He was unwilling to compromise his faith for the sake of the king. He resisted temptations and orders to defile himself at the table of the king (Dan. 1:8). He was spiritually and emotionally sensitive to God's voice (Dan. 1:17). He faced the lions in the den with a biblical passion. He was prepared to *suffer for* God, even unto death. He connected with God's Spirit in a way that allowed him to serve as one of the great prophets of all time. Through his witness Nebuchadnezzar ultimately praised God and exalted his name (Dan. 4:34–35; 6:26–27).

Though Daniel was a strong, powerful, charismatic figure of a man, his sensitivity to the feelings, fears, and needs of others was his strength. Though he was surely a capable leader and servant of the king, his humble, prayerful, worship of God was the source of his power. Daniel's prayer of petition and confession for the nation of Israel is packed with passion. He ends his plea for mercy:

> Now, our God, hear the prayers and petitions of your servant. For your sake, O Lord, look with favor on your desolate sanctuary. Give ear, O God, and hear; open your eyes and see the desolation of the city that bears your Name. We do not make requests of you because we are righteous, but because of your great mercy. O Lord, listen! O Lord forgive! O Lord, hear and act! For your sake, O my God, do not delay, because your city and your people bear your Name (Dan. 9:17–19).

Daniel lived a life of impassioned character for God. He influenced and drew untold numbers of people to God. He discipled prominent learner-leaders like Shadrach, Meshach, and Abednego. He led the king to honor God. God used the passion of Daniel. Daniel blessed God with his impassioned character.

Rightly dealing with feelings and passions is a necessity for effective discipling across cultural divides. First, we must be honest with ourselves. Then, we must be honest with God. And finally, we must be honest with those we serve. We must remove the religious masks that hide our vulnerability and depend on the only sinless one, Jesus Christ. We must not allow others to put us on a false pedestal.

For most of us this impassioned character does not come easy. We can develop and maintain impassioned character by staying immersed in the biblical models and examples of the Bible. The Bible defines passionate character for us. It sets the bar. The Holy Spirit requires that we seek this impassioned character. The good news is that the Holy Spirit will lead and direct us along the journey. Finally, we are inspired by the body of Christ, the lives of those who have gone before us. The examples of the martyrs of the faith, then and now.

Like Daniel, we can humbly seek impassioned character from the Lord. When we live and walk alongside those we disciple, they will see that our faith and commitment are real. And they will know that the object of our faith, our passion, Jesus Christ, is worthy.

Rick's Reaction

Hate? I was struck by Mike's opening story. Is it possible that missionaries can actually hate the people and culture they've been called to serve? We hear so little of this dark side of ministry, but it is indeed true. I have seen deaf workers who detest the deaf people they serve. I shared in another chapter the story of missionaries who openly admitted to hating the food, the customs, the lifestyles, even the language of the people they claimed God called them to serve.[8]

Workers such as these are antipassionate or negatively passionate, cancers in Christ's teaching ministry. They sow seeds of distrust, frustration,

---

8 There will be parts of any culture that we do not like and probably never will like. Our choice is what we do with these dislikes. Try to find what can be valued about the culture, and determine what you do not need to value. Find ways to love the people even if you don't like the way some things are done. We often go swimming with our Russian and Belarussian brothers and sisters. The outfits worn by nonbelievers and some believers do not meet our family's standards for modesty. What should we do? We respond to the people and not to the outfits. We relate to them as they are. Over time we can find a way to dialogue about the issue and solve it for God's glory. However, if we choose not to love, not to relate, we will not help them, nor will we continue to grow as learners. We are all in this together. AL

conflict, and division in the very field they've come to plant with the gospel. My experience mirrors Mike's: such workers have become trapped, by their own choices or the requests of others, in situations to which God has not called them. They served in their own power, a power now dissipated by disappointments or hardships. Mike's advice to this couple was to withdraw, pray, seek God's face, and find where God wants you to be and serve. Go to another country. Learn another language. As children of God, we are never truly trapped in dead-end ministries. "Humble yourselves . . . under God's mighty hand, that he may lift you up in due time" (1 Pet. 5:6). When God lifts us, he lifts us to a passionate calling and an impassioned purpose. He gets the glory, and we get the joy!

Deceive? Mike makes a powerful point concerning self-deception. How often have I "come to myself" and realized how much I have deceived myself about circumstances, possibilities, and even successes. Such self-deception prevents honesty before God. Mike wrote, "I've actually seen people who try to be honest with God but cannot *because they have deceived themselves."* Failure to be honest with ourselves leaves us vulnerable to that which defeated the missionary Mike quoted in *True-Faced:* "I was a failure, doing my best to break out of my junk and hiddenness."[9] In such a state there is no capacity for impassioned living.

Develop? Mike asks the key question of the chapter several times: "How do we develop and maintain impassioned character?" He gives us several answers—all helpful. The one that touched me most was this: "The Holy Spirit fills and fires us to be effective cross-cultural disciplers." I can read the Bible, say my prayers, schedule quiet time, attend services, and do a dozen other good things, and still miss the Spirit-filled passion so often displayed in Scripture and mission ventures. The essential action is surrender to the Lord. To give up my religiosity in favor of God's agenda, his Word, his call, and his anointing. Impassioned ministry is his fruit, produced in and through me by his presence and power. It is not my work, done for his glory. "All to Jesus I surrender, all to Him I freely give. I will ever love and trust Him, in His presence daily live."[10]

Mike reinforces this: "[The Holy Spirit] carries us through the challenges. He is our number one coach, counselor, and cohort as we suffer for the sake of the name of Jesus Christ. He expects, requires, that we live lives of impassioned character." And that which God expects, he empowers us to do, as we depend on him and not on ourselves.

---

9 Thrall, McNicol, and Lynch, *TrueFaced,* 59.
10 Judson W. Van DeVenter, "I Surrender All."

There is nothing more depressing or futile than to be trapped by a dead-end ministry. There is nothing more exhilarating and blessed than to be lifted into a supernatural ministry—to serve in his name, by his power, and for his glory. The passion that flows from the heart of God through our own hearts, and then out to those around us, transforms us into Christ's image in ways that little else can do.

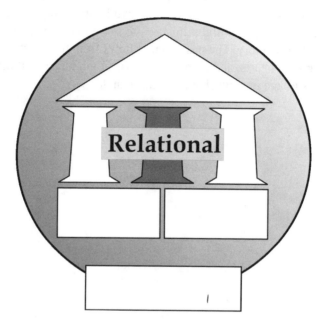

The Relational Character
of cross-cultural
Disciplers

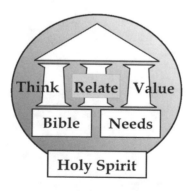

Disciplers' Model

7

Developing a Relational Character
Rick Yount

"The kings of the Gentiles lord it over them; and those who exercise authority
over them call themselves Benefactors. But you are not to be like that."
Luke 22:25–26

"A new command I give you: Love one another.
As I have loved you, so you must love one another.
By this all men will know that you are my disciples,
if you love one another."
John 13:34–35

The body is a unit, though it is made up of many parts;
and though all its parts are many, they form one body.
So it is with Christ. For we were all baptized by one Spirit
into one body—whether Jews or Greeks, slave or free—
and we were all given the one Spirit to drink.
1 Corinthians 12:12–13

Relational character is devoted to building bridges of mutual relationship, building ministry teams, and equipping bridge builders among national learner-leaders. Disciplers who develop a relational character connect with learner-leaders in life-changing ways. Simply stated, disciplers love their learners. Chapter 7 defines the role of relational elements of discipleship—"people with people with Jesus in the middle"—which are essential in discipling across cultures. We then describe how to develop a relational character as a pillar of discipling ministry.

The Toxic Flip Side

Building "my way" streets rather than "our way" bridges.

A Battle in Bishkek

He sat in the back of the Kyrgyz classroom, one of fourteen Russian-speaking students. It was the first hour of the course. I shared a little about my family and began my introduction to the course. I used

John 20:31, "But these are written that you may believe that Jesus is the Christ, the Son of God, and that by believing you may have life in his name," to make a simple point: the kind of teaching that transforms learners focuses on life.[1]

Sasha's hand went up into the air. "That is not John's only focus!" he said brusquely, almost angrily. His outburst took me by surprise so early in the course, and so I asked him what he meant. "John focuses on other themes in his writings!"

"Such as, what?" I prodded.

"In 1 John, he emphasizes the importance of fellowship!" The class had become quiet, just waiting to see what would happen, wondering what I might do.

"But isn't Christian fellowship part of spiritual life?" I asked.

"Well, yes."

I proceeded to the next point. A few minutes later I drew the Disciplers' Model on the board and began to define it as a central frame for the course.

His hand shot up again. "Where did you get this model?" he demanded to know.

"What do you mean?" I asked.

"I'm asking you where this model came from!"

My mind fell back into 1998, to another Russian class in another Russian city. For two weeks I battled with an embittered student leader and his two main supporters. He had wanted to travel to Germany but was required by the seminary president to stay in the city and attend my class. He made the two weeks as difficult for me as he could and succeeded in learning little. Did I have another like that in this present class? I decided to nip his angry interruptions early. And so I responded: "If you will wait just a little while, some of these questions will be answered in turn. For now, please do not ask any more questions." He did not like my response and pouted during the rest of the lecture, but he did not ask any more questions. The rest of the class relaxed and began to participate in more positive ways. Still I was left with the fact that my relationship with this student had been broken before it had a chance to grow.

A Battle in the Church

The one thing I felt I knew as I began my education ministry in late 1976 was work with the deaf. I had nearly eight years of church experi-

---

1 God's kind of life (*zoē*) rather than biological life (*bios*).

ence working with the deaf. Now I looked forward to working with the group my wife and I had established before heading off to Fort Worth for seminary training in 1973.

I was blocked from doing this early on. The deaf man who had taken my place as director of the ministry was not at all interested in working with me. In fact, over the next two years, I found myself in a contentious battle with him. As minister of education for the church, I was responsible for deaf ministry planning, and he was the lay leader in charge. It was important that we work together, but he would not. He spread rumors about me throughout the deaf community. He refused to report ministry activities. He blocked my efforts to engage the deaf group directly.

Word of the contention made its way to the personnel committee, and the decision was made that we should meet together to make peace. After a lengthy discussion with the pastor and chairman, the chairman suggested a solution: "Rick, why don't you and Brian meet together—just the two of you—and work this out as brothers in Christ? This would be the best way to solve this problem."

Brian and I were left alone, "as brothers in the Lord," to "work out our differences." I felt completely defeated. I had done everything I knew to do to engage Brian for the good of the ministry among the deaf, but he was not willing. I had little hope that having this private talk would help. After all, we had had many talks over the past year. The pastor and chairman stood and walked out, closing the door behind them.

Brian and I looked at each other, and he said, "Well, it looks to me like the pastor and the committee want you to work with me. So, Rick, what are you going to do now?" And then he smiled.

We are called by God to be "one in the Lord." We are the Father's family, brothers and sisters in Christ. But relationships, finding common ground and mutual trust, are difficult to form and harder to maintain. Personal agendas, egocentric thinking, ambition, and self-promotion war against the harmony of community. The task is made more difficult across cultural barriers. Can we really trust each other? How do we form social and emotional bonds with people who see the world through filters different from our own? It must be possible because Jesus commanded it. The question is how we develop a relational character that not only builds bridges to others but also helps our learners to build bridges with those they lead.

The Center Pillar: Helping People Relate

When Jesus was challenged to declare which commandment was the greatest, he condensed the Law and the Prophets into two statements of relationship: "'Love the Lord your God with all your heart and with all your soul and with all your mind.' . . . And the second is like it: 'Love your neighbor as yourself'" (Matt. 22:37, 39).

Our personal relationship with the Father ("Love the Lord your God") begins with faith in Christ. Spiritual power for worship and service, praise and thanksgiving, repentance and renewal, ministry and missions comes through this vital link with the Lord.

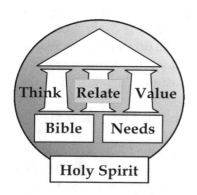

Disciplers' Model

Relationships with others ("Love your neighbor") energize our ministries of equipping, befriending, evangelizing, and discipling—reaching across cultural barriers to build bridges in Jesus' name. *The central pillar of the model is the central focus of church: to establish and strengthen relationships vertically (with the Father) and horizontally (with the family).* It is central not because I say so but because Jesus said so.

The relational focus of the model emphasizes the growth of relationships among believers as we worship God and share our joys and concerns with fellow members in Bible study, fellowship, ministry, and outreach to the unchurched. Our lives become joined together. "People with people with Jesus in the middle" as a friend of mine once said. We build community, the body of Christ, the church family. We remove our masks and share ideas and understandings, joys and hurts, triumphs and failures, happy times and sad. Not with superficial emotion but realistically. Not with cold intellectual detachment but with warm regard for others. Not behind the protection of "my kind" of cultural walls but with open arms to the nations. As we do this, we build a network of relationships, a family, which sustains us through life. The family strengthens us to live and work and minister in our world. The family overcomes cultural divides through the unity of the Spirit. Jesus prayed, "My prayer is not for these [eleven disciples] alone. I pray also for those who will believe in me through their message, that all of them may be one, Father, just as you are in me and I am in you" (John 17:20–21).

Relational Problems in Established Churches at Home

How sad to see people live on the fringes of the church, even in the relative safety of American freedom. They come to services from time to time but never plunge into family life. They keep up appearances but never build bridges. They join no group where emotional masks can be laid aside and the real discussed.

Then some tragedy strikes: a death, an illness, a divorce. They search in vain for the church and for God and wonder why neither can be flipped on like their cable TV. The *koinonia* of Scripture and of the church grows over time. There are no shortcuts.

The Apostle Paul and Relationships: "Social Garments." Paul wrote to the Christians in Colossae and warned them about characteristics which could either hurt or help their community of faith. He listed hurtful characteristics that Christians should remove from their lives, much as someone would take off dirty clothing: anger, rage, malice, slander, and filthy language (3:8). *Anger* is an outburst of temper toward another. *Rage* is a long-standing evil temper toward another and can be thought of as settled anger or hatred. *Malice* is wishing harm toward another. *Slander* is hurting another's reputation through gossip. *Filthy language* is unclean talk or abusive speech, akin to browbeating.

Paul then lists helpful characteristics that Christians should develop in their lives, much as someone would dress themselves with clean clothes: compassion, kindness, humility, gentleness, and patience (3:12). *Compassion* is the heartfelt desire to help another who is in need. *Kindness* is responding to another's need with specific action. *Humility* is a proper mental attitude toward others. Humble people think about themselves correctly. They do not think too highly of themselves (No one can do this as well as I can!), nor do they think too lowly of themselves (I can't do anything for the Lord. I have no gifts.). *Gentleness* grows out of the proper mental attitude of humility. Gentle people help others succeed without feeling superior to them. They praise others who succeed without feeling inferior to them. *Patience* means restraining oneself in the face of injury or insult from another.

Why would a clean person want to wear dirty garments? We have been washed from our sins. Now we should remove from our lives the "dirty garments" which belong to our former life and clothe ourselves in the spotless spiritual garments that build Christian community. But how do we do this? What is the mechanism that allows us to become socially mature and build *koinonia* with others, even those from other cultures?

The Secret of Changing Garments. We find the answer in Jesus' raising Lazarus from the dead. In John 11 we read, "Jesus called out in a loud voice, 'Lazarus, come out!' The dead man came out, his hands and feet wrapped with strips of linen, and a cloth around his face. Jesus said to them, 'Take off the grave clothes and let him go'" (John 11:43–44).

Who gave Lazarus new life? *Jesus.* Who removed the old grave clothes of Lazarus and set him free? *His friends.*

Who gives *us* eternal life? *Jesus.* Who removes *our* old grave clothes, our "old garments," and sets us free? *Our brothers and sisters in Christ.*

Each of the characteristics listed by Paul is social in nature. We cannot grow spiritually without brothers and sisters in Christ. We take off the old and put on the new *as we learn and live and work with others.* Embracing brothers and sisters in Christ across cultural divides makes the process of "family" both deeply frustrating (conflicting perceptions, values, and skill sets) and richly rewarding—for us, for them, and for the kingdom. We will investigate this further in a moment, but the fact remains: Jesus established the church to reach the nations. An integral part of that mission is to help change the way people treat one another. The church is a living laboratory of human relationships.[2]

I used to wonder why churches suffer so much turmoil. Since we are commanded to love one another, why do we find so much contention and fighting? But the irritations, conflicts, and confrontations that occur to some degree in every congregation of believers are a normal part of Christian growth—the *social dimension!* Interpersonal conflicts are an essential part of the growth of *koinonia,* of relationship, of family. We are called into the family because of a mutual love for Jesus. Yet we are people with varying backgrounds, cultures, languages, and interests. Our conflicts are part of the process of becoming one family in him. These social dilemmas and people problems are the raw materials of Christian character and community. God works in and through these human situations to grow us into the image of his Son, for "in all things God works for the good of those who love him, who have been called according to his purpose" (Rom. 8:28).

---

2 Cross-culturally it is so important to discover who will help you remove your grave clothes and whom you must help remove grave clothes. The task before us is far too great for any of us to accomplish it alone. AL

Smooth Stones—Rough Stones. This social dimension of change reminds me of the day my wife and I walked down a beach in Florida. We noticed people bending down and picking up something. We looked around and found, to our amazement, small stones in the sand. We picked up several for a closer look. The rocks were polished and smooth, just beautiful. As we walked around the beach into a small bay, we noticed that the rocks on the shore were rough and dull. They were the same rocks, but they lacked the crucial ingredients that would make them all they could be: the pounding of the surf and the grinding of the sand. Social conflicts and disputes pound us and grind us toward maturity in relationships as we depend on the Father of the family.

On the other hand, believers forfeit the opportunity to experience God's fatherhood and care when they choose to remain aloof, neglect their gifts, and refuse to join brothers and sisters in ministry. They are like the stones in the bay, undisturbed and unchanging. They stagnate in the status quo.

Christians experience deep satisfaction and fulfillment as they learn to share with others, to serve with gladness, to use the gifts God gave them for the good of the family, to pull with Jesus in the comfortable yoke he offers (Matt. 11:28–30). As we trust him for strength and guidance, we are able to tackle larger tasks with confidence. The work brings frustration as well as joy; but this bittersweet mix, the surf and sand, matures us. Those who tackle new tasks, face new challenges, and elect the greatness of service become as "polished stones," a prized possession in the kingdom. Spiritual unity develops in believers as they gather to worship, to study the Bible, to share with one another, to affirm one another, and to minister to one another.[3]

Flip Sides of Relationship: The Positive and Negative in Review. So we find in the relational focus two aspects: one is positive, the other negative. We find the positive aspect of relationships in the growing *koinonia* of the church family. Getting to know and learning to love brothers and sisters in Christ. Building a network of authentic relationships, which

---

3 Polishing takes on a special aspect among missionary colleagues. Missionaries end up spending more time with their colleagues overseas than we would in the States. Holidays, birthdays, free time, and even vacations are spent with the same people we work with. Often our boss, team leader, spiritual leader, good friend, and surrogate relative is the same person. This can lead to conflict and problems when our relational "stones" are rough and unpolished. Some are afraid of this process or unable to withstand the heavenly "polishing" and resign; others see it as a holy process and become true family members following the Father. Part of being called to reach is being called to polishing. Are you ready for the task? AL

gives real support to life in good times and bad. This has been our focus to this point in the chapter.

We find the negative aspect of relationship in the grinding and clashing together of personalities within a congregation. It is *putting up with* unlikable brothers and sisters in the family ("forbear . . . one another," Col. 3:13 KJV). It is struggling with fellow members on a committee. It is wrestling with difficult and divisive issues (and people) in a business meeting. These two aspects of relationship mature us.

Small Groups, Cells, and Sunday School. The best place in the church to develop these required relational skills is in a small group of believers—a home study and prayer cell, or Sunday school class, or an active committee. Here we find a small group of caring persons who give and receive, who comment and listen, who minister and are ministered to. Here members learn to share ideas and experiences openly. Here learners come to know one another and trust one another as persons of worth. Here believers pray for and support one another. In this kind of group, believers have opportunities to receive from others—learning and growing in a safe environment, and gaining confidence and encouragement to share the good news with others. We cannot replace this small-group honing with television or radio religious programming, no matter how entertaining the personalities.

Relational Problems in Cross-Cultural Settings

The goal of family expressed above is no less true in cross-cultural settings but is far more difficult. There are deep differences in the way people of various cultures think, value, and behave; but there are even more subtle complications in the various ways we communicate.

The nuances of language distort our message, even when the message is well intended. On my first trip to Ukraine, I found myself sitting outside the dining room. I had spent six months studying Russian, memorizing phrases and greetings. I had forgotten everything I learned in my college Russian classes thirty years before. Though I had yet to meet my class for the first time, I recognized one of the students walking toward me as a member of my class. I decided to put my practice to the test; and so, as he walked by, I looked at him and said *"Zdrast-vui-te!"* (Hello!) He stopped and looked at me hard.

Tentatively, almost questioningly, he said, *"Zdrastvuite."* I continued with the next phrase commonly found in textbooks: *"Kak vi pozhivaete?"* (How are you getting along?) He shifted from one foot to another, looked me squarely in the eye, and said in broken English, *"Ve dant say zat heer."* Then he walked off, disgusted. I later learned that this last phrase, so common in American greetings, is properly used in Russian only between friends who have not seen each other for a while and want to find out how life has been treating them. It is inappropriate (and simply incorrect) for strangers to use this phrase when meeting for the first time.

Facial expressions can provide miscues as well. You may have noticed in the above paragraph that I inferred two things from the facial expressions of my student. The first was his "hard expression." I read this as "unfriendly." I sensed that he did not like me. When he walked away, I thought he was disgusted with me. This was simply not true. It was a misreading on my part, a figment of my own imagination. A smiling stranger saying hello made him curious and cautious. It put him on his guard. His neutral expression merely *seemed* hard to me. Then I spoke to him poorly and incorrectly. He merely explained to me, *in my own language,* that what I said was incorrect.

I know I was mistaken in these readings because he proved to be both friendly and serious in the class. He was cooperative in every way and, by the end of the course, even appreciative of what I had come to teach. He invited me to his home for a meal, introduced me to his family, and asked me many questions about teaching and learning. In the privacy of his home, he opened his life to me, he laughed, and he shared experiences of pain and spiritual growth. Had I acted on my own miscues, I could have destroyed all chances for the relationship which developed.

At a deeper level, the triad points to cultural gaps in perspectives, values, and skills. While everyone in the world thinks, feels, and does skillfully, as we have said before, the content of these cultural thoughts, feelings, and skills differ from culture to culture. And these differences, if handled poorly on either side, can hurt relationships—and that, in an instant. These differences create barriers to relationship because they separate us into factions, into us-against-them divisions. As the famous chorus proclaims, "It only takes a spark to get a fire going."[4] How we handle the sparks we ignite determines whether the relational fire warms us or destroys us. Disciplers find ways to handle the sparks of cross-cultural conflicts so that "wildfires" are controlled and "campfires" are established.

---

4 Kurt Kaiser, "Pass It On," © 1969, Lexicon Music.

Differing Perspectives (Thinking). A Ukrainian friend once explained to me the "difference between Americans and Ukrainians." He said:

> Let's say there are five problems in a church. An American will see these five problems; but he will also find five more "maybe problems," situations which may develop into problems if nothing is done. The American will immediately set out to solve all ten problems as quickly as possible. He will not sit and drink tea, watch a sunset, smell the fragrance of flowers, or play with his own children. He will move heaven and earth to solve all ten problems, regardless of the additional problems he creates or the interpersonal damage which may be done to others in the situation.
>
> Now a Ukrainian will operate much differently. He will see the five problems. He will completely ignore the five "maybe problems." They have not yet developed into real problems, and therefore nothing needs to be done about them. Concerning the five real problems, the Ukrainian will do little. After all, perhaps, in time, some of these problems will take care of themselves. During this time he will do all the things of life the American misses while solving ten problems. In six months the American will have solved most of the problems but will have created several others in the process. The Ukrainian will find that three of the five problems have already solved themselves and will begin thinking about how to solve the remaining two.

An American missionary friend, living with his wife in a large city in Ukraine, also explained the main difference between Americans and Ukrainians.

> My wife and I live in a second-story apartment. The electric transformer for our building stands outside our bedroom window. We noticed one night that the transformer was damaged because our bedroom was lit up by electrical flashes. It was like a lightning storm outside our window. The next morning I discovered that the transformer was hanging from the pole to which it was attached, and the pole was leaning over a school yard. The transformer was dangling dangerously over children playing at recess during the day. I called the power company and, after telling the official the problem, was asked, "Are

you in the city or in the country?" I told him I was in the city. "That is a different office. Here's the number."

I called the second office and, after telling the official the problem, was asked, "Is the pole wood or concrete?" I told him it was wood. "That is a different office. Here's the number." So I called the number and, after telling the official the problem, was asked, "Is the electricity 110 or 220?" I told him it was 220. "That is a different office. Here's the number." So I called the fourth number and, after telling the official the problem, was asked, "Is the transformer on the ground?" I told him that it had not yet fallen, but it was hanging over the playground and could cause injury or death if it fell. "When the transformer is on the ground, call me back."

The Ukrainian faulted Americans for their overactive can-do problem-solving perspective (and missing, as a result, all the joys of life). The American faulted Ukrainians for their underactive do-nothing indifference to dangerous situations. "Just do it!" versus *"Que sera sera."* It was obvious that both views, from opposite directions, frayed relationships between Americans and Ukrainians.[5]

Differing Priorities (Valuing). Americans tend to be punctual. Time is important. Begin on time and end on time. Most people of the world (with the possible exceptions of the British and Germans) are less tense about time. A woman missionary made plans to conduct a children's ministry conference at a large church in the region. She arrived early and set up her visuals. At the appointed time nearly a hundred people had gathered for the meeting, but the pastor had not yet arrived. The missionary waited ten minutes . . . twenty minutes. She asked several people present whether she should begin. They suggested she wait for the pastor to arrive. She waited another thirty minutes, but still the pastor had not come. She was afraid she would not have time to finish all she had prepared, and so she stood and began her conference. She noticed that the participants seemed a little agitated but assumed it was because they had all arrived on time and had been kept waiting for no reason.

---

5 Each culture also has variation among its peoples. It might be best to picture two ranges: one for Americans and the other for Ukrainians in this case. Within each culture there will be some that are more "just do it!" and some that are more *"que sera sera."* Be careful to distinguish between the two: just because one culture is more of one way than the other doesn't mean that everyone is that way. Some Ukrainians may be more action oriented than some Americans. The intention is always to look at each person individually with culture as a seasoning and not the main ingredient. God has made us all unique and uses cultures as flavoring! That is why we must be individually relational. AL

Ten minutes into her conference, the pastor and his wife arrived. Though he was an hour late, he was visibly upset that the meeting had begun without him. He stepped to the podium and made an official beginning to the meeting, including a long prayer for the missionary, the participants, and the material. She hurried through much of her material, and finished up at the appointed time. The pastor then stood and asked the congregation if they had questions. The Q&A session lasted more than an hour! Rather than becoming frustrated at the unannounced extension of the conference, everyone seemed to enjoy the interaction. No one was in a hurry to leave.

South African Christian believers place great importance on joyful celebration. They are enthusiastic in their singing, dancing, preaching, and witnessing. They express their joy openly through wide smiles and easy laughter. Northern Africans (Arab Muslims) are stoic. They focus on actions more than emotions and tend to distrust anyone who displays emotion openly. South African believers must learn to restrain their joyous outbursts if they are to build relational bridges to the stoic North African Arabs for the cause of Christ.

Differing Skills (Doing). Cultures place importance on different kinds of skills: task versus relationship, structure versus flexibility, praxis versus abstraction, results versus process. Cultures place different importance on competence, mastery, and excellence. While Americans admire these traits, other cultures view them as self-centered and arrogant. These differences plague us constantly as we attempt to build bridges of mutual trust and family.

The Relational Character of Jesus

Jesus crossed the greatest cultural divide in history when he "being in very nature God, did not consider equality with God something to be grasped, but made himself nothing, taking the very nature of a servant, being made in human likeness. And being found in appearance as a man, he humbled himself and became obedient to death—even death on a cross!" (Phil. 2:5–8). Let's look at how Jesus established relationships with others, especially those he called as disciples. In doing so, we will move beyond simple interpersonal skills to the relational character of the Leader of leaders.

The manner in which we lead others is an integral part of our equipping and discipling ministry. Whether we are a missionary or seminary professor, a pastor, staff minister, or lay leader, we will more effectively disciple God's people if we give attention to the relational implications of our leadership style. Further, if we wish to lead in a manner worthy of the Lord, we must understand how Jesus led and then follow his example.

When I think of Jesus, my first thoughts are Divine Logos, the Son of God, the Master Teacher, Lord. His words were sometimes harsh and biting. He denounced the indifferent (Matt. 11:21) and the self-righteous (Matt. 23:27). He called himself "Lord of the Sabbath" (Matt. 12:8) and equated himself with God (John 20:30). He drove the money changers out of the temple with a whip (Matt. 21:12). He taught in such a radical manner that people were "amazed at his teaching, because he taught as one who had authority, and not as their teachers of the law" (Matt. 7:28–29).

He demonstrated divine power through his ability to heal "all who were ill with various diseases, those suffering severe pain, the demon-possessed, those having seizures, and the paralyzed" (Matt. 4:24). He fed the multitudes of listeners on at least two occasions with small amounts of food (Matt. 14:15ff; 15:38ff). He taught spiritual truth with power and clarity (Matt. 13:54). Jesus was, and is, one who has authority and power. It is fascinating, however, to watch how he used that power!

Jesus was also a human leader as he walked this earth. He led men and women in a way that energized them to become all they were intended to be. He chose twelve unschooled men and in three years had molded them into the leaders of his church. He drew them together into a spiritual family, a team, and ignited them with a passion for God's kingdom. Jesus' favorite title for himself was "Son of Man." He used his power not to rule but to serve his Father and minister to people—Jews, Romans, Samaritans, Phoenicians—as he announced the coming of the kingdom of God. No other person in history has so perfectly meshed leading and serving, power and love, integrity and forgiveness, the rod and the staff! With sensitive awareness that we tread on sacred ground, let's look closely at the relational principles of how Jesus led the twelve.

1. The Individual Is Important

At a time when power politics was the norm, enforced through the military might of Rome, Jesus exalted the worth and dignity of the individual. He loved persons. He ministered to them one by one, despite their social rank. Think how he spoke with the Samaritan woman, how he praised the faith of the centurion, or how he embraced those hated tax collectors Matthew and Zacchaeus! For Jesus, one soul is worth more than the whole world (Matt. 16:26).

Crowds surrounded Jesus on every side. They wanted him to be their King. They wanted the Teacher to protect them and feed them and heal them and, most of all, to free them from the Roman yoke. But he did not adjust his message to please the crowds. He was interested in more than mere numbers. He ministered to persons at their particular point of need.

Principle One

Disciplers place importance on the worth of individuals. They see people not as groups or statistics but as persons of worth.

Cross-Cultural Implication

Disciplers reject the temptation to stereotype others by cultural generalities. They do not assume the perspectives, values, or skills of others but relate to each leader-learner individually. Disciplers must value and therefore honor everyone they meet.[6]

Disciplers take care to avoid cultural stereotypes and establish relationships with individuals in the culture one at a time.

2. Relationship Is Nurtured through Service

In every human organization there is a hierarchy of position and power. Moses discovered the necessity of hierarchical delegation when he was overwhelmed by details (Exod. 18:13–27). There are leaders and followers, employers and employees, directors and workers. The world places importance on the influential, the powerful, and the wealthy. But look what Jesus told his disciples! "The greatest among you will be your servant. For whoever exalts himself will be humbled, and whoever humbles himself will be exalted" (Matt. 23:11–12).

Jesus is Lord. He is Teacher. Leader. Servant. Friend (John 15:15). All of us who name the name of Jesus serve him as Sovereign. We teach in order to obey him. We lead in order to follow him. We minister according to his example. Then how should we lead? Or teach? Or minister? Jesus

---

6 Each person we meet is created by God and therefore very valuable. When we honor their worth as a creation of God, we honor God, his works, and his kingdom. I have found in my missionary career that the more ways I can find to value a person as God values them, the more God will use both of us to accomplish his purposes. Valuing or honoring is the best way I have found to show each individual's importance. AL

answers: "You know that the rulers of the Gentiles lord it over them, and their high officials exercise authority over them. Not so with you! Instead, whoever wants to become great among you must be your servant, and whoever wants to be first must be your slave—just as the Son of Man did not come to be served, but to serve, and to give his life a ransom for many" (Matt. 20:25–28).

The greatest leaders in the kingdom are those who give themselves away—in terms of time, talent, and resources—as a ransom for others. The only valid hierarchy in Christ's kingdom is the hierarchy of serving others.

Service, not credentials, builds relationship. A dangerous misconception seminary graduates can carry to their first field of service, at home or abroad, is that their degree gives them both the authority and the ability to lead. People tend to look on educated beginners with suspicion. There is the distinct possibility of the new—by having knowledge without wisdom, shine without substance. This natural resistance from followers can frustrate the best efforts of the enthusiastic young missionary or minister.

Disciplers give people time for relationships to develop through ministry, through sacrificial service. Jesus, of course, did more than teach servanthood. He set the example for it. He washed the feet of the disciples (John 13:2–15) and prepared them breakfast on the beach (John 21:12–14). He prayed for them, instructed them, corrected them, and even rebuked them at times through their three years together. His supreme sacrifice was his willingness to bear in his body, as Leader, the sins of his followers, and of the whole world.

The message of servanthood can be drowned out in the drumbeat of me-first religion and success-oriented ministry. Still, the message is clear: service to others, in Jesus' name, on the basis of their need, rendered out of sincere gratitude for what Christ has done, is the only route to a life of relational influence for Christ's kingdom, for "whoever loses his life for me and for the gospel will save it" (Mark 8:35). Mutual service among the individuals of a mission team, congregation, or Christian school draws the church family together. The discipling leader enhances the growth of relationships through service.[7]

---

7 Living cross-culturally means that we will almost always be outsiders and not insiders. This is God's plan for missionaries. As outsiders, the most enduring way to be used by the Lord among our national brothers and sisters is to serve first. Outsiders are accepted by insiders when the insiders see missionaries placing the insider's greatest needs as their first priorities. People are willing to listen to outsiders after they know they care about them. Serving shows our care. AL

Principle Two

Disciplers patiently build *koinonia* among
individuals through sacrificial service.

Cross-Cultural Implication

Disciplers reject self-serving models of power over those of
other cultures. They earn credibility for leadership by enduring
hardships and serving others.

Disciplers do not serve in order to gain power over people. This is nothing more than self-serving manipulation. Disciplers serve others out of heartfelt love which is produced through surrender to the Holy Spirit (chapter 2).

3. Relationship Is Nurtured through Humility

Despite his obvious power and authority, Jesus discarded the tinsel trappings of powerful people. He shunned pomp. He possessed a dynamic humility. He taught us to serve others but not for the public recognition this service brings. The best kingdom service is hidden service. Jesus said:

> "Be careful not to do your 'acts of righteousness' before men, to be seen of them. If you do, you will have no reward from your Father in heaven. So when you give to the needy, do not announce it with trumpets, as the hypocrites do in the synagogues and on the streets, to be honored by men. I tell you the truth, they have received their reward in full. But when you give to the needy, do not let your left hand know what your right hand is doing, so that your giving may be in secret. Then your Father, who sees what is done in secret, will reward you" (Matt. 6:1–4).

Jesus describes two levels of hidden service here. The first is service which is "hidden from others." We do not call attention to ourselves in order to be honored *by others.* The second is service which is "hidden from self." We do not call attention to ourselves in order to be honored by *ourselves!* When disciplers live "in Christ," when the Spirit is in control, the supernatural things that he does through them do not register consciously. The Lord can speak powerfully through a kind word, a pat on the back, a prepared meal, a written note, a silent presence. Disciplers serve the Lord without noticing they are doing anything special or out of the ordinary.

Jesus certainly lived this way. His actions, as well as his teaching, demonstrated humility. Upon healing two blind men, he "warned them sternly, 'See that no one knows about this'" (Matt. 9:30). After his transfiguration Jesus told Peter, James, and John, "Don't tell anyone what you have seen, until the Son of Man has been raised from the dead" (Matt. 17:9). Again Jesus showed radical humility when he restored the man possessed by demons. He cast the demons into a herd of swine which were owned communally by a nearby town. They immediately ran down a steep embankment into the lake and drowned. The townspeople were so angry over their loss, and so afraid of the power of Jesus, they demanded that he leave immediately. Without apparent personal defense of any kind, "Jesus stepped into a boat, crossed over and came to his own town" (Matt. 9:1). How many times have I tried in vain to explain the rightness of my actions when confronted by disgruntled church members?

The dynamic humility of Jesus was neither self-depreciation nor self-glory. He did not kick the dirt apologetically when he was praised. "Oh, it was *nothing!*" He did not discount his abilities. Nor did he brag about his abilities or power or wise interpretation of Old Testament Scripture. Self-depreciation questions God's creative wisdom and will. Self-glory presumes upon one's own goodness and ability. Self-depreciation makes one hypersensitive and critical. Self-glory makes one proud and insensitive. Both attitudes hurt one's ability to build and maintain relationships.

Biblical humility grows from a balanced and realistic appraisal of one's strengths and weaknesses. Disciplers are aware of their abilities and use them to further the kingdom of Christ anywhere in the world. They are also aware of weaknesses and apply God's power and promises to decrease their harm. By cultivating a proper mental attitude of humility, disciplers are freed from insensitivity (the result of self-glory) and defensiveness (the result of self-depreciation). This proper attitude undergirds conscious efforts of building relationships with those they lead.

Principle Three

Disciplers employ their gifts and experience with humility. Disciplers humbly maximize their gifts and experience. The resulting dynamic servant-leader style strengthens relationships.

Cross-Cultural Implication

Disciplers teach others with humility, rejecting all forms of innate superiority. They teach as servants and ministers, not as masters. Disciplers learn from others with humility—language, perceptions, procedures—and use what they learn, with gratitude, to improve ministry effectiveness.

Disciplers reject the manipulation of others through tasks or programs that spotlight themselves. They understand the long-term benefits of the more gradual process of equipping others. Disciplers use their abilities and influence to further the kingdom of Christ rather than gain public recognition for themselves or build a personal kingdom.

4. Jesus Met People's Needs

In chapter 6 we focused on compassionate character. One powerful by-product of compassion is the foundation it lays for meaningful relationships. Jesus was quick to help people in need. One day he was teaching on the subject of fasting. Suddenly, servants of Jairus, ruler of the synagogue, interrupted Jesus' teaching. Jairus's daughter was ill, and the servants had come to summon Jesus for help. At this interruption Jesus ended his teaching session and went with them immediately (Matt. 9:18–19).

On the way to the religious leader's home, Jesus was interrupted again, this time by "a woman who had been subject to bleeding for twelve years" (Matt. 9:20), making her ceremonially unclean (Lev. 15:19–27) and a social outcast among her people. Jesus gives no evidence of irritation at these interruptions to his ministry plans (teaching, healing). Jesus knew his Father was in control, even in interruptions! Jesus stopped to help the woman and healed her of this physical and social ailment. Then he continued on to Jairus's house and brought his daughter back to life. Interruptions to our primary agendas, especially in terms of the spontaneous needs of others, are often the best opportunities for discipling ministry.

Jesus was moved with compassion as he considered the masses of people (Matt. 9:36; 14:14; 23:37). He did not condemn them for their lack of faith. Rather he strengthened what little faith they had, and in so doing he fulfilled Isaiah's prophecy: "A bruised reed he will not break, and a smoldering wick he will not snuff out" (Isa. 42:3; Matt. 12:20).

One example of this faith-strength...
sation with the pagan Syro-Phoenicia...
and granted the request to heal her dau...
harsh words to the woman[9] are explaine...
who could not understand Jesus' messiar...
to heal. He could not yield to her request...
real meaning of Messiah. Her response (v. ...
ing that God was Master over Jew and Gree...
manner, she is no longer "under the table" (li...
sat at the table with Abraham, Isaac, and Jaco... ...s
bread. Disciplers demonstrate compassion tow...   ...r faith in
learners, not frustration at the lack of raging fire... ...us told the confident
rich young ruler, "One thing you lack." And then he provided the remedy.
Disciplers do the same.

Repeatedly we find Jesus using his power and authority to serve the
Father and meet people's needs. He did not exalt himself with his authority though he was tempted to do just that at both the beginning and the
end of his earthly ministry. At the beginning Satan showed him a scene
ripe for personal glory. The morning sacrifice had been offered by the
priests. The huge gates to the temple slowly opened, allowing the faithful to appear before the Lord. Silver trumpets summoned them. Here,
surrounded by the pomp of temple ceremony and the gathering crowds
of worshippers, what a welcome Jesus would receive as he, the long-
awaited Messiah, descended in the air. What shouts of acclamation and
praise would he receive! How he would have been worshipped! And
crowned king of Israel. But this was not the divine goal or God's plan.
"And thus once more Jesus is not only not overcome, but He overcomes
by absolute submission to the will of God."[10] And the purpose for this
was our need of salvation: "While we were yet sinners, Christ died for
us" (Rom. 5:8 KJV).

Again, at the end of his ministry, he is confronted by the temptation
to save himself while hanging on the cross. Religious leaders challenged
him. "He saved others, . . . but he can't save himself! He's the King of

---

8 Mark 7:26—the woman was a Greek, born in Syrian Phoenicia. She begged Jesus to drive the
demon out of her daughter.

9 Mark 7:27–30: "'First let the children eat all they want,' he told her, 'for it is not right to take the
children's bread and toss it to their dogs.' 'Yes, Lord,' she replied, 'but even the dogs under the table
eat the children's crumbs.' Then he told her, 'For such a reply, you may go; the demon has left your
daughter.' She went home and found her child lying on the bed, and the demon gone."

10 Alfred Edershiem, *Life and Times of Jesus the Messiah,* vol. 1 (Grand Rapids: Eerdmans, 1967),
304.

…wn now from the cross, and we will believe in … What more proof of his messiahship could Jesus ren-…ously to come down off the cross? But this, too, was not … Jesus' road to glory led through death for the *needs of people.* …s met the needs of people in life and in death. He used his power …authority to that end. He continues to do so today. Disciplers are more concerned about their flocks than their own careers. They serve people because, in serving others, they serve Christ. Even if that service should lead to their own death.

Principle Four

Disciplers respond to the needs of people, actively reaching out in love. They maintain priorities in ministry that are person-centered.

Cross-Cultural Implication

Disciplers care about people more than agendas, persons more than arbitrary goals. They endure interruptions, hardships, and setbacks in order to meet people's needs and introduce them to the King and the kingdom.

Ray of Hope Ministries in Bishkek, Kyrgyzstan, is a German-Russian mission. They open the door to sharing the gospel by distributing clothes, food, and hope. They have provided medical supplies to lepers and leadership training to Kyrgyz pastors. They work openly and honestly in a former Communist, predominantly Muslim country, and have earned the respect of governmental leaders for their humanitarian efforts. Thousands have come to faith in Christ through their efforts.

5. Jesus Supported His Followers

Jesus did not use his disciples to make a name for himself[11] or exploit them to establish his program. He gave himself for them. He supported them and strengthened them. He grew them through practical teaching and daily experience to the place they were able to sense the dynamic

---

11 But we all know that Jesus' name is the "name above all names." How can you say Jesus did not make a name for himself? Paul answers, "And being found in appearance as a man, he humbled himself and became obedient to death—even death on a cross! Therefore God exalted him to the highest place and gave him the name that is above every name, that at the name of Jesus every knee should bow, in heaven and on earth and under the earth, and every tongue confess that Jesus Christ is Lord, to the glory of God the Father" (Phil. 2:8–11). Disciplers work for his glory, not their own.

of his kingdom. For Jesus, people are the ends, not the means, of God's kingdom. The kingdom is more process than product. Making disciples and growing them into the image of Christ. How we do this is the heart of the model and the triad.

Matthew records for us the instructions Jesus gave before sending the Twelve on their first evangelistic campaign (Matt. 10). He did not send the Twelve out to do his work so he could rest. He did not stop at supervising the work of others. When he had sent them out, "he went on from there to teach and preach in the towns of Galilee" (Matt. 11:1). He led by example and shared in the work. His actions reinforced the sharp contrast between his kingdom and the religious establishment. He said:

> The teachers of the law and the Pharisees sit in Moses' seat. So you must obey them and do everything they tell you. But do not do what they do, for they do not practice what they preach. They tie up heavy loads and put them on men's shoulders, but they themselves are not willing to lift a finger to move them. Everything they do is done for men to see. . . . They love the place of honor at banquets and the most . important seats in the synagogues; they love to be greeted in the marketplace and to have men call them 'Rabbi'" (Matt. 23:2–7).

Jesus gave his disciples a different model: Do not bind heavy burdens on people in the name of the kingdom but serve the King by washing feet and binding up wounds.

Jesus' support permeated the group. One evidence of this personal support is the *climate of freedom* the disciples displayed in his presence. They freely chose to follow Jesus (Matt. 4:18–22; 9:9) even when the requirements were harsh (Matt. 8:18–22 and Matt. 10:16–23). The rich young ruler was sincere in his behavior and attitude (running and kneeling), reverent in addressing Jesus ("Teacher"), upright in his lifestyle ("All these I have kept") and religious in his question ("What must I do to inherit eternal life?"). Yet he freely chose not to follow Jesus, and Jesus allowed him that choice! No guilt trip. No pressure. Jesus let him go.

Beyond the freedom of choice to follow Jesus, we find personal freedom in the relationships of the disciples. They clearly enjoyed the freedom to speak their minds, even if at times their words revealed personal arrogance. When Mary of Bethany poured precious ointment over Jesus' head, the disciples were "indignant. 'Why this waste?' they asked. 'This perfume could have been sold at a higher price and the money given to the poor'" (Matt. 26:8–9). Peter's rebuke of Jesus (Matt. 16:21–22) and the request for heavenly positions by James and John (Mark 10:35) affirm the *freedom of expression* enjoyed by those closest to the Master. Had Jesus been an autocratic ruler, his disciples would have been less free in their speech and behavior.

Two of the disciples provide a vivid contrast in their response to the loving leadership and support of Jesus. As Judas approached Jesus to betray him in the garden, Jesus called him "friend" (Matt. 26:50) and accepted his kiss of greeting. Peter denied knowing Jesus though he had bragged earlier of his devotion (Matt. 26:69–75). Both betrayed their Leader. Judas never really understood who Jesus was and in desperation hanged himself (Matt. 27:3–5). Peter lived to experience forgiveness and a recommissioning to kingdom service ("Feed my sheep," John 21:17).

This example of Jesus as Servant Leader burned so deeply into Peter's soul that nearly forty years later this rugged fisherman would write to church leaders, "Be shepherds of God's flock that is under your care, serving as overseers . . . *not lording it over those entrusted to you*" (1 Pet. 5:2a, 3). How often have I heard it said that fast-growing churches require autocratic pastors. Here we see the wrong goal tied to wrong method. From these ideas of support come three principles.

Principle Five

Disciplers support their leader-learners. They do not use them merely to accomplish their program goals but nurture them into the service of the kingdom.

Cross-Cultural Implication

Disciplers protect and strengthen learners. They give their own lives, in terms of time, talent, emotion, and energy, for the benefit of leader-learners.

Disciplers are willing to work as a member of the team and multiply their ministries by delegating specific responsibilities to organization leaders.

Principle Six

Disciplers fight the tendency to become self-centered and self-important.

Cross-Cultural Implication

Disciplers avoid the temptation to bind burdens upon people through rigid rules, human hierarchy, and arbitrary structure, which is subtle and pervasive in every organization.

While it is easier to make rules than nurture relationships, disciplers support their leader-learners through flexible structures which enhance relationships.

Principle Seven

Disciplers build an atmosphere of freedom
and trust among their followers.

Cross-Cultural Implication

Disciplers are mature enough to accept praise (humbly) or criticism (thoughtfully). Such leaders encourage frank, open discussion with others.

6. The Disciples Were Organized

Jesus' focus on individuals and his desire for relationship among them drew the disciples into an organized group of apprentices.

The Twelve Organized. It appears that the disciples were organized into smaller groups, each group having its respective leader. These Gospel lists present the disciples in stable groups of four. The first group consisted of Simon Peter, James, John, and Andrew. *Peter* is always listed first among the Twelve and these four. The second group consisted of Philip, Bartholomew, Matthew, and Thomas. *Philip* is always listed first in this second group. The third group consisted of James the son of Alphaeus, Thaddeus (Luke calls him Judas, the son of James), Simon the Zealot, and Judas Ischariot. *James* is listed first in this grouping. (See Matt. 10:2–4; Mark 3:16–19; Luke 6:14–16; and Acts 1:13)

Special Attention to Three. Of the Twelve, Jesus gave special attention to *Peter, James,* and *John.* All four Gospels list these three disciples in the top four positions. They were present with Jesus when he healed the daughter of Jairus, ruler of the synagogue. The other disciples apparently remained outside (Mark 5:37–38). These three witnessed the transfiguration of Jesus while the others remained at the foot of the mountain (Matt. 17:1–9). These three were asked to accompany Jesus into the garden of Gethsemane and there to watch and pray with him, while the others remained just inside the gate (Matt. 26:36–38).

It is interesting to me that these three overcame short tempers and large egos as they were loved by Christ and as they loved him. Peter, James, and John—the brash fisherman and the "sons of thunder." *It was not the annihilation of their egos, but the reining in of their egos, for Christ, that made the difference in their lives.* These three made significant contributions to the spread of the gospel around their world. Peter evangelized the Jews, James pastored the church in Jerusalem, and John pastored in Ephesus. Their letters of encouragement to the churches strengthened the faith of millions in Jesus Christ and, as part of our New Testament, continue to do so.

The Special Status of Peter. Then further, Jesus concentrated his teaching and leading most directly on one of the three: Simon. He gave him the new name of Petros ("the rock") which symbolized what he would become (Matt. 16:18). He allowed Peter to do an adventuresome thing and fail (that is, walk on water; see Matt. 14:29–33). He rebuked Peter when he resorted to violence (John 18:10–11). As we've noted already, we see the climax of Jesus' earthly nurture and training of Peter on the beach as he forgave and recommissioned Peter to kingdom service. Notice the progression. *As the group gets smaller, the relationships grow deeper.*

From Many to One. Jesus taught the multitudes. From these he chose seventy to send out witnessing. From these seventy, he chose twelve "to be with him" for special instruction. Of the Twelve, he chose three for intensive training. And of these three he concentrated on Peter. The group was one. It was a body of several members, fitted together with Christ as head. The group, thus organized, trained, and led, marched out to turn their world upside-down with the gospel, with the exception of Judas, who sought to use the family for his own political purposes but never actually joined the family heart, soul, mind and strength.[12]

---

12 I really like the way this point was developed. I haven't seen it brought out this clearly before. Any lasting ministry must work from many to one. Missionaries must focus on a select few. How do you select these few? One easy method would be to find those who will in turn influence and disciple others. Too often missionaries focus either on the many to the exclusion of the few or on one or two people who take more than they give. When we focus on needy people who are not going to share what God has given to them, we are more often meeting our own self-esteem needs and not seeking the kingdom first. Our focus must always be on people who are about the kingdom's work of reproducing themselves. AL

Principle Eight

Disciplers organize their ministries to give attention, support and training to leader-learners who will, in turn, disciple others.

Cross-Cultural Implication

Disciplers serve the masses by equipping
small groups of leaders who are ready to learn.

Disciplers multiply their effectiveness by equipping equippers and discipling disciplers in order to minister to people through people.

7. The Authority to Relate and Lead

The authority Jesus possessed for life-giving ministry had two major sources. The first source was his union with, and total dependence on, the Father (John 5:17–19, see "Spiritual Character," chapter 2). The second source was Jesus' profound and intimate mastery of Scripture ("Biblical Character"; see chapter 3). Jesus' mastery of Scripture is displayed prominently in the Gospels as a weapon against Satan's attacks (Matt. 4:4, 7, 10), in his condensation of the Law and the Prophets (Matt. 22:37, 39) and in his personal fulfillment of the letter and spirit of the Law (Luke 4:16–21).

These two sources of authority allow disciplers to be consistent in their dealings with others. Spirit and Scripture establish a common ground across cultural divides. The Holy Spirit speaks to the hearts of Americans, Russians, Koreans, Kenyans, or Spaniards. By seeking the Spirit's direction together, we reduce cultural barriers and reinforce spiritual commonalities. Whether the Scripture speaks in English, Russian, Korean, Swahili, or Spanish, it proclaims God's message. By anchoring our teaching and leading in Scripture, we reduce cultural barriers and reinforce spiritual commonalities. Three principles derive from the consideration of authority issues.[13]

---

13 This is an excellent point, and further explanation might benefit readers. *Our authority as leaders is dependent on our ability to follow God,* by how we depend on him in all things and allow his word to master our lives. Hosea 12:6 says this clearly in the New Living Translation: "Act on the principles of love and justice, and always live in confident dependence on your God." God calls us to depend confidently upon him. Dependence on other things instead of God is never confidence, and confidence without dependence on God is overconfidence. We can only be confident when we truly depend on God, and we can only be truly dependent when we depend on something that is confident and true—the Word of God.

The more of our life that we pour into the Bible, the more God's Word will become a lamp to our feet and a light to our path. We should not just be concerned with how much of the Bible we know

Principle Nine

Disciplers are firm in their personal relationship with the living Word, and in their conviction concerning the written Word. Spirit and Scripture establish common ground across cultural divides.

Cross-Cultural Implication

Spirit and Scripture provide strength for daily living and daily leading. Such spiritual and biblical authority provides a solid platform on which to build family.

Disciplers do not confuse spiritual authority with a dominating attitude over others, which ultimately destroys relationships.

Principle Ten

Disciplers have a fluent [articulate, well-versed] mastery of the Bible and make decisions in light of that understanding.

Cross-Cultural Implication

Disciplers employ biblical principles in everyday situations, illustrating that the kingdom of God is above every human culture. Disciplers are known more for how the Word of God has mastered them than how they have mastered the Bible.[14]

Disciplers' mastery of the Bible is living knowledge—objective (true), subjective (personal), and behavioral (active)—that expresses itself in transformed living. Such living knowledge allows disciplers to solve problems and make decisions in line with spiritual truth.

---

but how much of the Bible serves as the lamp and light of our lives. We can master the Bible in knowledge and understanding, but our desire is for the application and power of God's Word to master us. We must seek his Word not as advice from a consultant but as the will and way of our Master.

Our authority to lead and to guide others' lives only comes from the authority of Scripture. We disciple people because the Bible gives us a clear image of what a disciple looks like. In the Gospels disciples are those that follow Jesus; in the epistles the characteristics of disciples are clearly explained. These are true in all cultures.

The Bible also shows us many different examples of disciplers. We can find postmodern disciple-making and enlightened disciple makers, stories and lists, literate followers, and illiterate followers. Today we have postliterate followers, and they too are found in the Bible. The Bible and not our personal preferences or worldview is the standard for disciplers. AL

14 Second implication offered by Andy Leininger.

Principle Eleven

Disciplers see themselves as perpetual learners.

Cross-Cultural Implication

Disciplers view their own spiritual status as "in process." This dynamic spirituality produces fruit in their lives and ministries as they surrender daily to the lordship of Christ.

Disciplers live on the cutting edge of faith and draw others to join them in "family." This self-perception of "learner" increases their influence.

8. Dealing with Failure

Jesus taught a multitude of people who followed him and listened to him. They wanted him to be their king (John 6:14). Who could throw off the Roman yoke and reestablish David's kingdom better than the one who healed diseases and infirmities, fed thousands with a small lunch, and spoke with unrivalled authority?

But Jesus rejected the call of the multitude to kingship. From that point until his death we see with human eyes his downward plunge into failure. He was attacked by the educated and religious. He was rejected by the masses. He did not fit their notions about God's plan. Even his own disciples, with the single exception of John, deserted him in the end. Turned over to pagan authorities, he was tried, scourged, and crucified. He hung on rough nails driven into raw wood between two criminals. No one seemed to understand him or the gospel he had proclaimed for three years. What a failure!

But wait! The story isn't finished. Jesus did not measure success by the masses, religious leaders, or disciples! He measured his mission's success by the Father's will for his life (John 5:30, 36–40; 6:38; 8:28–29). Failure would come only by acting outside God's will to attempt to reach spiritual objectives by human means.

Earlier in the chapter we noted Jesus' triumph in three major tests: the temptations in the wilderness, the prayer struggle in Gethsemane, and the taunts of the crowd at Calvary. Each time Jesus weighed the evidence and found nothing more important than doing the Father's will. On one arm of the balance lay rejection, persecution, abandonment, and the agonies of an unjust and cruel death. On the other lay the resurrection! There was no failure in the life of our Leader! There was only success as he faithfully carried out God's will.

We would lead more consistently, we could join with others more humbly, and we could strengthen family more confidently if we measured our ministry more according to God's will for our ministry and less on the inevitable criticism, misunderstanding, confrontation, and miscommunication that occurs when people work together in a common cause. We pray for sensitivity to the "still small voice" that leads us.

On the other hand we should guard ourselves against the danger of mistaking emotional or social or political pressure as God's will. Jesus knew the Father's will precisely. We struggle by faith to know even part of his will for us (1 Cor. 13:12). Therefore we must exercise great care lest we mistake our own personal feelings (or ego needs, or materialistic desires) or pressure from supervisors, colleagues, or members in the church for the will of God.

Further, we have the promise that, though we will inevitably fail in some aspect of our work ("for all . . . fall short of the glory of God," Rom. 3:23), he can work all things together for our collective good (Rom. 8:28). The events of our lives are like beads on a string. We tend to look at them one at a time. This one's good. This one's not so good. The good events lift us up, and the bad events tend to depress us. But when we look at the entire string by faith, we can see how all the beads together produce a beautiful necklace of life.

The resurrection gives us hope if we will but receive it—not only hope for the future in heaven but hope for daily living right here and now. Whether we face unjust criticism or gossip that undermines reputation or outright opposition, whether we fall into sin or become misdirected in priorities, *God can resurrect us to his service,* just as Jesus did with Peter. He can give us greater resources, more influence, and a deeper understanding of family and Christian leadership if we will trust in and cling to him day by day.

Principle Twelve

Disciplers view failure redemptively.

Cross-Cultural Implication

Disciplers retain active hope in the Lord even when they fail because they know and follow the risen Christ.

Disciplers know that when failure finds meaning, it is no longer failure. It is rather the means to greater effectiveness. They do not lose heart in the face of failure, real or perceived, but rather trust in the one who called them and wait patiently for him to "lift them up in due season."

How to Develop a Relational Character

While overarching principles are helpful in developing a proper perspective, what practical steps will help us make an immediate relational impact? We could list hundreds of such steps, but I will mention those I've noticed as most helpful.

On Initial Contact

The power of first impressions is well-known. The first impression we make is the most lasting. But some worry so much about first impressions that they make the long-lasting mistake of assuming the need to sell themselves, or their organizations, in that first meeting. We have only one chance to make a good first impression.

A fundamental question is this: what constitutes a good first impression to people of other cultures? In most cases it is concern for others. The apostle Peter reminds us to "love each other deeply, because love covers over a multitude of sins" (1 Pet. 4:8). Listen before talking. Observe before suggesting. Ask questions before giving answers. Fit in before standing out. Make a good first impression by accepting others as they are.

Building Relational Ties

In subsequent encounters build on initial positives by emphasizing commonalities. Learn from them before attempting to teach them. Engage with their opinions before stating your own. Intentionally work behind the scenes, a servant leader who promotes others. Let the leader-learners have the spotlight in their own context.

Strengthening Family Bonds

Deepen relational ties with individuals and groups over time by means of *patient giving*. Overlook minor frustrations, forbear (that is, "put up with") various cultural perspectives, values, and procedures. Walk the second mile as a lifestyle. Engage others with humility. "Let your conversation be always full of grace, seasoned with salt, so that you may know how to answer everyone" (Col. 4:6).

Deepen relational ties with individuals and groups over time by means of *patient receiving*. Scripture teaches that *"it is more blessed to give than to receive"* (Acts 20:35). We can then bless others and strengthen family by allowing others to give to us. Not selfishly, or subserviently, but with a heart to help others, we can encourage others to help us with their language, their customs, their common practices. By encouraging others to become our teachers, we gain influence for our ministry, especially as we practice what our learners teach us! I'll never forget the interpreter for the deaf who told the deaf members of the church to stop correcting the way she signed the sermons, "After all, *they* don't know anything about interpreting." She missed the blessing of being taught, as well as the blessing of building family between herself and the group.

Extending Principles to Relational Team-Building

Relational ministry goes beyond our personal relationships with individuals. Model the role in team-building by drawing individuals together into communities. Demonstrate team-building skills through consistent, positive actions. Referee conflicts within groups, helping each group member to esteem the other more highly than himself (see Phil. 2:3). Help demolish the barriers of conflicting ideas, priorities, values, and actions, "speaking the truth in love" (Eph. 4:15)—that cause divisions and dissensions in the group, as they arise. Encourage lay leaders in their leadership.

Equipping Learner-Leaders to Build Bridges and Develop Teams

Multiply effectiveness in team-building by intentionally spinning off teams under the supervision of leader-learners. Prompt learners to become leaders of other groups which grow out of the central community.

Caution! Do this within the context of the surrounding culture. Do not violate relational principles in order to build relationships! In Ukraine, for example, it is difficult to plant a second church in a town or city. It is usually the pastor of the one church who opposes establishing a second. "What if the second church takes away some of my members?" Time is required to help the pastor, through relational teaching, see that the short-term loss to his church, if it happens, will result in long-term gains for the kingdom as the two, three, or more churches work together to reach into different areas of the region.

Set Aside Every Hindrance to Relational Ministry

Take off pride, which prompts us to focus energies on ourselves. Take off busyness. Adjust agendas to include relational time. Take off demanding workloads. Make relational activities part of the central ministry task. Take off inflated expectations. The disappointment which wells up when such overexpectations go unfulfilled can destroy vital relationships.

We Americans are task oriented. We point to our accomplishments as evidence of the value of getting the job done. We point with pride to our megachurches, which have the human and financial resources to do great things. But just what is the real job we are trying to get done? Most of the rest of the world is oriented more to community than task, more to being than doing. We find this same order of priority in the Ten Commandments and the Sermon on the Mount:[15] who we are must precede what we do.

What is the evidence that we are Christians? Our wealth? Our know-how? Our many programs? Our slick publications? Our can-do spirit? Our success by worldly standards (fame, possessions, power)? John tells us, "We know that we have passed from death to life, because *we love our brothers*. Anyone who does not love remains in death" (1 John 3:14).

The central pillar of the model is "relating" because it is the central pillar of the church. The central discipling characteristic is "relational character." Not because I say so but because Jesus said so. "Jesus replied: "'Love the Lord your God with all your heart and with all your soul and with all your mind.' This is the first and greatest commandment. And the second is like it: 'Love your neighbor as yourself.' All the Law and the Prophets hang on these two commandments'" (Matt. 22:37–40).

These two statements of relationship—vertical: *loving God,* and horizontal: *loving neighbor*—form the central focus of the church, of the Disciplers' Model, and of this text. "And they'll know we are Christians by our love, by our love. Yes, they'll know we are Christians by our love."[16]

---

15 In both the Ten Commandments and the Sermon on the Mount, God tells us what to *be* before telling us what to *do*. We see the same in Paul: "I can do all things through Christ." Who I am in Christ must precede what I do for Christ. We Americans often short-change the *becoming* in our rush to *produce*.

16 Peter Scholtes, "They'll Know We Are Christians by Our Love," ©1966 by F.E.L. Publications, Ltd./ASCAP.

A Battle in the Classroom

Sasha sat silently in the back of the classroom for the rest of the first session. At the first break students filed past me as they made their way outside. I watched as Sasha approached me, wondering what I could do to repair the damage of our emotional skirmish and build a bridge. I prayed for Russian words to say, for grammar. The sentence formed from somewhere, and I scrambled to practice it several times in my mind. As he passed, avoiding my eyes, I reached out and touched his arm. When he turned toward me, I said, "I want you to know that I am still your friend." It was a strange thing for me to say, but at that moment I wanted more than anything to keep the skirmish from escalating in open warfare. He thanked me and went on out.

In the next session he began to ask questions again, but his attitude had changed. Now his questions were more honest and less combative. We talked over meals, and the more we talked, the more positive he became. He invited me to speak to his church on "why teaching is important in the church." By the end of our two weeks of courses, he had become a close friend and brother in the Lord. The bridge of mutual trust and friendship allowed us to learn from each other.

A Battle in the Church

Brian had me in a difficult political bind. If I refused to come to an agreement, I would be seen as uncooperative at best, and perhaps even un-Christian—not a good position for a staff minister in a local church. If I agreed to make peace, then Brian would win the challenge, and his dysfunctional behavior would continue to plague me and the deaf ministry as a whole.

The problems had been reported, and here I sat with Brian. As I prayed about what to do, the Lord brought to mind his promise: "Humble yourselves, therefore, under God's mighty hand, that he may lift you up in due time" (1 Pet. 5:6). I could not get away from the stark reality: to refuse to make peace could only be seen by my pastor and the personnel chairman as obstinate pride.

Brian knew he had me in a no-win situation. It came as no real surprise when I relented and agreed to make peace. Brian smiled again and underscored his victory. "You had no choice." We called the pastor and chairman back in and shared "our agreement" with them, much to their relief. As far as they were concerned, the problem had been solved. Brian and I both knew politics had won over truth.

I continued to pray for Brian, asking the Lord to make a way for an improved relationship; but things only grew worse. I was powerless. All I could do was pray.

Weeks, months went by. And then word came. Brian had checked into a mental health clinic with a nervous breakdown. No visitors. I began working with the deaf group directly; and with Brian out of the way, bridges quickly developed. As one story after another surfaced, I was able to explain exactly what I had done and why. Truth replaced rumors. Clarity replaced confusion. For the first time in three years, I was able to work with the deaf members directly, and it was such a blessing.

Then one day I received an ominous phone message. Brian had been released after several months of treatment and was on his way to see me. I prepared myself for battle in the only way I knew: I prayed very hard! The appointed time came, and Brian walked into my office. I offered him a chair, but he refused; he wanted to stand. I stood with him. He looked at me for a long time and began to sway back and forth. It was obvious he was agitated. I tried to say something to him, but he motioned me to remain silent. He continued to sway, farther and farther, until I thought he would fall down. To be honest I began to wonder if this big man was going to kill me!

Finally he spoke, hands jabbing and piercing the air. "You like seeing me like this! You think you've beaten me, and you like it, I know!" A part of me agreed. He had lied and had acted shamefully and gotten away with it for a long time. While he had been out of the picture, the deaf ministry had thrived. New leaders had been equipped and a new Bible study class started. Ministry projects had been planned and carried out by folks now free to lead. Members who had dropped out returned, and visitors had begun to attend again. Part of me took joy in the fact that finally truth won out.

But when Brian said this, something snapped inside me. Seeing him broken like this was not pleasant. In a moment the disappointment, frustration, and bitterness which had grown over the years were replaced with empathy. Watching him sway, seeing his fear, did something to me. For me the battle was over. All I could think was, *How can I build a bridge?* I told him truthfully that I did not like seeing him like this, that I had wanted nothing more than to work with him in our ministry with the deaf community. I told him that in his absence we had not replaced him as the deaf ministry director and, as soon as he was able, I wanted him to come back and continue his work. (The Lord gave me the grace to say these things because my head was telling me I had lost my mind.)

Brian stopped swaying. "Do you mean this? After all I've done to you. All I've said about you?" His eyes welled up, and tears flowed. I'd never seen Brian weep. I told him I meant every word of it and that I had been praying for him for years.

As tears continued to flow, he looked at me and said, "I'm so sorry." He stepped forward and wrapped his big arms around me. I embraced him as he sobbed uncontrollably. His power plays had broken him. After a moment we stepped back and then prayed together.

Brian did not accept the position of director again. He continued to work to support his family and continued to attend counseling sessions. Not long after this the Lord called me away from the church to another ministry position. Just before I left, some of the hearing workers in the deaf ministry invited Barb and me for dinner. Over Chinese food I learned just how much things had changed. Brian had been visiting friends and church members to apologize for his battle with me. There were even a few stories about how he defended me against others who were found repeating some of the rumors Brian himself had started. I never saw him again, but it was a blessing to know we parted as friends. It had been a long, painful three years, but the Lord had brought about peace. "Inasmuch as it is possible, live at peace with every man" (see Rom. 12:18). Through this experience I came to understand that sometimes it is not possible for one side of a relationship to make peace. I also learned the power of God's love to transform people, relationships, and situations. Relational character allows God's love to flow through us to those we teach and lead. "A new command I give you: Love one another. As I have loved you, so you must love one another. By this all men will know that you are my disciples, if you love one another" (John 13:34–35).

Mike's Reaction

Rick gave us some dynamic metaphors for understanding how relationships are central to God's mission. "Jesus established the church to reach the nations. An integral part of that mission is to help change the way people treat one another. The church is a living laboratory of human relationships." The church is a living laboratory! I like this. I became a follower of Christ as a young nineteen-year-old college student. I was discipled by campus ministries. It was a rich time of developing spiritual and biblical character. But for the first seven years of my life in Christ, I was a lone-ranger Christian. Not much development of relational character. I didn't want to have anything to do with the church. I was hypercritical of the hypocrisy of the local church. I was like those believers who "forfeit the opportunity to experience God's fatherhood and care when they choose to remain aloof, neglect their gifts, and refuse to join brothers and sisters in ministry." Of course, I was focused on what *I* wanted versus what *God* wanted.

Today I realize the mystery of God's kingdom plan to work through the church (Eph. 3:10). Isn't it ironic that through the years God has used me most to start new churches and equip others to do the same. Yes, Rick, the church is exactly that, a laboratory where God tests and develops us into Christlike disciplers. He grows us up through church relationships.

Rick also pinpointed a key strategic concept that seems to be experiencing a revival in twenty-first-century church growth and kingdom expansion. He points out that "the best place in the church to develop these required relational skills is in a small group of believers—a home study and prayer cell, Sunday School class, or an active committee." In the next chapter we will look at some examples of churches God is using for his kingdom—small congregations and megachurches alike. But each of them has small groups at the center of their strategies. Even in a megachurch of twenty-five thousand members, one-to-one relationships provide a platform for serving Christ. Remember, Jesus' plan is a "people-to-people" plan (chapter 3). It's all about relational character.

I really like the eight categories (twelve principles) of relational character. This is good stuff. I need to reread and chew on some of these concepts. For example, in the third category, "Relationship Is Nurtured through Humility," Rick described how Jesus demonstrated two levels of humility. "The first is service which is 'hidden from others.' We do not call attention to ourselves in order to be honored *by others*. The second is service which is 'hidden from self.' We do not call attention to ourselves in order to be honored by *ourselves!*" This is profound. We must not allow others or ourselves to put us on the pedestal. Relational character grows out of this Christlike attitude of humility that impacts ourselves as much as others. Well done, Rick! Well done, Jesus!

You almost lost me when, referring to Jesus, you exclaimed, "What a failure!" You really had me going there. But your point was well taken. Jesus *was* a failure in normal human terms. That's the point, isn't it. We must rearrange our thinking, our feeling, and our doing to match God's terms. In that sense, as Rick puts it, "There was no failure in the life of our Leader! There was only success as he faithfully carried out God's will." Amen and amen.

In leadership and team theory we talk about two different approaches to working together. One is "transactional"; we sometimes say "task oriented." The other is "relational"; we sometimes say "people oriented." As the task-oriented doer/thinker that I am, Rick helped me understand how Christlike relational character is vital for effective discipling across cultures.

The Relational Character
of cross-cultural
Disciplers

Discipler's Model

8

Developing a Maturational Character

Mike Barnett

Speaking the truth in love, we will in all things grow up
into him who is the Head, that is, Christ.
Ephesians 4:15

The discipler who develops maturational character—a perspective devoted to equipping and maturing national disciplers in order to fulfill God's kingdom mission—is better able to connect with learner-leaders than those who do not. Chapter 8 defines the role of maturational growth—"grow up . . . into Him who is the head, even Christ" (Eph. 4:15 NASB)—which is essential in discipling across cultures. We then discuss how to develop maturational character as the capstone of discipling ministry.

The Toxic Flip Side

Pursuing worldly success rather than Christlikeness.
Measuring accomplishment in terms of bigger rather
than better.

Liang, a Cross-Cultural Discipler in East Asia

I first heard the story of Liang in 1996 at a meeting in Thailand. Her story has been told around the world.[1]
Old Wang winced in pain as the creaking bus bounced along the dirt road. The pain from his broken ribs was excruciating, but he was better off than his coworker Cai Wen. He looked at Cai Wen, who was weak from blood loss. He had closed his eyes and was cradling his broken arm. The ten-hour trip was long, but Wang wasn't eager to get home. How would he face little Wang's wife, Liang, and her ten-year-old son? He

---

1 Liang's story was adapted from *12 Case Studies: Toward Church Planting Movements* (Richmond, Va.: Overseas Media Services, International Mission Board, SBC, 1998), 22.

wondered how he would break the news to her that her husband (his son) had been killed by an angry mob of Zhou people the night before.

He could still hear their accusations: "The spirits of the Liushou Mountains rule our land. Your tribe of dogs has only been here five hundred years, and you know nothing. You have stolen our land, and now you wish to steal our gods as well. You will pay for this!" The mob proceeded to beat Old Wang and his companions with sticks and farm implements. One particularly fierce young man continued to beat Little Wang. When the crowd dispersed, Little Wang was motionless. He had paid the ultimate price. He and his family had only been believers for five months.

The Capstone: Helping People Grow in the Lord

There are four basic ways of talking about church growth. The most common type of church growth is *numerical* growth, the rate of increase in membership. Numerical growth refers to church *size*. A second kind of church growth is *organic* growth, which refers to the strengthening of the internal structure—leadership, organization, vision—of the church. Organic growth refers to church *efficiency*. A third kind of church growth is *incarnational* growth, which refers to the church growing in Christlikeness. Incarnational growth enables the church to *influence its culture,* to make a difference in its community in Jesus' name. The fourth kind of growth is *maturational* growth, which concentrates on the believer's

Type of Growth	Expected Result
Numerical	Larger church
Organic	Strong internal structure
Incarnational	Enhanced cultural influence
Maturational	Increased personal Christlikeness

Disciplers' Model

personal growth in Christ. While all four kinds of growth are important in the kingdom, the capstone of the model represents this last type of growth, the process of growing individual believers in the Lord, of helping them become like Christ. It moves beyond individual growth to include the personal growth of the church in inculcation of Christlike characteristics in the body.

Paul's Treatise on Growth

Paul's treatise on church growth in Ephesians 4:11–16 fastens on this maturational theme. Christ gifts the church with four kinds of leaders. Apostles, prophets, and evangelists are itinerant disciplers who travel, proclaim the gospel, and plant churches. Pastor-teachers are local church disciplers who have as their main task the responsibility "to prepare God's people for works of service" (v. 12a). From these churches come future apostles, prophets, evangelists, and pastor-teachers. Why does Christ give these gift-disciplers to the churches?

"So that the body of Christ may be built up" (v. 12b). This term "built up" does not refer to size but to maturity, as Paul stresses in the next verse ("until we all reach unity in the faith and in the knowledge of the Son of God and become mature"). Paul did not focus on churches *getting bigger* but *becoming better.* The implication is that Paul's idea of church growth has little to do with buildings, budgets, or chandeliers; it is tied to the spiritual health of the church, reflected in the self-sacrificing love, ministry, and outreach of its members.

How mature does the church have to be? Paul says our task of discipling is done when everyone in the church is as mature as Jesus, "attaining to the whole measure of the fullness of Christ" (v. 13b).

What results from this growing maturity? Paul says the result is believers who are no longer childish—fickle or gullible—tricked by religious con artists (v. 14) who mouth spiritual words but lust after worldly power. Instead, Paul points to a higher goal: believers who know and understand the truth (left pillar), and speak it in a loving way (right pillar).

By doing this we all grow up into Christ (capstone). Further, Christ, the head, draws us together into oneness, a *koinonia,* a community, the Father's family, a network of relationships (center pillar) "as each part [of the body] does its work" (v. 16).

How Do I Measure This Growth?

Perhaps numerical growth is popular because it is easy to measure. Churches with the highest body count win. What did *body count* do to America during the Vietnam war? Didn't we learn anything? What has *viewer count* brought to television? What has *ticket count* done for football or the movie industry? The philosophy of body count has led churches into all sorts of demeaning activities, all for "ten more next Sunday." A youth minister shaves his legs and wears jams to church because the youth group reached an attendance goal. A pastor jumps into a vat of grits after Sunday morning worship because their Sunday school goal was reached. This is circus, not New Testament churchmanship. Such tactics, taken for granted back home, can easily be carried overseas, resulting in wrong ends being pursued by wrong means, failing Paul's standards two ways simultaneously.

> Such tactics, taken for granted back home, can easily be carried overseas—resulting in wrong ends being pursued by wrong means, failing Paul's standards two ways simultaneously.

In his letter to the Galatians, Paul gives two lists of traits, a spiritual yardstick, by which we can measure the spiritual growth of those we teach. One list contains traits that believers should put away. These works of the flesh include "immorality, impurity and debauchery; idolatry and witchcraft; hatred, discord, jealousy, fits of rage, selfish ambition, dissensions, factions and envy; drunkenness, orgies, and the like" (5:19–20). Some of these personal traits, like debauchery and witchcraft, should suffer a quick death in the newborn believer. Others, like selfish ambition and discord, refuse to die and keep plaguing us like some kind of spiritual nutgrass. We overcome them a little at a time, day by day, as we continue to grow in the Lord.

The second list contains traits that should increase in Christians over time. These "fruit of the Spirit" include "love, joy, peace, patience, kindness, goodness, faithfulness, gentleness and self-control" (5:22–23). These traits are not religious practices that can be learned from books or lectures. They are spiritual traits infused by the indwelling Spirit, developed only by *surrender to him* (chapter 2), strengthened by following the one who lives within, "Christ in you, the hope of glory" (Col. 1:27).

Disciplers measure spiritual growth by evidences of decreases in fleshly behaviors and increases in godly behaviors. The pillars of thinking, valuing, and relating—anchored in God's eternal truth and the particular needs of leader-learners in the group—culminate in a discipling process that allows the Spirit to reduce the fleshly and increase the heavenly. This type of measurement is, admittedly, subjective. But focusing on the spiritual changes in the lives of learner-leaders is far more productive than simply counting heads in a crowd.

Make no mistake about what I am saying here. Numbers are people. More people coming to Christ, more people growing in him, more leaders being equipped, more churches planted—this is our desire. We want the church to grow numerically. We give our lives to considering prayerfully ways to improve the quality of discipling in classes, churches, and seminaries, as well as teaching stations around the world. As ministers of education, we keep and study attendance records to locate weaknesses in our reaching/teaching efforts. As church planters, we develop strategies for growth, for reaching specific people groups and populations. But the abuse of God's flock through guilt and manipulation for the sake of reaching strangers, whether at home or abroad, is unscriptural. Jesus' command was clear: "Feed my sheep." We tend the flock, care for the lambs, provide nourishment, and in his time God brings the increase.

We carry these principles with us as we leave our homes and move into the world, people group by people group. We go not to conquer but to free. We go not to use but to equip. We go not to dominate but to nurture. We go not to spread our culture but to enlarge God's kingdom. We are God's ambassadors—his equippers, disciplers—ready to do whatever it takes to accomplish the great mission he has called us to fulfill in his strength and in his way.

Maturational Kingdom Growth

We think of maturity as a good thing. When we say something has matured, we mean it has developed to its full potential. Mature fruit has ripened and is tasty and nutritious. Mature plans are fully developed, fine-tuned, ready to be realized. Mature people have grown up physically, emotionally, and even spiritually. One of the core values at Columbia International University is the "victorious life in Christ." We realize we will never be perfected in Christ this side of eternity; but we want our students, staff, and faculty to hold one another accountable always to reside in Christ. This mutual accountability changes, transforms, grows up, matures our lives to be more Christlike for the sake of his reputation and glory. Maturational character is the capstone of the development of an effective cross-cultural discipler. It is the result of our discipling.

The Kingdom within Us

Jesus taught more about the kingdom of God than anything else with the possible exception of money. He focused on the mission of God—to be glorified by the entire universe. He was on mission with the Father to fulfill his kingdom purpose. His ministry on earth was about communicating God's kingdom in a way that it would grow (mature) throughout all people on earth. When the Pharisees asked him when the kingdom of God would come, he replied, "The kingdom of God does not come with your careful observation, nor will people say, 'Here it is,' or 'There it is,' because the kingdom of God is within you" (Luke 17:20–21). The kingdom of God is within us!

God's reign in our lives allows us to participate in his kingdom here and now on earth. Jesus said he came that we might "have life, and have it to the full" (John 10:10). We do not have to wait for this "abundant" (NASB) life. It reigns in our lives and world today as we are transformed, matured in Christ. It is reflected in our love of God and one another. It is gloriously displayed by the fruit of the Spirit (Gal. 5:22–23) through our changed lives.

Paul encouraged the believers in Ephesus, "And you also were included in Christ when you heard the word of truth, the gospel of your salvation. Having believed, you were marked in him with a seal, the promised Holy Spirit" (Eph. 1:13). And what difference does this Holy Spirit make? Paul says we receive "wisdom and revelation" in order to know the Lord Jesus Christ better. He prays that we might "know the hope . . . the riches of his glorious inheritance in the saints, and his incomparably great power" (Eph. 1:17–19); this is truly a foretaste of God's heavenly kingdom.

This is how God brings about his kingdom. Remember his people-to-people approach? As disciplers follow him. As we rely on his Spirit (chapter 2). As we depend on his Word (chapter 3). As he develops our minds (chapter 4) and hearts (chapter 5). As we serve alongside others (chapter 7). As we suffer with others and *suffer for* him (chapter 6). He grows us up in Christ internally, within us. And the same transformation takes place in the lives of those we disciple. *This transformation within us communicates across culture.* Others understand such character in spite of language and customs. We connect with our leader-learners at these points of life change. Our national friends see the reality of the message. They see it right there in our lives. And their lives are grown as well. We all grow up in the Lord together in the kingdom within us.

The Kingdom Community

Maturational character is about much more than individual growth! It is about much more than our one-to-one relationship with Jesus. It goes beyond our personal understanding and even personal worship of God. It impacts the whole body of Christ, the church. Again Paul explains to the Ephesians how this works. He has just revealed, once again, the mystery that this powerful good news about Jesus Christ is not just for the nation of Israel. This good news is, indeed, for all peoples—for the Gentiles as well as the Jews. We must pause here. I fear we cannot imagine what is so mysterious about God's inclusion of the Gentiles in his plan. But to Israel and to the Gentiles, Paul's mysterious claim was truly mind-boggling! Is this not the God of Israel? Are they not God's chosen people, his holy nation? Did God not promise that he would be *their* God and they *his* people? And yet here is Paul, of all people, a Jew's Jew, claiming that God's plan includes Gentiles? Mysterious.

But there is more. Allow me to paraphrase Ephesians 3:9–11: "Not only is God going to reach the Jews and the Gentiles through Jesus Christ, but he will reveal himself to the entire universe! After all, he created the entire universe. So he will be known by the entire universe. He will be glorified by all creation—even the heavenly beings beyond the earthly realm. And how will he do this? *Through the church,* the body of Christ, those on earth who know him personally and follow Messiah—the one and only Lord and Savior."

Now that *is* mind-boggling! Not only is God set on connecting with every people on earth, but he is going to reveal himself to the entire universe. And he will do it through the body of Christ, the church. It is as though the entire universe, creation itself, is standing by watching the church to see, to know, who is God. And you can bet that they are watching to see how the church matures in Christ, how God uses such clay vessels for his glory and honor.

You ask, which church are they watching? Paul's point is that they are watching the church of the Ephesians—the local church! This is why he continues in his letter to pray that God will strengthen them in their inner being (the kingdom within, 3:16) so they might live worthy of being identified as Christ followers ("prisoner[s] for the Lord," 4:1). This is where Paul teaches the church about unity of faith, mutual love, respect, working as a team together, based on individual call and the community of faith. This is where Paul again refers to the church as a body, made of distinct but interdependent parts, functioning as a whole (4:16). This is where he explains how the church is made up of equipping ministers who disciple the disciplers, the saints, for the work of the church (4:11–12). This is where Paul explains how the church will be united in its faith and witness of Jesus Christ, Son of God. And this is where Paul says the church will "become mature, attaining to the whole measure of the fullness of Christ . . . speaking the truth in love, [and] will in all things grow up into him who is the Head, that is, Christ" (4:13, 15–16). This is maturational character within the kingdom community.

Was Paul's message just for the local churches of Ephesus? Absolutely not. The plan includes all local bodies of believers. When we disciple others effectively, the churches they plant, serve, and lead will reflect maturational character. They will be biblical, obedient, Great Commission churches. And the universe is watching! That raises the bar a bit, doesn't it?

The Kingdom of All Nations

But wait. We're not finished with this character capstone of effective disciplers yet. If we are encircled by the Holy Spirit. If we are growing in our understanding and dependency on God's Word. If we are developing Christlike character in our thinking, feeling, and doing. If we passionately commit ourselves to serve Christ according to his plan, not ours, will it make any difference to the nations? It better.

This is the most critical issue regarding maturational character from my point of view. If we cannot see how our identity in Christ impacts more than our individual lives, more than our own church, then something is wrong. Something is missing. God's mission is to be glorified by all peoples on earth. *However* we serve him, *wherever* we serve him, in *whatever role* we serve him, we must be able to know, to see, how it connects that service with his mission to all peoples. Unfortunately, this is not always the case.

I will never forget that day in Beirut when I asked the church leader about his church's mission. He was one of many established church leaders in a land where evangelical congregations are scarce. He and his colleagues represented the best of the legacy of twentieth-century missions throughout the Middle East. Dozens of churches with thousands of members were struggling to survive in a world dominated by non-Christian leaders and worldviews. It was a time of change, of transitions from foreign-led and supported missions structures to nationalized, hopefully more indigenous, missions strategies and ministries. We had been dealing with tough issues regarding changing leadership, ownership, and partnership. I'd been waiting for the moment to challenge this brother concerning his church and their sense of mission. So I asked, "Over these past decades how many missionaries has your church convention sent to other countries, to other people groups, to preach and teach the gospel of Christ?" He stopped and stared. It was a deafening moment of silence. I could see the wheels turning in his mind. A slight frown, then a growing smile. I watched for that "aha!" light in his eyes. I thought I saw a twinkle when he cleverly, carefully, responded in that delightful, upbeat way of his culture. "Ah, but you are the missionaries, not us!" We both had made our points.

For him and his church, a new day was dawning. Through the preceding decades my church had failed to nurture a mature kingdom character that empowers God's people to be on mission with him. The story was similar throughout this region and across mission agency lines. Maybe it had been too much about *our* mission rather than theirs or even God's. After all, we had been successful, sort of. At least we were as successful as any Western mission in the Near East. But in the process of developing new churches, new ministries, new hospitals, new agricultural programs, publishing houses, and even seminaries, we failed to give away God's call upon his church. We failed to pass on the challenge, the blessing, the mission of the Great Commission. We short-circuited that process whereby he grows and matures his church to reach the nations.

The good news is that God is not finished with either of us. He continues to grow us, mature us. We as a church of the West, as a mature mission, have refocused on his purpose of reaching all nations through his church. Today our workers in that part of the world are committed to facilitating movements of churches planting churches in ways that all nations will be involved and impacted. We are seeing the "new" churches of the non-West mobilize their own people to go on mission with God. By the way, this pastor and his peers are now leading others to take the gospel from the Middle East to Africa and beyond. This is God's plan. This is his mission. This is how he grows his church. This is maturational character that impacts the kingdom of all nations.

The Heavenly Kingdom

As effective cross-cultural disciplers, we all will one day experience the maturation, the perfection of Christlike character. We will be there in the end and forever. We will join the elders and the heavenly beings in praising and serving our Lord Jesus Christ. "Holy, holy, holy is the Lord God Almighty, who was, and is, and is to come. . . . You are worthy . . . because you were slain, and with your blood you purchased men for God from every tribe and language and people and nation. You have made them to be a kingdom and priests to serve our God, and they will reign on the earth" (Rev. 4:8; 5:9–10).

We, believers from all nations, will reign on earth. We will give glory to God. We will be a kingdom of priests, according to God's plan, his mission—the same plan that calls us as disciplers to teach all nations to obey all that Jesus commanded. As we obediently serve him according to his plan and purpose for our lives, we will grow up in Christ. We will mature in our individual relationship with him. And he will use us as he grows up our communities of believers, as he works through the church for the entire universe to witness. Finally, he will use us as he grows up, matures, and perfects disciplers from all peoples on earth. As cross-cultural disciplers, we must never forget this. May your heavenly kingdom come—even now Lord!

How to Multiply Maturational Character

In previous chapters concerning the character of the discipler, I asked the questions, "How do we get it and keep it? And how do we develop and maintain it?" But those questions don't exactly apply to the characteristics of maturational character. This character trait is really the consequence of the others. It is the final product, the end result, the completion of the growth process in the dynamic relationship of discipler and leader-learner. My question for maturational character is, how do we multiply it? It is an appropriate question since God's purpose throughout his mission to the nations is to multiply followers of Christ, increase worshippers of the one, true, living God, and establish and grow his kingdom on earth and for eternity.

Multiplying Individual Maturity

The first step in this multiplication process of Christlike, maturational character starts with us—you and me. We must first establish where we fit in this master plan of God. You say that sounds simple enough. Maybe not. Are we all called to be frontline apostles—missionaries—discipling across the most extreme cultures of our day? Is everyone supposed to be learning another language, living a radically different lifestyle, moving to the ends of the earth in order to teach and mentor new believers into mature disciplers? Probably not. Remember, Paul said, "He [Christ] . . . gave some to be apostles, some to be prophets, some to be evangelists, and some to be pastors and teachers, to prepare God's people for works of service, so that the body of Christ may be built up . . . and become mature, attaining to the whole measure of the fullness of Christ" (Eph. 4:11–13). So *some* are called to be apostles—missionaries—not all. But wait. Don't miss the point. Paul says others are called as proclaimers (prophets), communicators (evangelists), pastors and teachers (leaders) of the gospel. These all fit, along with the missionaries, in the role of equipping the rest—the workers ("saints," NASB) of the church. In other words, we all fit somewhere in God's master plan, either as equippers or as workers. In fact, most of us are the actual doers or workers of the gospel. A few are equippers. (By the way, even equippers must serve as workers.) All fit. All are a part of his strategy for the nations and the universe.

Where do you and I fit? I always ask this question of my students and colleagues. It is, I think, the most important strategic question we can answer as individual Christ followers. Yes, I am talking about "the call" but not in some "once in a lifetime," memorable-moment way. This question is one we must regularly ask ourselves as we journey our way through life and work as disciples of Jesus Christ. I give my students some basic choices. I ask them, "At this point in your life, *choose one* category that most identifies where you fit in God's mission to all peoples on earth."

1. *Advocate*—one who consciously prays, encourages, motivates, and mobilizes believers and resources to be on mission with God among all peoples.
2. *Supporter*—one who is specially endowed with financial, logistical, and/or resources of influence and is committed to making them available for God's mission among all peoples.
3. *Worker*—one who is on the front lines of God's mission to all peoples, whether in their home culture or crossing culture.

4. *Equipper*—one called to teach and lead others to know where
    they fit and to serve well on mission with God among all peoples.

There is nothing sacred about these four choices. This is what has
worked best for me throughout the years of coaching and discipling.

You might ask, "But you are a missions professor, an equipper of missionaries, what about those of us who are not called to be missionaries?"
This is exactly my point. Though not all of us are called to be missionaries, all of us are called to be a part of God's mission, to make him known
among all peoples on earth, to be glorified by all of creation. That is his
mission. That is what he reveals to us through his Word, from Genesis
to Revelation (chapter 3). That is the reason for church, for the body of
Christ. You and I *must* know where we fit into this mysterious, miraculous plan of God. Anything less robs us of our inheritance, the full and
meaningful life that Christ has promised.

And so I ask you, just as I ask my students who are preparing for the
pastorate or church staff positions right here in America, you must lead
your church members to know where they fit in God's mission. Pastors,
if the church secretary, the landscapers, the ushers, and the ones who
care for the infants in the church nursery do not know how what they do
in the church and the marketplace fits into God's master plan among all
peoples, then shame on you! If the elderly members of your congregation
no longer see how they can serve on mission with God, then woe unto us!

We all play our part. We are all parts of the body, with Christ the head
(Eph. 4:15–16), on mission with God to reveal and redeem all peoples
unto him. Preachers, medical doctors, worship leaders, craftsmen, Bible
study teachers, accountants, lawyers, choir and band members, benevolent ministry workers, police officers, church ushers, political leaders,
parking attendants, small group leaders, military soldiers, retirement
home dwellers, youth workers, schoolteachers, businessmen and women,
seminary professors, and yes, even missionaries—we all fit into God's divine strategy. It is central to our healthy understanding of who we are in
Christ. It is vital if we are to be obedient Christ followers. It is the most
fulfilling life experience we will ever have. It is nonnegotiable if we are
to grow and mature in our relationship with him.

Who are the disciples/disciplers? Jesus focused his ministry on the
twelve disciples, but he taught hundreds if not thousands of disciples during his three-year ministry. The very word *disciple* comes from the word
for apprentice or student or follower. This means that if you are a follower of Christ you are commissioned to "disciple all nations." When he

tells his disciples that they will be his witnesses in Jerusalem, Judea and Samaria, and the ends of the earth (Acts 1:8), he's defining who you and I are to be as his disciples.

We are his witnesses. We are called to share the gospel with others—to tell our story, to tell his story. All of us are to lead others, to encourage one another, to be a part of his great mission. The short-term missionary in Somalia, the medical missionary to India, the young businessman in Houston, the benevolent ministries worker in the local church, Russian educators in Kazakhstan, the young Chinese widow in rural East Asia. We are all disciples and disciplers of Jesus Christ. We are all a part of his master plan of multiplication of Christ followers and worshippers around the world. Wherever we fit into his plan, if we remain faithful and follow him, we will bear fruit. We will mature in Christ. And that maturational character will be multiplied.

Multiplying Maturational Character in Community and Beyond

When God grows us as individuals, his church is transformed. If we as individual disciplers know where we fit in God's mission. If we realize the part we play. If we pass this Christlike character on to our leader-learners. If we are faithful to the call and mission of Christ, then our churches will grow up in the Lord as well. They will reflect maturational character.

I hear many negative comments about churches in the West. Some churches are hopelessly stuck in the evangelical glory days of the past century. They don't know how to engage the new global culture of postmodernism. They are hopelessly bound to outdated traditions and forms of worship. They are dying a slow death, perpetually stuck in their bureaucratic denominational structures and methods. They are doomed to attrition as they fight their personal and political power wars over issues that aren't even on the radar of twenty-first-century evangelism and missions. Well, I disagree! Just take a look around, and you will be amazed at how God is maturing his church. As Jesus said, "The gates of Hades will not overcome it" (Matt. 16:18).

Hill of the Lord University Church, Columbia, South Carolina. God is mobilizing churches in the West to multiply. Cindy and I attend Hill of the Lord University Church, a church plant that serves the gospel through word and deed to university students in our city. It is a fun ride with these young people and our Lord! We never know what to expect.

Worship services are fresh, creative, original, and generally contemporary but traditional at times. A lot of the church programs that we grew up with are missing, but whether we are with the fifty to seventy worshippers on Sunday morning, at our midweek leadership meeting in a home, attending a baptismal service on the shores of the Saluda River, meeting in one of the weekly small groups, or just hanging out at the worship pastor's house every Sunday night, we are a church on mission with God. We are growing in character, in Christ. I hear from my students about hundreds of other such authentic communities of Christ followers. No, I'm not discouraged.

Xenos Christian Fellowship, Columbus, Ohio. This church was one of those university-based movements before its time. What began in 1970 as an underground newspaper on the Ohio State University campus has grown into an interdenominational evangelical church of some forty-five hundred members. Xenos's home churches are still the center of gravity of their fellowship today. They are known for their discipling culture. No wonder God matured the character of this congregation to become a global discipling base.[2] Here is just one example. Xenos has a partnership with World Team, an international missions agency, that includes thirty full-time missionaries deployed in five different fields around the world. Xenos Christian Fellowship is another example of a community of disciples with maturational character.

Willow Creek Church, South Barrington, Illinois. I admit that I've never been a part of a megachurch. Cindy and I are most comfortable in a smaller congregation, even a house church. Still, I am amazed at how some of the most famous megachurches in America are reflecting maturational character as they go to the next level of being the body of Christ. "The next level?" you say. How could they get any higher? Think about it. Willow Creek Church in the Chicago area continues to connect creatively with tens of thousands of people through their famous seeker-sensitive services. But they have become more than that. Today they coordinate hundreds of ministries around the world. Perhaps their best-known and most far-reaching ministry is Leadership Network with its global satellite broadcasts to thousands of emerging leaders. Bill Hybels explains this best-kept secret about the ministries of Willow Creek.

---

2 From the Xenos Christian Fellowship Web site, http://www.xenos.org/aboutxenos/history.htm, cited on 26 November 2005. See also the World Team Web site, http://www.worldteam.org/church-link/partnerships.htm.

What visitors usually notice first is the large number of people who attend our weekly services and the more than 100 ministries that meet a wide range of needs. Our size has benefits: we're big enough for you to blend in and investigate the claims of Jesus Christ anonymously, if you choose to.

But if you look closer, you'll find that in many ways we're small. In fact, we're actually a network of small groups. And if you'd like to develop authentic and enduring relationships with others, then you'll be glad to know that new groups are forming all the time.[3]

Saddleback Church, Lake Forest, California. This world-famous church is another example of a congregation that is maturing in character in a way that touches all peoples on earth and multiplies disciples of Christ. Led by senior pastor Rick Warren, this giant of a megachurch is actually comprised of about two thousand small groups where one-to-one discipling takes place. Following their now-famous purpose-driven strategy, Saddleback recently launched a new initiative called PEACE. It is a global, holistic mission that seeks to engage and defeat the world's greatest problems or "giants": spiritual emptiness, self-serving leadership, poverty, disease, and ignorance/illiteracy. The vision is truly world changing. The method is to mobilize the resources of Saddleback to catalyze tens of thousands of churches around the world to take on these giants. It is interesting, and surely no accident, that this megachurch's macro-strategy resembles the capstone we are calling maturational character. Here are the PEACE[4] basics:

Personal P.E.A.C.E.—Your personal mission to the people around you. Jesus calls us to love God, to love our neighbors, and to go and make disciples, in our everyday lives—with our neighbors, co-workers, classmates, friends, and family.

Local P.E.A.C.E.—Your small group's mission in your region of the world. Together with your small group you can make a difference. Evaluate opportunities in your immediate community. Explore

---

3 From the Willow Creek Church Web site, http://www.willowcreek.org/welcome.asp, cited 26 November 2005.
4 The acronym PEACE identifies the five major elements of Saddleback's global missions' initiative: **P**lant churches, **E**quip servant leaders, **A**ssist the **P**oor, **C**are for the sick, and **E**ducate the next generation. These five elements attack five worldwide giants: spiritual emptiness, lack of servant leaders, poverty, disease, and ignorance. "Mobilizing a civilian force of compassion using the worldwide distribution network of millions of local churches."

opportunities to assess "at risk" population segments in our extended community. Consider reaching out into other cultures locally.

Global P.E.A.C.E.—Our church's mission to the world through small groups. Our church is a part of a global plan to care for people who face the difficulties of spiritual emptiness, egocentric leadership, extreme poverty, pandemic disease and crippling illiteracy around the world.[5]

PEACE begins with individual, personal growth that takes place in the midst of community—in this case Saddleback. It multiplies itself throughout the body, to transform their congregation and the community that they touch. And at the same time it impacts God's mission to all peoples on earth, in this case PEACE to overcome the global giants of evil. Now that's mega-maturational character!

Northwood Church, Keller, Texas. I first met Bob Roberts, senior pastor of Northwood Church in 2001 when he spoke in my church planting class. I remember his catchy term for the strategy of Northwood. It was a "glocal"-minded church. It focused on local and global all at once and continuously. I liked the sound of that. I spoke in one of the mission churches of Northwood and was amazed at the fact that a brand-new mission church with fewer than a hundred in attendance had already engaged a least-reached foreign field in missions involvement.

Bob started this suburban church in 1985 with a vision to grow Northwood into one of the new breed of megachurches. They grew quickly, and soon more than five hundred worshippers were attending Sunday morning services. The future was bright. In the midst of this ascent to the pinnacle of what he retrospectively calls "Bob's kingdom," God got Bob's attention. Through Bob's own personal "brokenness" and subsequent struggles at Northwood, God refocused Bob's attention on God's kingdom, not Bob's. Today Northwood averages around two thousand in attendance on Sunday, but their reach and impact are truly global. Bob explains the transformation:

> Instead of being the biggest church in the area, we were going to church the area. Little did I know then that a series of decisions would soon lead to our churching entire communities and nations. We began to go glocal in our focus—locally and globally—and God began to do things I'd never dreamed. Today, our church has started over 80 churches—that's over 20,000 people who are in church. Because each

5 From the Saddleback P.E.A.C.E. Web site, http://peace.gs/Public/LocalPeace/Site.aspx?xdft=c579 06c4bd304696a21ef7f0178de2f6, cited 26 November 2005.

of our church plants believe in church multiplication, it is part of their DNA. We have many granddaughter, great-granddaughter and great-great-granddaughter churches for a total of over 30,000 people in worship every single week. 3,600 new people are in churches now that didn't even exist 12 months ago. And most of those churches average 50 to 100 in attendance. Four years from now, they'll all quadruple (at a minimum), making it possible for another 15,000 to 20,000 people to be in church, just from that crop. A single local church.[6]

Northwood is a community of believers plugged in to God's mission. As they journey with him, God multiplies maturational character in their lives in a way that transforms and matures churches around the world.

Whether a small, upstart congregation of university students, a suburban congregation that intentionally multiplied rather than "mega-tized" itself, or the largest most famous congregations on earth, when God grows Christlike character in individual disciplers and disciples, it results in the maturing and multiplying of his churches, locally and globally.

Simply speaking, when disciplers follow Christ, when we encircle ourselves with the Holy Spirit, depend on his Word, grow in our minds, hearts, relationships, and commitments to serve him, he produces fruit. He grows character that reflects Christlikeness and influences others to be on mission with God. When we are on mission with God, he uses us and our leader-learners to influence and multiply the disciplers among the nations! This is how God multiplies maturational character.

Maturational Character, Stephen and the Disciplers' Model

One of my favorite biblical models for Christlike character is Stephen. In the 1990s I led a team of strategy support workers that provided necessary logistical, financial, and administrative support for hundreds of missions workers throughout the heart of the least reached parts of the world. Together we transformed the paradigm for providing support from

---

6 From the GlocalNet Web site, http://www.glocal.net/enews/may2005.htm#whatwould, cited on 26 November 2005. See also Bob Roberts Jr., *Transformation: How Glocal Churches Transform Lives and the World* (Grand Rapids: Zondervan, 2006).

a heavy-handed, top-down, prescriptive methodology to a culture of strategy-driven empowerment and servanthood. Stephen was our model. We called what we did "Stephening." Stephen is one of our best examples of the complete, mature, Christlike character of an effective cross-cultural discipler.

How did God use Stephen in his mission to the nations? What characteristics of an effective cross-cultural discipler do we find in the life and work of Stephen? He obviously had encountered Christ, if not personally, then spiritually. The influence of the body of Christ, the church of Jerusalem must have had an impact. Acts informs us that Stephen was "a man full of faith and of the Holy Spirit" (Acts 6:5). God had grown this spiritual character in Stephen before we meet him in Scripture. We can say that Stephen was encircled by the Holy Spirit. He was more than an effective administrator of the resources of the church. He was Holy Spirit led. He had *spiritual character.*

I think Stephen also had *rational character.* The qualifications for these first deacons of the church were that they be "full of the Spirit and wisdom" (6:3). This biblical word "wisdom" means "insight, intelligence, knowledge." The implied meaning is that he had the wisdom of God, the kind of mind that made decisions according to God's purposes and plan. He was a thinker who connected with thinkers. He was the kind of leader who inspired godly obedience in those he led. He was a teacher who modeled Christlike character to his learner-leaders.

What was Stephen's primary role in the church of Jerusalem? To administer the distribution of food and services to the widows. He was focused on serving the felt needs of the community. This was one of the distinctives of the first-century church. They served the needy, the poor, the widows and orphans. This is one of the reasons they were "enjoying the favor of all the people" (Acts 2:47). They were a church with compassion. They *suffered with* others. And Stephen led them in this effort. Stephen had *compassionate character.* He connected with people's hearts, with their feelings.

Stephen must have also been the kind of person who inspired unity in others. Remember that part of the problem of distribution of church resources was clouded in the ethnocentric tensions of the day. Greek members of the church felt that the Jewish leaders were neglecting the needs of their Greek widows. Whoa! Sounds like a church controversy was stirring. But Stephen and his colleagues were able to redeem this situation in a way that restored the health of the church. They were able to motivate others to relate to their fellow believers in a way that honored

God and was a positive testimony to the larger community (Acts 6:7). Stephen demonstrated *relational character*. Again he connected with the emotional side of people, with their feelings.

Now for my favorite side of the character of Brother Stephen. The man had *biblical character*. He was an active discipler, a powerful witness for the Lord Jesus. Eventually those who opposed these Christ followers of the Way began attacking Stephen. They plotted against him. They enlisted false witnesses to frame him. He was brought before the Sanhedrin religious leaders of the day and accused of blasphemy. So what did he do? He told them God's story! He began with Abraham (Acts 7) and worked his way right through the good news of God's redemptive mission to Joseph, Jacob, and Moses. He proclaimed God's Word. He pointed unbelievers to the answers in the Bible. To the Holy Spirit, the glory of God, the Son of Man (7:51, 55–56). Again he used his mind to communicate the gospel to unbelievers. And of course, he did more than talk; he walked the walk as well.

Stephen had *impassioned character*. Remember what happened to him? After hearing his defense of the faith, the Sanhedrin and their people took action.

> At this they covered their ears and, yelling at the top of their voices, they all rushed at him, dragged him out of the city and began to stone him. Meanwhile, the witnesses laid their clothes at the feet of a young man named Saul.
>
> While they were stoning him, Stephen prayed, "Lord Jesus, receive my spirit." Then he fell on his knees and cried out, "Lord, do not hold this sin against them." When he had said this, he fell asleep. And Saul was there, giving approval to his death (Acts 7:57–8:1).

Stephen was committed to the cause of Christ, whatever the cost. His passion was complete. He was a man of action. His example still connects with those of us who are doers today. He followed in the steps of his Lord and Savior.

Finally, what about *maturational character*? If our analysis of the life and work of Stephen is accurate. If he had spiritual character. If he was a good rational thinker. If he really felt for and *suffered with* those he served. If he was a peacemaker with relational character. If he relied on the Bible as his manual for life and work. And if he was willing to pay the ultimate price for Christ, what was the capstone of all this character? What was the fruit, the produce, the point?

After his martyrdom, the Bible says that "all except the apostles were scattered throughout Judea and Samaria" (Acts 8:1). The rest of Acts tells the story of those who were scattered, how they fulfilled their role in God's mission. They planted churches throughout the Near East and eventually Asia Minor. Who knows the impact of Stephen's testimony and stoning on the young religious persecutor Saul who eventually matured into Paul, apostle to the Gentiles? God used Stephen's life to grow up his body—the body of Christ throughout the Roman Empire. God also used the witness and life of Stephen as an instrument of developing maturational character among the nations. Stephen was the catalyst for a movement that continues to this day. Stephen still inspires disciplers and the church. He knew how to connect with thinkers, feelers, and doers. He was a man of *maturational character.*

Liang—a Cross-Cultural Discipler in East Asia

As soon as Old Wang and Kai Wen arrived home, they began to prepare for their return to the Zhou village. They made arrangements for others to assist Liang, the new, young widow, in their absence. Neighbors agreed to help with the farm and provide necessary meat and eggs. On Sunday the church gathered, determined to send Old Wang and Cai Wen back to the Zhou people. The need was great. The Zhou had no believers or churches among them. There was no one to tell them the good news! Someone had to take the message of salvation to them.

The church grew silent when Liang rose and requested that she be allowed to accompany her father-in-law and Cai Wen on their return trip to the Zhou. They worshipped for hours that day, praying fervently for the trip and for the salvation of the Zhou villagers. Other house churches in the county were notified to pray and fast for the first three days of their evangelistic efforts.

When the three arrived in the Zhou village, it was evening. They slept beside a pigpen just outside the village. They were restless throughout the night. The next morning they walked into the market. Soon word spread of their return. A mob quickly formed, and people began to yell threats. Old Wang felt fear sweep over him.

Suddenly Liang stepped to the front and spoke up. "I am the widow of the man you killed less than three weeks ago. My husband is not dead, however, because God has given him eternal life. Now he is living in paradise with our God. My husband came here to tell you how you could have that same eternal life. If he were here, he would forgive you for what you did. I forgive you as well. I can forgive you because God has forgiven me. If you would like to hear more about this God, then meet us under the big tree outside of town this evening."

The crowd had grown quiet and gradually dispersed. That day Old Wang instructed Liang as to what she should teach that night. Most of the village gathered to listen to her. Each day Old Wang and Cai Wen taught Liang what to teach. As the Zhou heard the good news about this Almighty Creator God who sent his Son to save all peoples, including the Zhou, many were drawn to Jesus. After a couple of weeks, Liang returned home with Cai Wen. Old Wang remained with the Zhou and baptized and taught the new believers.

Two months later Old Wang returned to his home village with two leaders and a young man from the new Zhou church. During the Sunday worship the two leaders brought their greetings and expressed their appreciation. The young man stood to speak. "I am the man who murdered Little Wang. The Lord has graciously forgiven me, and I ask your forgiveness as well. I and our entire church owe an eternal debt of gratitude to Little Wang and Liang for bringing us the message of life. We want to give this love offering to help support Liang. This is the least we can do to show our appreciation."

Four months later word came from the Zhou church that they had planted another Zhou church, two mountains over in the same county. When this word came, Old Wang silently mused over the truth of the hymn that Liang had recently written. It said, "It is through difficulty and suffering that we must follow. Our Lord has prepared the way, and it leads to glory. He is glorified in our obedience, so take courage. He will be glorified in all the earth, and we will be glorified in him."

This true case study illustrates what maturational character means. The gospel was communicated through the Christlike character of Little Wang and his father. The church among Old Wang's people was planted in a way that each believer knew where he or she fit in God's mission. They learned it from participative Bible study as the sole authority for their faith. They understood the importance of loving God and one another. They stepped up to assist their sister Liang in time of need. They *suffered with* Liang and her family; they walked the walk. They prayed for leadership and power from the Holy Spirit. Though it was a relatively new church, it was a church with maturational character.

Old Wang's church knew they were on mission with God to the nations. They were committed to communicating the gospel to neighboring tribes no matter what the cost. No matter that Liang was less mature in her understanding of the gospel. She was used in a most powerful way. This tribe was impassioned to serve Christ. Little Wang paid the ultimate price. Ultimately, the kingdom expanded to include the Zhou people. In fact, it expanded in a way that led naturally to the Zhou multiplying themselves—their church, their character as Christ followers—to the next village. This is the fruit of effective discipling. This is the result of Christlike character being taught and lived out. This is the point, the product of maturational character. It will be a glorious celebration when we sing praises to God with Little Wang; Old Wang; his people, the Zhou; and the multitudes!

God is on mission to reach all peoples on earth with the good news of his Son Jesus Christ. He will be glorified by the entire universe. His plan is to use you and me. He desires to grow us up in him to develop Christlike character that connects with others and multiplies itself into mature believers, disciplers, churches, and the kingdom among all peoples on earth. No matter where you and I fit into God's master plan, we can celebrate the fact that he will use us. He will grow in us maturational character for his name's sake.

Rick's Reaction

The story of Liang touched me deeply because it illustrates in stark black-and-white relief the distinction between New Testament discipleship and modern-day churchism. She had little in this world except her husband, and even he was taken away. Yet her response was to give all she had to the Lord, and the result was a breakthrough for the gospel. Such is always the case in spiritual maturity. It is not a matter of what we have or how much we have (money, education, experience); it is a matter of how much we give ourselves to be used by the Lord.

Mike's emphasis on "the kingdom within" resonates in me powerfully. I have recently discovered Dallas Willard's book *The Divine Conspiracy* and have been gripped by his vibrant explanations of the kingdom within. Mike carried this idea beyond self to church, from church to community, and from community to all nations. As we cross cultures in Jesus' name to disciple and equip, we go where God has already gone, and the connections we make with leader-learners build the kingdom from two directions. I have seen this time and time again: no matter how far out into the countryside I travel, at the end of my journey is a small village church where faithful believers have worshipped for years. We share Jesus together from different sides of cultural divides—two cultures, one kingdom.

I learned a lot from Mike's use of real-world churches who display, regardless of size, a maturational character. I was particularly taken with Northwood Church and the testimony that "God refocused Bob's attention on God's kingdom, not Bob's." Perhaps it is a natural progression: I accept the kingdom. I begin to work in the kingdom. I create my own kingdom within his kingdom. I surrender my kingdom for his and serve at his command. This last step is a good indication of spiritual maturity.

Finally, I applaud Mike's insight that maturational character grows as a by-product of the other elements. As we grow biblically and compassionately, as we develop rationally, passionately, and relationally, as we anchor ourselves spiritually in the living Lord within, we will mature. Growth in maturity may not come easy. There may be disappointments and deaths, illnesses and attacks, misunderstandings and abuse among family, friends, and even among the people we've been called to serve. But through it all, God uses the pressures of life and mission to transform our coal into his diamonds.

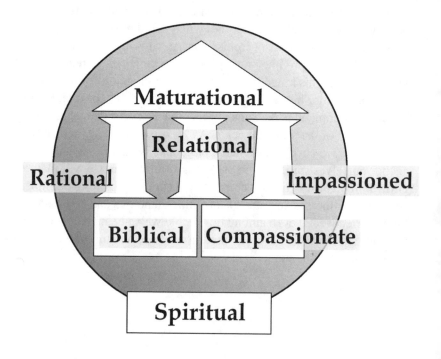

Character Traits
drawn from the
Disciplers' Model

9

Godly Influence:
The Synergism of Discipling
Rick Yount

"Not by might nor by power, but by my Spirit," says the LORD Almighty.
Zechariah 4:6

And Jesus grew in wisdom and stature, and in favor with God and men.
Luke 2:52

For whoever wants to save his life will lose it,
but whoever loses his life for me will find it.
Matthew 16:25; Mark 8:35; Luke 9:24

D isciplers project godly influence as they eschew personal power, priorities, and self to engage others for the kingdom of God. They humbly serve the Lord by serving others. By provoking national leader-learners to engage with the Lord, his Word, and his kingdom—head, heart, and hand—cross-cultural disciplers give themselves away and find life.

The Toxic Flip Side

Building one's own kingdom through
personal power, priorities, and self.

The Dark Side of Trait Theory

Leith Anderson stepped up to the microphone to begin his second and final session on leadership. He was addressing nearly two hundred participants in the annual meeting of the North American Professors of Christian Education association.[1] Anderson, one of two keynoters for the meeting, is senior pastor of the vibrant Woodale Church in Eden Prarie, Minnesota, where he has served since 1977.

---

1 Annual meeting of NAPCE, Rochester, Minnesota, October 2005. For more information on this vibrant organization for evangelical Christian educators, go to http://www.napce.org.

211

His introductory remarks sent a chill through me. "Trait theory—the idea that possession of specific traits guarantees success as a leader—was thoroughly debunked in the 1940s." He went on to lament that one can still find support for traitlike theories in many circles, including the church. My mind was racing. This manuscript was nearly complete. Was our focus on "discipling characteristics" the same as the trait theories Anderson was dismantling before my eyes?

Things grew darker the longer he talked. "Wouldn't most agree that honesty is a desirable trait for leaders? Yet Abram, the father of Israel, lied to Pharaoh about Sarai, claiming she was his sister and not his wife. Wouldn't we agree that marital faithfulness is an important virtue for leaders, especially in the church? And yet King David, a great leader and a 'man after God's own heart,' not only committed adultery with Bathsheba but killed her husband and took her as his second wife. Wouldn't one agree that kindness is a desirable trait for leaders to have, and yet how many successful pastors have you known who were more driving, demanding, and determined than kind?"

He continued to pound the theme. "Trait theory is demoralizing," said Anderson, "because no one possesses all the traits or fully possesses any of them. If success depends on developing multiple, sometimes conflicting, leadership virtues, then who can succeed? But worse, we look around us and find many examples of successful leaders who lack this or that required trait and are left confused."

The profound dissonance between Leith's critique and our five-year journey to develop this text would not let me go. Had I not written down what I had experienced in the Lord? Didn't Mike and I resonate with these principles, these elements? Hadn't we experienced successes in ourselves and in others when these elements were at work and failure when they were violated?

I wanted to hear more of what he was saying about leadership challenges, so I determined to lay aside the war of ideas clashing in my mind and put aside the knot in my stomach. *I decided to see him after the session.* I would swallow my pride and my experience and lay these ideas out before him. I'd let him evaluate our approach. Let the chips fall where they may. At least I was able to tune into his address.

Jesus, Our Example

Jesus is our example, but as the divine Son of God, second person of the Trinity, he was then and is now far above us. He understands us, having been tempted in every way like us, and yet he did not sin (Heb. 4:15).

The skeptic would mock Jesus. "You call Jesus kind," he might say, "and yet would you call the words of Jesus in the following dialog *kind?*"

A Canaanite woman from that vicinity came to him, crying out, "Lord, Son of David, have mercy on me! My daughter is suffering terribly from demon-possession."

Jesus did not answer a word. So his disciples came to him and urged him, "Send her away, for she keeps crying out after us."

He answered, "I was sent only to the lost sheep of Israel."

The woman came and knelt before him. "Lord, help me!" she said.

He replied, "It is not right to take the children's bread and toss it to their dogs."

"Yes, Lord," she said, "but even the dogs eat the crumbs that fall from their masters' table."

Then Jesus answered, "Woman, you have great faith! Your request is granted." And her daughter was healed from that very hour (Matt. 15:22–28).

The skeptic continues, "You call Jesus loving, and yet would you call the actions of Jesus in the following encounter *loving?*"

When Jesus heard this, he said to him, "You still lack one thing. Sell everything you have and give to the poor, and you will have treasure in heaven. Then come, follow me." When he heard this, he became very sad, because he was a man of great wealth. Jesus looked at him and said, "How hard it is for the rich to enter the kingdom of God!" (Luke 18:22–24).

The skeptic taunts us. "Here comes a man asking for advice on receiving salvation, a man who had kept the Law his whole life. 'Loving' Jesus ignores his good work, his good intentions, his heartfelt desire for salvation and skewers him with the one thing he still lacks. Again, you call Jesus patient, and yet how does the explosion of emotion in the following passage correspond with patience?"

When it was almost time for the Jewish Passover, Jesus went up to Jerusalem. In the temple courts he found men selling cattle, sheep and doves, and others sitting at tables exchanging money. So he made a whip out of cords, and drove all from the temple area, both sheep and cattle; he scattered the coins of the money changers and overturned their tables. To those who sold doves he said, "Get these out of here! How dare you turn my Father's house into a market!" (John 2:13–16).

The skeptic mocks. But we know that in each of these incidents, Jesus was sinless. The Canaanite woman had to understand that Jesus was not merely a Jewish Messiah, a local god, but the Savior of the world. She had asked Jesus to help her daughter. She had put her faith in him. Her response to Jesus' sharp words demonstrated her faith; and Jesus, who knew what was in her, granted her request.

Jesus knew the young ruler was bound, physically and emotionally, by his wealth. As long as he trusted his wealth, he would never be able to trust God. He gave this ruler the conditions that would set him free. Mark tells us that "Jesus looked at him and loved him" (Mark 10:21) before he set the requirement before him. "One thing you lack."

When Jesus saw how the temple grounds had been changed into an oppressive religious business, he responded in "holy anger." This was no adolescent temper tantrum—no self-serving, out-of-control demand. Jesus was not lost in a fit of rage. This was the Son of God reacting rightly to cleanse the Father's house of prayer of its commercialism. The disciples understood his motives immediately. "His disciples remembered that it is written: 'Zeal for your house will consume me'" (John 2:17, quoting Ps. 119:139).

Allow me to say this once again: Jesus is our example. But as the divine Son of God, second person of the Trinity, he was then, and is now, far above us. He understands us, having been tempted in every way like us, and yet he did not sin (Heb. 4:15). Jesus acted out of complete knowledge of persons, needs, histories, and context. We live and work with incomplete knowledge. Given our human inadequacies, we do better when we are kind than when we are unkind. Better when we are loving than unloving. Better when we are patient than impatient. Still, human inadequacies and sin fragment us. And in the process we naturally become distorted in our perceptions and unbalanced in our efforts.

How do we make our way back to balance? How do we put off our human fractures and put on God's image?

Sources of Imbalance

The Disciplers' Model provides a means to consider issues of imbalance and distortion in the ministry of teaching, discipling, and

214

equipping across cultural divides. As one element or another is ignored, synergy is lost and the model falls, indicating that spiritual growth of learner-leaders is hampered.

Biblical but Not Compassionate

Some people place more emphasis on the Bible than on the needs of the people they teach. In terms of the triad, they are thinkers, and such an emphasis comes naturally. Thinkers focus on historical context, word meanings, and theological concepts (see chapter 3). They reflect studies in Greek and Hebrew, systematic theology, philosophy, educational theory, and the English Bible. For these thinkers teaching is defined in terms of telling what one knows: explanations, illustrations, discussions of concepts, and objective questions. Such telling flows from teacher to learner; and since the emphasis is, intentionally, on the meaning of the text, there is little concern about the ones who receive the teaching.

Yet as we have seen clearly, Jesus went far beyond the meaning of words in his teaching. Before framing his explanations, parables, and illustrations, he analyzed his listeners. He knew what was in their hearts and minds and used that knowledge to find the best way to reach them with truth. He loved them, cared for them, and taught them out of his never-ending concern for them.

William Brown, president of Cedarville University in Ohio, addressed our students in chapel recently on this point. "You must do more in ministry than exegete the text. As important as 'rightly dividing the truth' is, it is equally important to exegete the culture. You must care about what listeners think and how they feel, what they believe and why. Only then will you understand how to frame the case for the gospel. Without this exegesis of culture, your preaching and teaching will be, for most, simply irrelevant."[2]

For years I have taught from the conviction that teaching the Bible without connecting biblical truths to learner needs can result in little more than "irrelevant history." I've found over the years that this is a provocative term. I'll never forget the night, over twenty years ago, when a retired Mississippi judge stood to his feet in front of three hundred conference participants, pointed his finger at me, and said in solemn, measured tones, "Young man, I'll have you know that the Word of God is never irrelevant!"

Three hundred pairs of eyes turned toward me to see how I'd respond. I quickly prayed for wisdom and then said: "Well, of course you're right. But if we merely talk about the Bible, if we never help learners see how the Bible addresses their own problems and needs, today, as the living Word, then they will come to *believe it's irrelevant.* And the result is to reduce the transforming Word of God to dry history lessons. That was my point."

To help the lost understand their need for the Lord and to help believers grow in him, we must do more than present an academic exegesis of the text or rehearse the details of history. Disciplers demonstrate the relevance of God's eternal Word to the contemporary needs and problems of our learners. As thinking disciplers, we push ourselves to exegete culture in general and our learners specifically. We will convey truth more effectively when we open our hearts to care for those we teach.

Compassionate but Not Biblical

Some people place more emphasis on the needs of the leader-learners they teach than on God's Word (see chapter 5). In terms of the triad, they are feelers; and such a warm, accepting emphasis comes naturally. They focus on the personal stories, testimonies, feelings, and values of their learners. For these feelers, teaching is defined in terms of openness, freedom, and minimal structure. The teacher serves as a facilitator of personal stories. Scripture is used as a catalyst for group sharing. Such sharing flows out of the interpersonal dynamic in the group; and since the emphasis is intentionally on the life experiences of learners, there is less concern about the text—its meaning, context, and actual message.

---

2 November 2, 2005. Chapel, Southwestern Baptist Theological Seminary. Quote is a paraphrase written from memory the same afternoon as the sermon.

We have emphasized the compassion of Jesus for his disciples and listeners, and yet Jesus never compromised truth. He engaged Jews, Samaritans, Galileans, and Romans; lepers, the deaf, the lame, and the blind; women, and even children on a personal level. He had compassion on them "like sheep without a shepherd" (Matt. 9:36). But he moved beyond warm human relationships to vibrant connections for teaching God's Word. It is fine to give clothes to the needy and food to the hungry, but it is not enough. Without sharing the good news of God's gift of salvation, our compassion amounts to little more than secular humanitarianism.

Learners who merely share concerns and needs with one another—a teaching methodology I call "group therapy"—without addressing those needs out of Scripture will not grow in the Lord. Group therapy is fine in its place, but it isn't Bible study. Sharing our experiences with one another doesn't provide answers to the questions which are raised.

Discipling feelers push beyond easy acceptance, warm sharing, and mutual relationships to connect learners with the eternal truths of God's Word. We become more effective in conveying biblical truths across compassionate bridges as we pay the price in biblical scholarship and analysis in order to speak clearly and credibly.

Rational but Not Passionate

Thinkers naturally prefer structure, conceptual context, principle and objective application (see chapter 4) to that of interacting with learners. It is not that they *dislike* people, but rather they prefer the challenge and joy of unlocking mysteries, solving problems, and developing new perspectives to the irrational chaos of emotion.

Time and time again when I have conference participants divide themselves into thinkers, feelers, and doers, the thinkers consistently agree on their favorite approaches to learning: a well-structured lecture, thought-provoking questions, objective discussions, profound discoveries. This is true whether the participants are American, Russian, German, or Brazilian. True whether they are old or young, rich or poor, male or female. Caucasian, Hispanic, African-American, or Asian. What do they dislike? "Sharing," "wandering," superficial stories, personal opinions, and excess emotion.

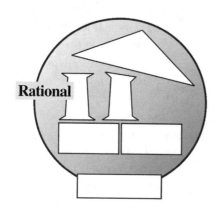

Over time thinkers' overemphasis on content and structure produces a cold, dogmatic approach to learning. Dispassionate. Controlled. Ordered. Such an approach may attract other thinkers, but it will not push out to engage the world. It will not convince. It will not last.

Jesus spoke the truth with quiet passion. He was not given to fits of temper or uncontrolled emotion, and yet he burned with an internal passion to do everything the Father had sent him to do. Raised a Jew in a devout Jewish home, Jesus broke with Jewish law and custom. He healed on the Sabbath day; spoke with a Samaritan woman; praised the faith of a Roman centurion; received with dignity the worship of the palm-waving crowds on Passover, the kneeling young ruler, and his own disciples. He engaged pagans, remained silent before a demanding King Herod, and endured both scourging and crucifixion, contrary to Roman law. And he died with the words "It is finished!" still hanging in the cold, dark air. In each of these instances (and many more besides), Christ demonstrated passion for his work: the Father's mission done the Father's way.

Thinking disciplers let go of the comfort they find in cold dogma and engage learners on a personal level, heart to heart in the Holy Spirit fires. Engaging God intellectually is certainly satisfying; but engaging him personally—from a position of total surrender to his cause, his kingdom, and his ways—is transforming. Discipling thinkers leave the safety of their libraries, with their overstuffed chairs and walls of books, and engage the world around campfires.

Impassioned but Not Rational

Feelers naturally prefer passion (chapter 6) over intellect. It is not that they dislike biblical truth, but rather they prefer engaging the personal humanity of others. They embrace the humanization of biblical truth as Scripture is filtered through personal experience. To see God's truth alive in the lives of others energizes feelers far more than a translation of the text or some wooden, impersonal illustration.

Time and again in conferences, feelers report their preference for the things thinkers disdain: sharing, wandering personal stories and opinions, and emotion. These are strengths for feelers not weaknesses. Sharing denotes equality among believers. Wandering equals freedom. Stories and opinions are the human products of truth, which energizes learning and living. Feelers dislike structured lectures, arbitrary authority, academic questions and discussions. Such methods constrict and control, stifle and mold. This is true whether the participants are American, Russian, German, or Brazilian. True whether they are old or young, rich or poor, male or female. Caucasian, Hispanic, African-American, or Asian.

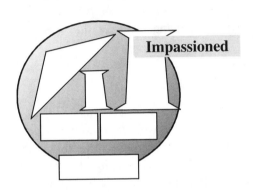

Over time feelers' overemphasis on freedom, opinion, and personal experience produces a warm but superficial approach to learning—nonrational, chaotic, unstructured. Such an approach may attract other feelers, but it will not push out to engage the world. It will not convince. It will not last.

Jesus was the impassioned Messiah, the anointed one, the Savior of the world. He lived passionately and died passionately, but he never let his passion undo his reason. The rich young ruler rejected Jesus. Jesus, knowing he rejected the truth, let him go. He forgave the woman caught in adultery—despite the Old Testament demand that she be stoned to death, along with her partner—but commanded her to go and "sin no more" (John 8:11 KJV). His passionate life and death tore open the wineskin of the Old Convenant and ushered in the new wineskin of the gospel; and yet he claimed, truthfully, that his teachings did not replace the Old Testament but fulfilled it. Though Jewish religious rulers tried, and finally succeeded, in having Jesus killed, he taught Israel to "do as they say," because they occupied Moses' seat, the place of authority within Judaism. In each of these instances (and many more besides), Christ demonstrated commitment to the truth: the Father's mission done the Father's way.

Discipling feelers let go of the comfort they find in warm fluff and group hugs to engage learners on a rational level, mind to mind in the Holy Spirit fires. Engaging God personally is certainly satisfying, but engaging him with one's mind, from a position of total surrender to his cause, his kingdom, and his ways is transforming. Discipling feelers leave the warmth of their cozy campfires and engage the world's ideas with God's truth.

Fellowship but No Koinonia

The central pillar of the model calls us to build relationships with those we teach (see chapter 7). We often use the word *fellowship* to refer to the interconnectedness of believers in churches and small groups. The word has taken on the unfortunate connotation of socializing. I have often heard a Sunday school director say, "We're going to have a few minutes

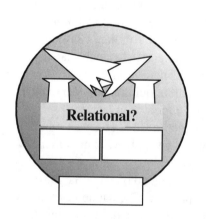

of fellowship before going to our classes" (to be interpreted, coffee and doughnuts). And a pastor announce an after-church fellowship, where members will remain after the service to eat ice cream or watermelon.

Socializing may be a first step toward biblical *koinonia,* but *koinonia* goes far beyond doughnuts. The New Testament term expresses the sense of togetherness or partnership in mission. "They devoted themselves to the apostles' teaching and to the *fellowship,* to the breaking of bread and to prayer" (Acts 2:42).

Koinonia also means "to give aid or relief." "And do not forget to do good and to share with others, for with such sacrifices God is pleased" (Heb. 13:16).

Therefore it is what we do with others, in partnership with them, that determines the quality of our fellowship. Providing aid and relief to their actual needs builds biblical *koinonia*. And what are their needs? We learn this by listening, by being approachable, available.

What American intends to offend the nationals with whom they work? I have met few, and those few soon find other work. But a question from a student in Moscow illustrates how easy it is to unintentionally destroy budding relationships. Dima asked me, "Dr. Rick, when Americans ask us how we are, they really do not want to know, do they?" It was spoken more as a statement of fact than a question. He was referring to our social practice of saying, "Hi! How are you?" and then moving on to other matters. For us, this is merely a form of greeting. But to ask Russians that question is to communicate that we really want to know! And they will begin to tell us in detail how their lives are going. When we quickly grow impatient with their long stories, they are offended. "Didn't you ask us how we are?"

An invitation by a national leader to a meeting, to a worship service, or to their own home is the single most important building block to *koinonia* we can receive early on in our ministry. "Would you like to visit the village church I serve?" "The brothers [pastors] would like you to come to their meeting Sunday night. Can you come?" "My wife and I would be most honored if you would have tea with us at 10:00 p.m. Thursday. Is this convenient for you?" There is only one acceptable answer to these invitations: "Yes!" I usually add from the heart my deep gratitude for their invitation. I may be put in awkward situations. I may be called on to pray or say a few words. In meetings, especially with pastors, I may be completely ignored. I may be asked a multitude of questions. I may even be asked to preach! As a thinker, such situations are naturally uncomfortable to me. But they are essential to *koinonia*. Every good work I have been allowed to do in the former Soviet Union—every single one—has come out of some previous surrender to an invitation. Through these meetings and meals, coffees and teas, prayer times, and discussions, I make connections to individuals who are present or future leaders. As they grow to trust me as a person of faith, they open doors to further ministry with others: *koinonia*.

Unfortunately more than a few Americans kindly refuse such invitations. Nationals observe the priorities of these few Americans. "Most Americans do not like to come to village churches because they are too small. They prefer to preach in the large downtown church."

Such an attitude speaks a loud negative to those who give their lives to minister in their small places. I am reminded of the Russian-Kazakh pastor and his wife, students of mine in a weeklong course in Tyumen. They live with their two children in a home with a dirt floor and without running water. Their village is inaccessible except in winter when the surrounding swamps are frozen or in summer by helicopter or boat. He graduated from a Soviet university where he majored in physics. She graduated with a degree in mechanical engineering. They came to faith in Christ and answered God's call to leave the comforts of Almaty, Kazakhstan to live in central Siberia. There they minister to thirteen believers (2001) in a hard-core Russian Orthodox village.

Americans themselves report frustration with these invitations. "I simply do not have time to drive out to the villages. These people spend the whole day going from one church to another. How many three-hour worship services in a day does one need?"

Yes, they do, without pay, because they love the Lord and love their brothers and sisters in these churches. It is unknown how much impact one might have for the kingdom through *going* and simply sitting with these believers in worship.

"Yes, I went to the pastors meetings a few times, but I was never asked to do anything, and so I quit going. I had better things to do." They were watching you, to see how you reacted to the meetings. Did you engage the speakers with your eyes? Did you show your interest in them before and after the meeting? Or were you bored because you had no standing in the group? Had you shown yourself faithful and engaged as a visitor, you would have earned credibility to be invited to a larger role. You proved your lack of interest in them by finding other things to do with your time. And then you wonder why you cannot build a relational bridge to the leadership? *You abandoned the one best way to do so!*

"I feel awkward going into people's homes. And one never knows what might be put on the table! I feel more comfortable in large group meetings. I have more freedom to meet people and select the foods I know." Nothing is more valuable to our ministry with others, *koinonia,* than to place our feet under their kitchen table, sip tea, and talk. We spoke of "removing emotional masks" in chapter 7. The kitchen table is the best place for this to happen. Those who exchange these invitations for

> Every good work I have been allowed to do in the former Soviet Union—every single one—came out of some previous surrender to an invitation.

other activities turn their backs on the most effective means to biblical *koinonia*.

Feelers embrace relational activities more enthusiastically than do thinkers. But the best relationships are anchored in both truth (honesty, integrity) and *agape* love. Godly influence flows across these relational bridges in both directions! Recall Paul's powerful conclusion to his passage on "equipping the saints for works of service": "Instead, speaking the truth [chapter 4] in love [chapter 5], we will in all things grow up into him [chapter 8] who is the Head, that is, Christ. From him the whole body, joined and held together [chapter 7] by every supporting ligament, grows and builds itself up in love, as each part does its work" (Eph. 4:15–16). Mutual self-giving relationships between discipler and disciple are central to the growth of *koinonia,* which lays at the heart of cross-cultural discipling.

Holy Spirit Versus Human Spirit

We began marching through the elements of the model with "spiritual character" (see chapter 2), allowing the Holy Spirit to teach and disciple through us. There we underscored the importance of prayer (ask God), position (servant, not boss), and priority (his will not mine) as tangible means by which we allow ourselves to be engaged by him for supernatural ministry. But there is more.

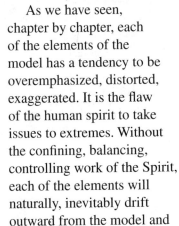

Spirit-led?

As we have seen, chapter by chapter, each of the elements of the model has a tendency to be overemphasized, distorted, exaggerated. It is the flaw of the human spirit to take issues to extremes. Without the confining, balancing, controlling work of the Spirit, each of the elements will naturally, inevitably drift outward from the model and eventually result in stagnation.

The Holy Spirit sets the boundary. As we have seen, there is great variety within the boundary. We can conduct a verse-by-verse exegesis of a specific passage. We can share with one another personal experiences in the Lord. We can test our understanding against that of others or share personal needs. We can meet in large groups, small cells, or one on one. The model displays the great range of teaching and learning preferences available to us in the Lord. But when we move beyond the circle, outside the Spirit's leading, we fall into extremes born out of the human spirit. We've already defined these extremes: excessive thinking leads to cold dogma. Excessive feeling to warm fluff. Excessive (shallow) relating to socializing. Excessive needs to group therapy. Excessive emphasis on the Bible lessons to irrelevant history. The excesses of the human spirit produce human (fleshly), not spiritual, work. Programs come and go; plans succeed and fail; gimmicks for "ten more next week" thrive and fade. But through all of this runs the golden thread of God's work: the drawing, winning, and maturing of people in Christ. This holy work proceeds only with surrendered disciplers.

Let us fasten our eyes on this golden thread and find true success. Ours is a higher calling than transmitting religious facts across cultural barriers. We are called to make disciples of all nations (Matt. 28:18–19) and "to prepare God's people for works of service . . . until we all reach unity in the faith and in the knowledge of the Son of God and become mature, attaining to the whole measure of the fullness of Christ" (Eph. 4:12–13).

This is an awesome task! But we need not fear the challenge. As we surrender our thinking, feeling, and relating to the Spirit, he will quicken them, order them, and anchor them for supernatural ministry.

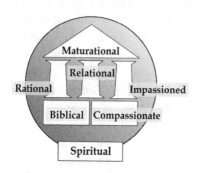

Character Traits
drawn from the
Disciplers' Model

Questions to Guide Synthesis

The following questions, and others like them, have helped guide me over the years to bring balance into my teaching.[3] On any given day, in any given teaching opportunity, I can revert to my own natural distortions and fail to create the best learning experience for those who sit before me. In those times I surrender my best attempts to the Lord and ask him to quicken my efforts for his kingdom's sake. Yet as I run my mind over these questions, as I take them to heart, I find that I am more likely to engage learners than when I do not. These questions have provided tangible ways to integrate the model into lesson plans, conferences, and chats over tea. I pray they will help you as well. I have divided them by model element.

Spiritual Focus

- How am I preparing spiritually (prayer, surrender, confession) to teach?
- Have I done all I can to prepare well while depending on the Holy Spirit to guide me?
- Have I prayed for the learners individually? Prayed for the session?
- How willing am I to cooperate with other leaders in order to increase harmony and build a spirit of teamwork?
- How dependent am I on the Holy Spirit as discipler in the group?

Biblical Focus

- How am I allowing the Bible to speak to those I teach? (in their language?)
- Am I merely talking about the Bible?
- How will *learners* use their Bibles in this study?
- Do I handle the Bible with reverence?
- Do I teach Scripture as God's guide, God's authority, God's lamp in my life?

---

3 While the "characteristics of disciplers" is a relatively new thrust of the Disciplers' Model, developed for this text, I have used the seven elements of the model to guide my lesson planning since it first came together in my early days as minister of education at Columbia Baptist Church, Falls Church, Virginia (1977).

Rational Focus

- How am I helping learners to think during this study?
- What am I doing to stimulate mental struggle with the passage and life needs?
- How do I encourage learners to study their own Bibles between sessions?
- How do I stimulate the desire for self-discovery and action?

Compassionate Focus

- How well do I know each person in my group?
- What are the specific needs in my learners that relate to this passage?
- How does this study help meet those needs?
- Do the teaching approaches I've chosen fit the way my learners learn best?

Impassioned Focus

- How accepting am I of my learners?
- How open am I to my learners?
- How do I encourage learners to share themselves—experiences and feelings—in class?
- How do I model the role of impassioned ministry?
- What opportunities do I give learners to share testimonies in class?
- What assignments do I make to prompt impassioned ministry outside of class?

Relational Focus

- How am I encouraging interaction—sharing, discussion—among learners?
- How am I helping learners to reach out to unsaved family, friends, and coworkers?
- How do I use small groups (one on one, triads, quads) in my teaching?
- What opportunities are there for ministry among learners?
- How do I help leader-learners build bridges to potential leaders?

Maturational Focus

- How is my group growing spiritually?
- What biblical goals have I set (Gal. 5; Col. 3; Heb. 11) for spiritual growth for the year?
- How do I demonstrate the struggles and blessings of spiritual growth in the way I live and work?

Throughout this text we have emphasized principles of cross-cultural discipleship. We have focused our attention on teaching, equipping, training, and nurturing others. But another dimension to cross-cultural discipleship needs mention before we close. The manner in which we lead either reinforces our words or undermines them. Space does not permit a full treatment of discipling leadership, but a quick look at Peter's reflections provide a foundation for what might become another text: "Called to Lead: Characteristics of a Cross-Cultural Leader"!

Disciplers as Leaders—Reflections from Peter

In the years following Jesus' ascension and the Spirit's coming, disciplers crossed national boundaries and cultural divides to plant churches throughout the known world. Problems concerning church organization and government began to rise when it became apparent that Jesus would not return immediately.

No disciple spent more time with Jesus or received more personal attention from Jesus than the apostle Peter. In writing guidelines to church pastors around AD 64, Peter recorded his perceptions of the major elements of Jesus' leadership style. Consider Peter's key emphases as they relate to cross-cultural discipling.

The worldwide church is the body of Christ. "A chosen people, a royal priesthood, a holy nation, a people belonging to God" (1 Pet. 2:9). The church is not intended to be a religious hierarchy whose power resides in the clergy. The church is composed of believers from all nations and tongues, with Christ as its Head.

The discipler-leader cares for and nurtures the church wherever it is found. "Be shepherds of God's flock that is under your care, serving as overseers—not because you must, but because you are willing, as God wants you to be; not greedy for money, but eager to serve" (1 Pet. 5:2). The Christian leader is a shepherd, not a hired hand, or worse, a hired gun. Jesus clarified the difference: "The good shepherd lays down his life for the sheep. The hired hand is not the shepherd who owns the sheep. So when he sees the wolf coming, he abandons the sheep and runs away. Then the wolf attacks the flock and scatters it. The man runs away because he is a hired hand and cares nothing for the sheep" (John 10:11–13). Cross-cultural disciplers are shepherds, not hired hands. They do not run from wolves.

The discipler-leader is an example. "Not lording it over those entrusted to you, but being examples to the flock" (1 Pet. 5:3). I can't help but wonder if Peter's mind went back thirty-five years to the day he heard Jesus say the same thing: "Jesus called them together and said, 'You know that the rulers of the Gentiles lord it over them, and their high officials exercise authority over them. Not so with you. Instead, whoever wants to become great among you must be your servant, and whoever wants to be first must be your slave—just as the Son of Man did not come to be served, but to serve, and to give his life as a ransom for many'" (Matt. 20:25–28). Cross-cultural disciplers minister in a way that serves as examples for others to follow, not religious rulers who make demands in their own power.

The discipler-leader is humble toward others. "Clothe yourselves with humility toward one another, because 'God opposes the proud but gives grace to the humble'" (1 Pet. 5:5b). Cross-cultural disciplers are confidently humble but not arrogant. They do not think too much of themselves and exude the sense that "there are others who can do more than I can." Neither do they belittle themselves, and they humbly recognize that in Christ "there are things I can do that others cannot." Disciplers think appropriately about their weaknesses (Lord, help me!) as well as their strengths (Lord, thank you!).

The discipler-leader is humble before God. "Humble yourselves, therefore, under God's mighty hand, that he may lift you up in due time" (1 Pet. 5:6). Cross-cultural disciplers are not self-centered. They do not rebel against God or chafe at the troubles which come to us all in life. Rather they celebrate the fact that, even in trouble, God's hand is on them. They find, as a result of surrender to the Lord, that God lifts them up to greater service and at just the right time.

The discipler-leader depends on God. "Cast all your anxiety on him because he cares for you" (1 Pet. 5:7). Cross-cultural disciplers depend on the Lord for strength as they work each and every day. They find that such dependence allows them to fly like eagles when life is going well, run with vigor when pressures mount, and walk without fainting when difficulties oppress (see Isa. 40:31). When I find myself unable to soar, or bowed down with weariness, or ready to give up and faint, I know I need to consider prayerfully when I stopped depending on the Lord.

The discipler-leader is in control of himself. "Be self-controlled and alert" (1 Pet. 5:8a). Cross-cultural disciplers are aware of the sinful environment that surrounds them, as well as circumstances that could harm them or their ministries. They are firmly in touch with reality. They see the world's subtle temptations for what they really are, Satan's bait-hooks.

The discipler-leader faithfully stands. "Your enemy the devil prowls around like a roaring lion looking for someone to devour. Resist him, standing firm in the faith, because you know that your brothers throughout the world are undergoing the same kind of sufferings" (1 Pet. 5:8b–9).

Cross-cultural disciplers resist the world's models of leadership that tout arbitrary power and material success. They resist Satan's offer of worldly gain—money, fame, pleasure, and power. Worldly models produce religious rulers who use gifts, training, and experience to dominate God's people for personal purposes. Jesus' example shows us the possibility (indeed, the necessity) of servant leading: using gifts, training and experience to free up God's people for kingdom purposes, despite personal cost.

"Teaching is more than telling what we know." This essential principle permeates every page of this text and is illustrated in the leadership principles Peter drew from Jesus, the Master Teacher. The manner of leading is a powerful aspect of our discipling ministry. *But can we succeed without developing these principles?* I am snapped back to my encounter with Leith Anderson.

Leith Anderson Revisited—the Lighter Side of Trait Theory

I thoroughly enjoyed Leith Anderson's presentation. My mind had returned to the dark side of trait theory only a few times as I listened. After the crowd dispersed, I made my way over to talk with him. I told him about this text and my experiences, and—I held my breath—I asked whether his comments about trait theory also applied to our "discipling characteristics."

He looked at me with a relaxed smile. "Are you saying in your text that one must possess these seven characteristics in order to succeed as a teacher or missionary?"

Were we? Just what were we saying?

"We believe we will grow more effective as disciplers as we develop in these seven areas. No one naturally possesses strengths in all seven areas, but as we grow in these areas, we will become more effective in ministry."

"Keep that focus!" he gently commanded. "The problem with trait theory is that it holds up a standard no one can achieve. Such a perspective completely demoralizes the one who desires to succeed. How can I possibly measure up to this? And many simply stop trying."

The pastor continued. "We all fail. And what do we do after we fail? Get up! Try again. And keep on trying. God takes our inadequate efforts and transforms them into progress for the kingdom.

"No, I think you have a good idea here. These are areas we must give attention to. So long as you do not present them as requirements for success."

He smiled and took his leave. He had blessed our perspective, and— should I admit this?—I felt blessed indeed.

We can succeed in ministry without one or more of these developed characteristics. But as we minister in Jesus' name, as we give ourselves to him as we are, as we depend on him to take our efforts and multiply them, we can also grow in these seven elements. Though none of us will ever achieve perfection in any of the seven, it is our heartfelt conviction that we will continually do better as we grow.

When he had finished washing their feet, he put on his clothes and returned to his place. "Do you understand what I have done for you?" he asked them. "You call me 'Teacher' and 'Lord,' and rightly so, for that is what I am. Now that I, your Lord and Teacher, have washed your feet, you also should wash one another's feet. *I have set you an example that you should do as I have done for you.* I tell you the truth, no servant is greater than his master, nor is a messenger greater than the one who sent him. *Now that you know these things, you will be blessed if you do them"* (John 13:12–17).

We are called as leaders. We are *called to lead* by a local church or missions agency that assumes we possess the gifts and sufficient knowledge, training, and leadership ability to contribute to, and perhaps even improve, their ministries. Our ministry training provides materials, patterns, and ideas which we use to strengthen the work of this church or mission. We are expected to be experts in our chosen field or at the very least expected to be willing to develop that expertise as we serve. We are called to lead in difficult times and places. It is a calling that implies a position out ahead of those who follow.

We are called as servants. We are called to serve by a church or missions agency that assumes we possess sufficient spiritual maturity and relational skills to help individuals and groups grow in Christ. We are expected to treat each person as an individual with unique gifts and minister to their needs as they live in a hostile world. We are called to minister. It is a calling that implies sensitivity and caring and giving.

The tension is resolved in Christ! We are pulled by these two roles—leader and servant—first one way and then the other. We may find ourselves (as leaders) in conflict with individuals as we attempt to make positive changes in organizations or operations. On the other hand, we may become so accepting of individuals (as servants) that organizations or operations lose their capacity to function, and we accomplish little for the Lord. In this tension we live and work; we cannot escape it if we are to be effective.

Paul wrote, "We proclaim him, admonishing and teaching everyone in all wisdom, so that we may present everyone perfect in Christ. To this end I labor, struggling with all his energy, which so powerfully works in me" (Col. 1:28–29).

We work with people (as servants) across cultural divides. We love them and serve them, minister to their needs, and help them discover and use their gifts to reach others in their cultural context. We humbly learn from them even as we teach them.

We work with people (as leaders), serving as examples of what Christ can do in a surrendered life. We teach as we want them to teach, encouraging them to teach others. We lead as we want them to lead, encouraging them to lead others. We build relationships in Jesus' name, encouraging them to build relationships with others. We love them, and we lead them so that "we may present [them] perfect in Christ."

May God richly bless you as you absorb the truths reflected in the Disciplers' Model and the Christian Teachers' Triad. May this text be a blessing to you, assisting you in the ministry of crossing cultural barriers every day. Open yourself first to the Lord and then to those you serve in Jesus' name. "Have I not commanded you? Be strong and courageous. Do not be terrified; do not be discouraged, for the LORD your God will be with you wherever you go" (Josh.1:9).

May God bless you on your journey!

Appendix 1
Insights into Cultural Differences
Rick Yount

In 1970, Barb and I moved to the campus of Gallaudet College for the Deaf, in Washington, D.C., to begin our work as dormitory counselors. We were twenty-two years old. The only training we had received was six months of sign language training at Westchester Baptist Church in Hartsdale, New York. Our teacher was a young missionary to the deaf of the Northeast, Rodney Webb.

Invited by friends to visit Columbia Baptist Church in Falls Church, Virginia, we were welcomed warmly by the pastor, Neal Jones, and the church as "experts in work with the deaf." We began our ministry with the deaf the next Sunday, with three coeds from Gallaudet. During this first year, the ministry grew to thirty-five deaf members—thirty-two of them making professions of faith. During this year we met with George and Lorene Joslin, missionaries to the deaf, Baptist General Association of Virginia.

Over the next three years, George became one of my most important mentors. He demonstrated great insight into deaf culture and language. In 1973, I left for seminary but returned to Columbia Baptist and Virginia in 1977 as minister of education. George continued to provide wonderful cross-cultural training. I will always be grateful for his discipling and equipping me in sharing the gospel with deaf youth and adults.

A few years ago George and Lorene were invited to leave behind their retirement and travel to Ecuador to live for six months, working with the deaf in that South American country. What follows are the discoveries he made as a missionary in a new culture. His insights are helpful for all of us but especially so for those preparing to go overseas for the first time.

Ambiguities and Absolutes

George Joslin

Retired Missionary with the Deaf
North American Mission Board, SBC

In many Third-World countries, such as Ecuador, life is made up more of ambiguities than absolutes related to daily life.[1] The point of this paper

---

1 Dr. Octavio Esqueda, assistant professor of foundations of education at Southwestern Baptist Theological Seminary, born and raised in Mexico, comments that these insights of my friend

233

is that ambiguous life experiences may make it difficult for them to accept the absolutes of the Bible regarding receiving Christ through faith or the eternal security of the believer. This is even more acute for the deaf members of that culture.

The culture of a nation is neither good nor bad; it just *is*. While there are many significant exceptions to these observations about a particular culture, there seems to be some validity in the observations and the resulting conclusion with implications for ministry. This is not to suggest that these examples of ambiguity are wrong. They are acceptable and expected within this culture. They do not bother anyone because that is how it is! This paper is not an effort to suggest that these things should be changed. They exist. They may change over time but not because of some outside force. They are understood by the people who live in this culture. Those people do not see these as ambiguities. The culture is what it is. What should we do to become more effective in presenting the gospel within this culture?

Note that these observations are made by a North American! Every effort has been made not to evaluate the culture of other people in terms of North American culture, but our own culture seeps through! Try hard to determine what the culture is, not why it is different from North American culture or why it should be different from what it is. Note also that you will know individuals in your culture who behave like this! However, the observations stated here are not of isolated individuals but describe the vast majority of the people.

Ambiguities Related to Time

1. Although some larger businesses function with fixed hours of operation, most smaller stores and businesses operate on an ambiguous time schedule. No "hours of operation" are posted. Generally they will be open by 9:00 a.m., close for a couple of hours between noon and 3:00 p.m., then open again until 6:00 p.m. or so. But it is impossible to depend on this. At 10:00 a.m. the local grocery store may be closed with no sign to indicate when it might reopen. (And that doesn't bother anyone because that is how it is!)

George demonstrate a strong North American perspective. Ecuadorans might well express these "ambiguities" differently or perhaps they might see Americans as "excessively rigid." Still, I believe these insights help us see firsthand the nature of "cultural divides" we address in the text, and I am grateful for his contribution. RY

2. Church services and other meetings are announced to begin at a set time but seldom start on time. And that doesn't bother anyone because that is how it is!

3. Appointments or activities scheduled in the home seldom happen at the times scheduled. The water man may come when he promised, or maybe two hours later, or maybe the next day. People invited to come at 2:00 p.m. may arrive at 1:00 p.m., or more likely 2:30 or even 3:30 p.m. And that doesn't bother anyone because that is how it is!

4. Many people do not have salaried employment and have no assurance from day to day whether they will work, how many hours they will work, or how much they will take home at the end of the day. And that doesn't bother anyone because that is how it is!

5. Many are employed in a family operation. For many of the deaf people, there is no wage. Someone, perhaps the father or an older brother, gives them money "as they need it." And that doesn't bother anyone because that is how it is!

Ambiguities Related to Location

1. Addresses are often given as an intersection between two streets, but the actual location of the house or store may be as much as two blocks in any of four directions. And that doesn't bother anyone because that is how it is!

2. Few streets have names posted at every intersection. Many buildings and houses do not have house numbers displayed. Maps do not show the block numbers for the streets. And that doesn't bother anyone because that is how it is!

3. Deaf people often do not know the address of their home. They can tell which bus to catch to get near it but cannot show on a map where it is or give the cross streets nearest their house. This is especially true for less well-educated deaf people. And that doesn't bother anyone because that is how it is!

Ambiguities Related to Laws

1. Driving laws exist but are generally ignored. Taxi drivers and other drivers regularly run stop signs. A taxi, driving down a two-lane street and the only vehicle in the block, will drive on the left

side of the road until he is within one hundred yards of where he plans to turn right! And that doesn't bother anyone because that is how it is!

2. Other laws are ignored. But when someone is apprehended by the police, interpretation of the law is up to the police officer. Many times arrest can be avoided by slipping the police officer some cash. And that doesn't bother anyone because that is how it is!

3. Permits are most often purchased under the counter rather than being granted according to established laws that are equal for all. A driver's license for one of the missionaries took two trips to a town thirty miles away where a friend knew someone and was able to persuade the one person with authority to grant the license. It was not a matter of meeting some established criterion but of knowing the right person. And that doesn't bother anyone because that is how it is!

Ambiguities Related to Cost and Availability of Items

1. Although some larger stores have fixed prices, the typical person buys what he needs in small shops and markets where prices are negotiable. And that doesn't bother anyone because that is how it is!

2. Grocery stores, even the larger ones, cannot be expected normally to have staples such as milk, coffee, or sugar. Smaller stores may have an item one week but not have it the next. Drug stores may have a common prescription medication one week but not have it the next and not have a definite plan for getting it into stock. Shoppers must go to one store, then another, until they find the item. And that doesn't bother anyone because that is how it is!

Ambiguities Related to a Person's Word

1. A person will agree to meet another at a given time though he knows he will not be able to do so. This is not a deliberate lie. He does not want to offend the other person by saying he cannot meet him as agreed so he agrees and then does not show up.

2. A person will promise to do something and never get it done for the same reasoning as above. And that doesn't bother anyone because that is how it is!

3. A person will give directions, even though he does not really know. He does not want to seem ignorant and wants to be helpful. And that doesn't bother anyone because that is how it is!

4. These are not seen as lying. This is just the way everyone handles these kinds of transactions. And that doesn't bother anyone because that is how it is!

Ambiguities Related to Family Relationships

1. Marriage vows are made in all sincerity, yet in many families it is understood that the man will have at least one mistress. His wife is aware of this. His children grow up and know this to be true. Unlike some of the other examples of cultural behavior that are just different, the Bible declares that adultery is sin and cannot be condoned.

2. Young people who live at home, even though they are forty years old, are subject to the authority of their father or mother. They can make plans to participate in an activity, but when the time comes, the parents say they must do something else. They are not independently able to plan their life until they move away from the home of their parents, even though they have their own job and are generally self-supporting. And that doesn't bother anyone because that is how it is!

Ambiguities Related to the Catholic Church

1. Deaf people usually have not had much indoctrination from the Catholic Church, but they are influenced greatly by their hearing parents and family members who are influenced by Catholicism.

2. In Catholicism there is no teaching of salvation through faith as an absolute or of the eternal security of the believer as an absolute. Certain things are necessary to maintain their salvation, and then after death there is still some degree of uncertainty or ambiguity. But the Bible speaks of certainties and absolutes. God is not ambiguous.

Ambiguities Related to Personal Responsibility

1. In South American culture no one accepts responsibility for what happens. If they drop something, the Spanish language has vocabulary to let them say, "It dropped itself." It is not easy for them to say, "I did it." Since everyone knows they dropped it, it isn't really a lie; it is just a way of expressing it. But this lends itself to their not accepting responsibility for their sins. Before a person can be saved, he recognizes that he is a sinner. He cannot dismiss his responsibility for his sin.

2. It is difficult for them to say, "I am a sinner." Compare this to the teenager who says, "All the rest of the kids smoke," as if that makes it right. Or the other expression, "Well, no one is perfect; I am only human." But they must recognize that their sin separates them from God.

Questions to Consider in Light of These Observations

1. How do people living in such a world of ambiguities respond to our teaching from the Bible that
   - salvation is through faith, only, and
   - that when a person repents and asks for salvation, it is given him, and
   - he is saved forever.

2. Are they able to grasp these absolutes, or do they see them as having as much validity as laws, prices, and hours that they meet every day of their life.

3. Do they see salvation as "maybe" instead of "truly"? Even though we tell them it is absolute, do they really grasp this concept?

4. How can we help them overcome this lack of confidence in the Word from God regarding their salvation?

Conclusions and Implications for Ministry

1. Our ministry is not to change their culture but to present the Word of God in a way that is understood within their culture.

2. In all teaching situations we must stress repeatedly the absolutes of God—all powerful, all knowing, always keeps his promises, is just in all his dealings with people, and that God hates sin but loves sinners.

3. We must stress that the Word of God has lasted through the ages and is still absolutely true.

4. We must always avoid as much ambiguity as possible. We must keep our word about appointments, always be on time, show no favoritism but treat all persons equally.

5. Encourage believers to give their testimony frequently, stressing that they have no doubt about their salvation.

6. Use drama to show that man may not always be dependable, but God is.

7. Use current events from TV or newspaper headlines, showing that people and things are not always what they should be. Then from the Bible stress that God never changes and is always the same.

8. Encourage believers to participate fully in activities.

9. While it is not important to change their attitude toward time (And that doesn't bother anyone because that is how it is!), it is important that they be involved in Bible study. It seems good and appropriate to have scheduled teaching and worship activities. If they arrive late, they have missed some of the teaching. Start as nearly on time as possible. Sometimes a meeting starts late because the people arrive late. Most of the time a meeting starts late because the starter starts late! Start with the dessert—something really good—drama, choruses, or something they really enjoy. Then if a person arrives after the meeting has begun, next time he just might try to get there for the "good part" at the beginning. But if they continue to arrive late, that doesn't bother anyone because that is how it is!

10. Remember that the Bible records more examples of Jesus teaching while he walked, sat, or ate with his disciples than at more formal class settings. If the people are not there when you are scheduled to teach, teach them when you are with them. Be prepared to teach in and out of season, in and out of doors, in and out of their homes. When two are gathered together in his name, Jesus is there! (see Matt. 18:20). When one or two are with you, teach them! When they come to a teaching activity late, start teaching again! There have been times when we have started again many as three or four times. Those who arrived first do not complain that we are being repetitious. And that doesn't bother anyone because that is how it is!

Appendix 2
Illustrations from Dr. Jeff Ritchey
Professor, Canadian Baptist Seminary, Calgary, Canada
Former IMB Missionary to Croatia

Croats often get together over a cup of coffee rather than a meal. Americans enjoy coffee but for the most part like to drink the coffee while it is still hot. Croats, on the contrary, see the meeting as a time for leisurely discussion and fellowship. They will literally sit for hours over one cup of coffee. It does not bother them in the least that the coffee is stone cold! It took us a while to realize that we were confusing our Croatian friends when we (in their minds) quickly gulped down our coffee. They thought that we must have a busy schedule and did not have time for conversation. We missed out on fellowship time by not letting the cup sit half full even though it was getting cold and (in our minds) no longer suitable for drinking.

Cheating on assignments and tests seems to be a common problem in Eastern Europe. We developed an interactive curriculum for pastors. The three major parts of the curriculum included input, learning activities, and feedback. The input was the content part of the workbook. The learning activities were written to correspond to the previous content. The feedback was written to help the learner gain further insight from the learning activities. The explicit instructions to the learners were to work through the learning activity before reading the feedback portion of the curriculum. When it came time to translate the curriculum, our translating team in Croatia decided not to include the feedback portions for the students. They made this part of the curriculum available only to the facilitators. The director of our distance education program was well aware of the attitude of the students toward "borrowing another's work."

My colleague and I were sitting in a local restaurant eating lunch. While we were enjoying our meal, we noticed that all of the other customers in the restaurant were eating "the European way" (fork in the left hand and knife in the right, using both utensils at the same time without laying them down throughout the entire meal!). Because I had come to live and minister in this part of the world, I desired equilibrium. During the next several weeks, I practiced the European method of eating until I was comfortable with the technique. Soon I was able to enjoy a meal in a restaurant without feeling like I stuck out like a sore thumb!

"To be Croat is to be Catholic." Most people in our part of the world tie their spiritual beliefs to religion and tradition. They tend to be concrete thinkers in terms of religious practices. A good Christian attends weekly Mass, goes to confession on a regular basis, and participates in Catholic holiday celebrations. Christianity is associated with religious deeds. The problem comes in trying to connect the religious deeds with the relevancy of religion in everyday life. Through small-group Bible studies, we emphasize the importance of a living relationship with Christ. Christianity involves more than religious deeds. The goal of Bible study is to take the truths learned from God's Word and understand how to use them in solving everyday issues in life.

About the Authors

Rick Yount has spent his adult life prayerfully considering ways to improve the quality of teaching and learning in Bible study groups, churches, seminary classes, and workshops. He

served as minister to the deaf in two churches (1970–1976), and minister of education at Columbia Baptist Church, Falls Church, Virginia (1976–1981). Since 1981, he has shared these principles with future pastors and Christian educators as professor of Foundations of Education at Southwestern Baptist Theological Seminary. Since 1996, he has discovered the joy of the Lord in carrying these principles to seminaries and Bible institutes in the former Soviet Union,[1] teaching national pastors and missionaries how God created us to learn and how to use those insights to teach and equip believers to grow in the Lord.

Mike Barnett has spent his adult life straddling the world of international business and ministry. He has used his business knowledge and

experience to provide strategy support and organizational development services to dozens of discipler teams around the world. He and his wife served for twelve years with the International Mission Board of the Southern Baptist Convention. He continues to serve as a strategy consultant and equipper on a global scale. In recent years he has discovered the joy of the Lord in sharing these lessons with students at Southwestern Seminary and, since 2004, at Columbia Biblical Seminary and School of Missions. Here he serves as Elmer V. Thompson Professor of Missionary Church Planting, equipping and connecting future discipling pastors and missionaries with God's mission among all nations.

---

1 For stories and pictures of these trips, go to The DisciplerZone at http://members.aol/wyount.

Index

A

Abdul-ahi 37, 38, 63
accommodation 81, 83, 93
accountability partner 57, 116, 118
adaptation 81–82, 98
ambiguities 233, 234, 235, 236, 237, 238
Anderson, Leith 211–212, 229–230
assimilation 76, 81, 82, 83, 93
authority 1, 22, 89, 90, 112, 149, 161, 163, 164, 167, 168, 173, 174, 175, 207, 219, 220, 225, 228, 236, 237

B

Bangalore Baptist Hospital 114
Bhojpuri-speaking people 51
Bible
  as an anchor 34
  defines impassioned character 140–141
  as God's Eternal Word 38–39
  how teachers use 40
  learning, not just knowing 49
  memorization of 59
  and missionary strategy 51–56
  as operating manual 41–44, 65
  and power for witness 50–51
  and renewal of missionary call 47–51
biblical character 37–65
  how to get and keep 57–59
  in Somalia 37, 63–64
  and the Teacher's Triad 61–63
Blackaby, Henry and Richard 137
Brown, William 215–216

C

call to missions 41–48, 198–199
campus ministries 199–200
Carey, William and Dorothy 110–111
Cedarville University 215
cell groups 156
character 9–11

Christian Teachers' Triad
  and biblical character 61–63
  circles 8–9
  and compassionate character 119–121
  and impassioned character 144–145
  as a reflection of God's design 6–7
  spiritual character and 24–33
church growth 188–189
cognitive development, stages of 84–87
cognitive structures 79–80
Columbia International University 191
compassionate character 105–125
compassion for the lost 127
compassion for the poor 105–106, 121–122
concrete operational 84
contextualization 83
cross-cultural communication
  with deaf people 75–76, 82
  and honesty 100–101
  and inner transformation 192
  nonverbal 157
  and relationships 156–157
  in Russia 67–69
cross-cultural disciplers
  in East Asia 187–188, 206–208
  in Ecuador 15–17, 33–34
  in India 51–52, 113–114
  in Iraq 132–133, 142–143
  in Kyrgyzstan 168
  in Lebanon 195–196
  in Russia 1–2, 68–69
  in Somalia 37–38
  in Ukraine 67–68
cultural differences 233–240
cultural mistakes 4
cultural shock xvi, 1
culture and missionary adaptation 127–130
cultures 156–160

D

Daniel 144–145
deaf people 15–17, 33–34, 68–69, 75–76, 82, 150–151, 180–182

Disciplers' Model
    central pillar of 152–153
    and character traits 3–5
    circle of 17–19
    as a framework 2
    left foundation stone of 38–39
    left pillar of 69–70
    and missions 3–4
    right foundation stone of 106–107
    right pillar of 129–130
    seven elements of 10–11
    and sources of imbalance in teaching 214–231

E

Elliott, Larry and Jean 132–133, 142–143
Equilibration 80–81

F

failure 175–176
fellowship 220–223
freedom, climate of 169

G

Gallaudet College 28
Graham, Billy 53

H

hidden service 164–165
Hill of the Lord University Church, Columbia, S.C. 199
Holy Spirit
    as Discipler 17–19
    versus human spirit 223–224
    requires impassioned character 141–142
    as teacher 98–100
honesty 100–101, 139
house churches 72–73, 200
humility 164–165
Hybels, Bill 200

I

imbalance in teaching, source of 214–223
impassioned character 127–147

indigenous churches 55–56
indigenous missions 195
influence, godly 211–232
information, overemphasis on 74

J

Jesus
  compassionate character of 112–113
  as cross-cultural discipler 111
  as our example 212–214
  focusing on needs 107
  and human needs 166–168
  parables of 87–88
  prayers of 20–21
  priority of 23–24
  relational character of 160–171
  as Servant Leader 170
  servanthood of 21–23
  as the smartest man in the world 90–91
  spiritual character of 19–24
Joslin, George 68–69, 80

K

kingdom growth
  and the church 193–194
  and church growth 188–190
  and the heavenly kingdom 193–194
  maturity and 191–192
  measuring 190–191
  among all nations 194–196
  Paul on 189–190
knowledge 70–73
knowledge, teaching for
  as a beginning point 73–74
  in China 72–73
  leading to understanding 75
  and levels of learning 70
  principles of 71

L

language acquisition 1–2, 55–56, 73, 156–157
Lea, Tommy 58–59
Leadership Network 200

learning, human vs. spiritual 26–28
learning environment 89–90
learning systems 6–9

M

man-of-peace strategy 52
Mary of Bethany 169
maturational character 187–209
maturity 197–199
McDonnall, David and Carrie 132–133, 142–143
memorization 73
missio Dei 42–44
mission, defined 42
Missionary Learning Center 49
Mission Columbia 111
Moon, Lottie 109–111

N

Naylor, Rebekah 113–115
needs of learners 107–108
Northwood Church, Keller, Tex. 202–203

O

optimal discrepancy 92–93
organization 79, 171–173

P

passion, defined 135
Paul
  as cross-cultural discipler xv
  on church growth 189–190
  global vision of 43–44
  and relationships 153–154
PEACE 201–202
persecuted Christians 187–188
Peter, James, John 171–172
Piaget 78–79, 84, 85, 91, 97, 101
position 19
prayer 18
priority 18

R

rational character 67–103
Ray of Hope Ministries 168
recall 71
reinforcement 82
relational character 149–185
relational ministry 179
relationships
  in cross-cultural settings 156–160
  maintaining 149–182
  and small groups 156
relationships, maintaining 179–182
Roberts, Bob 202

S

Saddleback Church, Lake Forest, Calif. 201–202
schemes, schematia 79–80
servant leadership 170
small groups 201–202
social garments 153
spiritual character 15–35
Stephen 203–206
strategy 51
Stroope, Mike 47–48

T

T4T 60
Taylor, J. Hudson 110, 123
team-building 178–179
techniques 9–11
temptations 21–22
Tertullian 142
trait theory 211–212, 229–231

U

understanding 75–76
understanding versus believing 83–84

V

victorious life in Christ 191–192
vocation 197–199

W

Warren, Rick 201
Watson, David and Jan 51–52
Watson, Karen 132–133, 142–143
Willard, Dallas 90–91, 208
Willow Creek Church, South Barrington, Ill. 200–201
Windham, Bill 111
wisdom 77

X

Xenos Christian Fellowship, Columbus, Ohio 200

Y

Yun 72–73